In a study which concerns itself with
Richardson, Goethe, Büchner, Dickens,
Poe, Hawthorne, Henry James,
D. H. Lawrence, Proust, Kafka, Musil and
Pynchon, the author examines the dialectic
of realism and fantasy in the novel and
demonstrates that the first premise of
realism is the fantastic belief that one can
know everything important about a person,
whilst the basis of fantasy is the realistic
conviction that one cannot. *The Realist
Fantasy* describes how, in an age whose lack
of security and fragmentation precludes the
formation of a stable ego, the novel assures
us we are wholes and thus furnishes us with
our fantasy of the real. The novelist is, as it
were, sacrificed on our behalf: he splits
himself in order to create images of people
as wholes. Paul Coates begins by showing
how this dialectic of wholeness and fragmentation is embodied in *Clarissa* and how
the modernist aesthetics of self-consciousness about writing derive from this novel's
epistolary form; how these aesthetics then
flower in the great modernist novels; and
how modernism in Europe alters and its
original ambitions are preserved only
among certain American writers, particularly Thomas Pynchon.

In an unusual juxtaposition of English,
German and American texts and an appli-
cation of the theories of Adorno and
Benjamin, the author throws fresh light on
works which may be in danger of being
submerged by the academic critical
industry.

Paul Coates works as a translator. He
studied German and Polish at Churchill
College, Cambridge, and then s
years in Warsaw where he succ
defended a Ph.D. written in P
Polish symbolist Bolesaw Lesm
shortly to be published in Pol
contributed to Polish journals
and the *Comparative Criticism Yearbook*.

THE REALIST FANTASY
FICTION AND REALITY
SINCE *CLARISSA*

PAUL COATES

St. Martin's Press   New York

ISBN 0–312–66524–5

Library of Congress Cataloging in Publication Data

Coates, Paul, 1953–
    The realist fantasy.

    Bibliography: p.
    Includes indexes.
    1. Fiction—History and criticism.   2. Realism in literature.
I. Title.
PN3340.C6   1983   809.3   83–8637
ISBN 0–312–66524–5

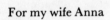

For my wife Anna

Wir haben das Gestalten erfunden:
darum fehlt allem, was unsere
Hände müde und verzweifelt fahrenlassen,
immer die letzte Vollendung.

(Lukács, *Die Theorie des Romans*)

Contents

Acknowledgements

Some of the material in this book has already been published elsewhere: 'Notes on the Novel', in *PN Review*; two or three paragraphs from 'The Illustrated Novel' and 'Mirrors, Paranoia and the Senselessness of an Ending', in the *Comparative Criticism Yearbook 4*, as part of an essay entitled 'Cinema, Symbolism and the *Gesamtkunstwerk*'; and the essay on 'Doubles', in my book in Polish about the Symbolist poet Bołeslaw Leśmian (the present version is partly a translation, partly a revision, of the Polish original). I would like to thank Michael Schmidt, the Cambridge University Press and the Państwowy Instytut Wydawniczy in Warsaw respectively for permission to reprint.

I would also like to thank Thomas Pynchon, the Viking Press and Jonathan Cape Ltd for permission to reproduce copyright material from *Gravity's Rainbow* in my essay on that novel.

In conclusion I would like to thank several people who have had an influence, direct or indirect, on the shaping of this book. Firstly, I must thank Rosemary Bechler for the enthusiasm with which she introduced me to *Clarissa*; I hope she does not feel I have abused the insights I so shamelessly appropriated from her. Secondly, Gabriel Josipovici, whose work has been an inspiration to me even when I have felt compelled to disagree with it. Thirdly, Macmillan's reader, whose light I am sadly unable to bring out from under the bushel of his namelessness, but whose suggestions were very helpful. Fourthly, Thomas Pynchon, whom I have never met, but who seems to me to be the major force keeping the novel alive today. And finally my wife Anna, without whose encouragement very little of what follows would ever have been put to paper; the dedication of this book is scant recompense for my debt.

Introduction

The title of this book is two-edged. It states both that the notion of realism is a form of fantasy; and that fantasy itself is a form of realism. It criticises the claims to objectivity made in the name of classic realism, and also reduces fantasy to the reality it flees and reproduces in the dark code of dreamlike distortion, symptomatic writing. Realism in prose is the fruit of a fantasy of omnipotence; the all-knowing narrator who directs his often shaky plot to the happy idyll of a siding in the best of all possible worlds is over-optimistic about the feasibility of dominating reality. The solipsistic fantasist and the first person narrator are in a sense more realistic than the realist, for they are conscious that other people are often opaque and that even the best-laid plot can miscarry. Realism and anti-realism are opposed in the same way as are the nineteenth and the twentieth centuries, the Victorians and the modernists. To say this is to repeat a truism. But the truism itself contains an element of falsity: it is too easy, too banal. For in actuality, realism and fantasy are both historically successive modes of consciousness (the self-proclaimed modernists swim with the tide of history even when they claim to oppose it), *and* two aspects of the same object. There is a dialectic of realism and fantasy, representation and solipsism, at the heart of all writing. The fact that one era accentuates one mode, another its opposite, means only that the inadequacy of any attempted resolution of this dialectic cries out for a correction that itself requires to be corrected.

Hillis Miller has given a definition of the Victorian novel that may appear seductively applicable to all novels.

Many characteristic Victorian novels show that society no longer seems to have a transcendent origin and support. This leads in turn to the discovery that the individual human heart generates the game of society and establishes its rules. Society rests on human feelings and on human will. It is created by the interplay of one mind and heart with another.[1]

The assumption that society is purely self-generating causes the Victorian novel to ignore the return of the repressed in the unforeseen

1

moments that question the continuity of a life, throw windows open on to other possible worlds: worlds governed by non-human orders, or by orders incomprehensible to men (as opposed to women) or to the men of a particular society (Ahab's misreading of the white whale in *Moby Dick* parallels the Western misinterpretation of the wandering South Sea islands in *Mardi*, the theme of Melville's earlier work). Although the shocks caused by industrialisation, centralisation and urbanisation were the fundamental experience of the nineteenth century, they are habitually ignored by the Victorian novel; perhaps there had not yet been time in which to assimilate the experience and devise aesthetic strategies with which to counter it. If this is so, the Victorian novelist is the baffled inhabitant of an interregnum. Perhaps only the female writers of the nineteenth century were able to perceive and thematise the shock – though insufficiently explicitly – for their very existence as novelists depended on changing mores and growing feminism. The degree to which their novels had to struggle into being is apparent in the way they only won their names by concealing them, by becoming Currer Bell or George Eliot. It is the radical novelists who require this cryptic coloration. Instead of surrendering their names in marriage, they give themselves away to their fictions, from which in turn they receive their true names. As women they are aware of the threat and benediction that inhere in a name; conscious of the way in which the need for a fictional name grounds the fiction itself in the violating moment of self-transformation. It is surely no accident that although Mary Shelley, unlike Charlotte Brontë and Mary Ann Evans, adopted no *nom de plume*, she was fascinated by the process of the transference of a name: in *Frankenstein*, the hero cedes his name to the monster he creates. In any case, 'Shelley', like 'Godwin', is almost a *nom de plume*; in both cases the name has a more renowned owner. Perhaps the women novelists of the nineteenth century were more aware of the fictional nature of identity than the men because, being women, they would expect to have to change their names at some point in their lives. Their identity itself was founded on the shock of monthly bleeding, of a continually repeated passage through the area of taboo. The pseudonymous isolation in which they worked precluded the classic Victorian novelist's identification with the mind of the community and acquainted them with self-alienation. In this they resembled the contemporaneous pseudonymous narrators of Kierkegaard. Their mannish seeming dimly prefigured the analysis of the nature of sexuality in Lawrence, Musil and Proust. In many respects the subterranean link between Romanticism and its self-critical resurgence as modernism lies in the work of the women novelists; Gothic was largely a woman's domain. The women with daggers who recur in George Eliot's novels have – like their pseudonymous author – appropriated the phallus. In many respects – they have been well described by Leavis and by Elinor Shaffer – *Daniel Deronda* is the ancestor of the modern novel. In speaking of the two novels it contains, Leavis responds to the self-unknowing aesthetics it practises, which distantly anticipate the modernist fixation on foreign culture in an era in which one's own culture had become foreign (for more remarks on this theme, see my essay on Conrad in Chapter 4). Like the great modernist novels, it is founded on a foreign culture. Its ultimate failure derives from its Victorian disbelief in the otherness of the other culture: its over-easy ingestion of the Hebraic simply swallows a projected mirage.

More successful, though equally stylistically discontinuous, is *Wuthering Heights*, in which Emily Brontë analyses the alien and alienating character of moorland culture, which arises on the stark edge of the world. Whereas Cathy's tragedy stems from an inability to recognise that her culture is a culture – an inability to accept the heaths and the cliffs, which become the alien gypsy child Heathcliff – an inability to accept the truth of her own remark that she *is* Heathcliff, for the remark itself is self-mystified and sounds absurd – Emily Brontë's triumph is to have re-defined the notion of culture to encompass both the Lintons and the Heathcliffs. Her Romantic respect for folk beliefs connects to culture what Cathy – born prematurely, in a pre-Romantic age – perceives as anticulture. *Wuthering Heights* is a tragedy of cultural history: of the prematurity of a birth signalled by the repetition of the name 'Cathy' in two successive generations. Even so, like *Daniel Deronda*, *Wuthering Heights* is an astonishing, prescient failure: it lacks the courage of its own insights into the nature of culture and refuses to break down the barriers between the narratorial meta-language and the language of the characters, as Lawrence was to do. Only the minor, stock relief characters speak in a Yorkshire dialect: on this level of the novel, Emily Brontë repeats Cathy's error. She cannot contemplate a rough-speaking hero; she can only preserve the heroic status of Heathcliff by rendering him silent. Just as George Eliot cannot hear Hebrew, so Emily Brontë is deaf to Heathcliff. The suppression of his language taints with violence the language of his deeds. Nevertheless, *Wuthering Heights* represented a phenomenal achievement in the context of the Victorian novel. It was the only Victorian English novel to earn the plaudits of the surrealists, or to be filmed by Bunuel. For by and large the Victorian novel ignores the transcendent experiences of disruption. These are the epiphanic moments of Musil and Proust, the inexplicable rendings of the weave of daily continuity in Kafka, the vertiginous violence of Clarissa's abduction, or the earthquakes of Kleist. Because it ignores these moments, the Victorian novel fails to grasp the connection between realism and fantasy (perhaps Dickens comes closest, but he is not close enough, for the upshot of his work is pseudo-realism and pseudo-fantasy): for in actuality the dialectical force of the unexpected event prompts one to ask which of two things is fantastic: the old life or the new? The order one has lost, or the force of the event that overturns it? For all its thinly spread religiosity, the Victorian novel is devoid of true religious feeling. This is as much as to say that it is without poetry. It ignores the way in which the force of the other can make a Paul of a Saul, render the old self fictive, and shatter the identity it shadowily preserves in the rhyme between the saint's Jewish and his Christian name.

In his study *Victorian Fantasy*, Stephen Prickett drew attention to the origin of the word 'fantasy' in a complex of words linked with the activity of visualisation. He suggested that Gothic fantasy in particular represented 'a very peculiar paradox: a literary medium that doesn't tell us a story so much as offer verbal *pictures*. The Gothic did not work by sequential arguments against the excessive rationality of the eighteenth century system-builders, but by flashes that haunt the waking mind like the images of dreams.'[2] He went on to say that 'those critics who, like Levine, complain that *Frankenstein* has no ending, are beside the point. What ending *could* there be after that opening vision of the monstrous pursuit across the ice?'[3] Prickett's remarks raise one of the key topics of these essays (focused most clearly perhaps in the chapter on the nineteenth century): the relation between visual reading and the endlessness of the text. The role of visualisation reflects the question of the status of perception of the external world and the role played by the imagination in perception (see 'Doubles' in ch. 4 of this book); it is also the problem of the relationship between the arts in a society in which labour – and thus the imagination – is divided. In a book which takes *Clarissa, Der Mann ohne Eigenschaften, À la recherche du temps perdu, Das Schloss* and *The Crying of Lot 49* as its exemplary texts, the theme of endlessness is unavoidable. (It reappears later in this introduction in the context of my partial indebtedness to the aesthetics of Bakhtin.) It can be argued that the near-interminability of these works is an aspect of their visionary pungency. Taken together, the themes of visualisation and endlessness reiterate the dialectic of my title: the conjunction poses the question of the relationship between the atemporality of the fantasy and the temporal structures of the realistic novel.

Critics often draw distinctions between realism and fantasy, generally as a move preliminary to declaring the one or the other the more 'novelistic' of the two. English writers lace the novel into leaden boots and place its feet in concrete, whilst continental theorists place it in a weightless zone where it hangs upside down, bat-like, a denizen of the night. However, what is typical of the novel is the way it enacts a dialectic of realism and fantasy, dream and disillusion, reproduction and distortion. One could say that the dialectic is founded on the interaction of 'poetry' and 'prose'. I retain these two words, despite their dubious nineteenth-century ring, because they are more honestly problematic than is the distinction between 'metaphor' and 'metonymy'; in many respects Jakobson's definition is a critical Ferrari with the engine of a model-T. It creates the illusion of precision in an area in which none actually exists, as becomes evident when one considers its fate in the criticism of Genette, which shows that in Proust it is impossible to separate the two terms. Pending the introduction of better terminology, I think it better to employ the older distinction: its very dubiousness is symptomatic of the degree to which the novel has questioned its dualism. For what is novel about the novel is its openness, the anti-formality that accompanies the general erosion of hierarchies after the sixteenth century. The fact that novels need not possess a rigid form does not make them fatally prone simply to 'happen', to stumble into the light as illiterate baggy monsters: rather, it allows them to provide a field for the clash and interaction of different forms.

The mix of poetry and prose characteristic of the great novels, the novels that exploit their freedom to bring two or more discourses into a space within which they deconstruct each other, is to a large, but incalculable, extent the consequence of the translation of the Bible into the vernacular. The Bible in Hebrew largely comprises verse. However, the verse-forms it employs – parallelistic and alliterative – had by the sixteenth century long ceased to be identified with verse in England. In *Euphues*, the devices of Anglo-Saxon poetry have become part of the panoply of prose, whilst the signifier of poetry is now rhyme. The Biblical language was neither one nor the other. What was new about the Reformation translations of the Bible was the way in which they created a text and a language in suspension, shot through with a powerful internal dialectic: on the one hand it possessed the hieratic quality of a sacred text, for even though no longer the sole preserve of the priest, it remained locked in the obscurity of prophecy and divine speech; but on the other hand, it was intended for the understanding and guidance of all men. In the countries of the Reformation the Bible in the vernacular created the language that seems to me to be the most fruitful for all novels: a language based on the mutual interrogation of poetry and prose, hierarchy and democracy. Pre-eminent among these countries were Germany and England – whence the main focus of this book – which were fortunate in the excellence of the translations made by Luther and King James's scholars. The novel both usurps hierarchies and undermines them. If it digs a tunnel under the castle, it generally removes the castle's wealth before blowing it up.

The Bible is the Book of the Protestant countries. The fact that it has never sunk deeply into the consciousness of the Catholic countries of Europe would suggest that the writers of those countries find it less easy to develop a language in which prose and poetry are held in mutual suspension. Thus the prose-poems of Baudelaire, Rimbaud and Mallarmé, the Whitmanesque lines of Verhaeren and Claudel, can be seen as an attempt to graft onto French the Biblical means of holding opposites in suspension. The self-conscious Satanism of the *fin de siècle* is part of its project to arrogate the Biblical style to profane life. If Edmund Wilson is right and the French were simply appropriating the stylistics of Shakespeare, they were also acquiring the stylistics of the late Elizabethan age, the age of the greatest English Biblical translations. If Proust is the greatest of French novelists, as I believe him to be, it is because he was the first inheritor of the newly won wealth. But he was able to exploit it to the full only because his Jewish heritage had made the prose-poetry of the Bible a near-natural idiom. Thus he can speak without strain of 'Sodome et Gomorrhe'. His continual procrastination before commencing *À la recherche* can be seen to stem from his lack of French precursors and mentors. Like the prophet Jonah, he shrank at first from the magnitude of the task laid upon him. For apart from a few vignettes by Nerval – himself largely extraterritorial to the French tradition and closer to the German Romantic one – there were no existing native resources for him to draw on. If his book is a modernist Bible, he is a reluctant scribe: the recalcitrant Jonah bearing a tallow lamp inside the whale.

Apart from Protestantism, there is of course another clear link between the German and the English literature juxtaposed within the confines of this book. Of the fiction concerned with the process of the composition and de-composition of the self, a strikingly large amount is influenced by or stems from German literature. One may think of *Frankenstein* or *Dr. Heidegger's Experiment*, in which the Germanic names of the heroes signal their intention to transmute the personality, just as the German personality was itself undergoing transformation and unification during this period. The influence of Hoffmann on Poe and Hawthorne is self-evident; but even the urbane Henry James selects gruesome motifs from the Gothic charnel. German literature evinces a profound fascination with the uncanny, an experience linked with post-Romantic reading, writing, and reading/writing, by the self-displacing nature of the reader's identification with what he reads. Where writing is inspiration, reading is possession. One may speculate endlessly on the reasons for this peculiarly Germanic experience, though to little avail. The German's sense of simultaneous identity and non-existence – the Romantic's proclamation of a national culture before the nation had come into being – may have caused his own selfhood to seem uncanny to him. The radical difference between German syntax and the syntax of the surrounding European nations may have induced a feeling of otherness among men; the more so since the pre-programmed patterns of this syntax often allow the individual to feel that he is less the master of his self-expression than the grease to its inevitable wheels. And for English and American writers in their turn, the Germanic may have seemed demonic because a resurgence of the Saxon element within the. English language would be tantamount to a return from the dead, to share power, by the language defeated during the Norman conquest; though perhaps a writerly fear of the untutored mob – and of the industrialising North – identified with the Saxon strain in the language, also played a part here. But, as I have said, these are merely speculations. If there is a deeply Germanic element at the heart of modernism – where the primary texts are Hegel and Freud – then any attempts to place a tourniquet around Germany to prevent it spreading must be abortive. As Poe said in his preface to the *Tales of the Grotesque and Arabesque*, the horror of the self 'is not of Germany, but of the soul'. If the German influence was so great, it was because in other countries the spores – forgive the pun – were ready for germination. There was a German Empire long before Bismarck: an empire of the mind, the ideal, and of the most non-conceptual, least realised, of all the arts: music. When the Empire descended into terrestrial reality, the mental kingdom was first aggrandised and then – in the Thirties – destroyed. May not the destruction of that intellectual kingdom – the burning of the books in German streets and in Canetti's *Die Blendung*, which bids farewell to the Germanic dream of the encyclopaedic novel, *Welt im Kopf* – have entailed the end of modernism itself? And may it not be only those, such as Pynchon, who rake over the Germanic ashes, who are able to rekindle some of the perished fire?

Perhaps this is a good point at which to say what I consider the word 'modernism' to mean. I use the word with reservations. Other words overlap with its frame of reference: 'neo-romanticism' and 'symbolism' are among the more closely conjunctive. Moreover, critical practice has stretched it to near-meaninglessness. One working definition of a modernist text would be that it mixes styles with the aim of subverting both realism and fantasy (*pace* Lukács); that it is in a sense Utopian in positing the existence of a language beyond its own mutually cancelling components. The subversion of styles prompts it to review its own status as language, and hence to use the artist- or writer-hero. The theme of writing links *Clarissa* and Kafka. Because there can be no satisfactory synthesis between the constitutive opposed terms of such works (in *Clarissa*, between the Bible and secular romance), these texts are endless. They are fragments, completed by history, or by the reader. But if the word 'modernism' is worth retaining, it is because it suggests a commitment to the novelty that is 'the novel'.

The great Russian aesthetician Mikhail Bakhtin has described the novel as a form committed to de-centralisation: it 'arose historically within the framework of de-centralising, centrifugal forces.'[4] It grew out of a picaresque play with speech, for which 'all "languages" were masks and there was no undisputed linguistic face.'[5] The parody depends on the form that pre-exists it; in this sense the novel is a late, a modern, even a decadent form, and Bakhtin rightfully distinguishes between its multiplicity and the monumentality of the epic; he is correct to defend the novel against those dogmatists like Lukács who would wish to transform it into a univocal epic. But the novel's parody of existing language is not simply play, and Bakhtin is wrong to overlook the extent to which it stems from a purely negative sense of identity. For the 'low' genres he praises belong by definition to those who are excluded from the high estate in which the forms they parody prevail. The parodic carnival is also the (democratic?) nightmare of the man without a social face.

The greatest novels are those which are conscious of the necessity that they be endless, for even their completed forms are but fragments. They cannot end, for they cannot allow any one idiom to achieve dominance. The texts of Musil and Kafka will their own incompletion; those of Richardson and Proust are rebuffed by their own endings and the energy that tended to rupture closure recoils back into the text in an endless trouble of revision, alteration and correction, and so the very fixity of the ending is disturbed as it is pushed further and further away by the intervening text. Pynchon, Hawthorne and John Fowles leave their texts in a state of deliberate suspension. The novels I consider in this book evince a growing self-awareness and a growing awareness of the premises of the medium. To begin with they are entangled with older forms of art, with allegory, religious tract and poetic epic. To begin with many of the novel's self-subversions are merely unconscious. In Hawthorne however – who is a key figure – the self-deconstructing nature of the medium begins to circle semi-visibly below the conscious surface of the text. In what is generally termed 'modernism' this aspect of the novel clearly ruffles the surface. Here the novelist realises that the fictionality of the identity of his own characters entails the fictionality of 'his own' identity. The growth of this awareness is essential to the passage from Victorian to modernist aesthetics; to repress it is to fall into inauthenticity, like Thomas Mann in his early books, or into blind monotonous egotism, like Dickens. As the novelist questions the unity of his own self, he is driven to test and verify his words against other art forms; hence the illustrated novel is a precursor of the works of the painter-writers, writer-musicians and writer-philosophers of the turn of the century. For the turn of the century represents a moment of general realisation that the novel is too serious a matter to leave to the novelists. (It is Mann's isolation of the novelist, his merely decorative use of ideas, that renders so much of his work debilitatingly frivolous.) The writer becomes conscious of a need to test his fictions, not simply indulge them. That is why much of the greatest modernist fiction is para-fiction, a testing of fiction against autobiography, against philosophy, against religion, against history and science. This is the strength of the greatest of the modernist writers, Musil, Kafka and Proust.

Raymond Williams has stressed the degree to which novelists in the nineteenth century are concerned with the problematic status of the 'knowable community': with the bewildering community of Dickens's city, with the circumscribed, phenomenologically isolated community of Conrad's ship or Hardy's Wessex. During the nineteenth century the knowable community first becomes semi-knowable and then finally evaporates. As industrialisation, urbanisation and colonialism do their work, people are prised out of the closed shells of their communities and pass through various semi-transparent social groups into the isolation of the opaque community. This passage through the semi-knowable to the opaque is documented in the stages of the attenuation of the genius of Henry James in particular, as he passes from the wisdom, beauty and absolute linguistic rightness of the early novels to the frustrations of the late style, in which content slides away under the cover of a wondering detachment. The passage from the semi-knowable to the opaque necessitates a shift in the foundations of the novel, from the realism of the nineteenth century to the fantasy of the twentieth, in which fantasy comes to fulfil the function of presenting a realistic image of the baffling momentariness of phenomena. It is the inability to lift his anchor from the bed of realism that causes the terribly sad deterioration of the work of James. James is the stepping-stone from the realism of the knowable community to the opacity of the fantastic one; he reaches the world of blankness by shuttling perpetually back and forth between two communities which are only semi-comprehensible to each other, between America and Europe. At points one can hear the machinery of the transition creaking, as when he refers to a character seeking the right word in French or Italian, although there had been no previous indication that any language other than English was being spoken; here the realism contradicts itself, without gaining the freedom of fantasy.

In the course of the century, the fictive element that accompanies the sociological one in the novels of Emily Brontë, Hardy, and the other novelists of the latter nineteenth century, gradually dislodges the social reality that is the basis of the realist style, thus generating the more purely fictive, more attenuatedly 'realistic', style of the modernists, for whom the knowable community has all but disappeared in the phantasmagoria of the city: the 'fourmillante cité, cité pleine de rêves'. Thus it is instructive to observe the fates of the three major English novelists who span the period of the transition: James, Conrad and Hardy.

In James, life in the city – the London of *The Awkward Age* – becomes life in a void against which collective narcissism, the fatuities of mutual self-admiration, provides insufficient protection. In Conrad the sense of community is preserved only artificially, by isolating people on a ship or behind a mountain range, as in *Nostromo*; yet it is the measure of his greatness that the deliberately isolated community is not a point of nostalgic repose, for that community itself is a microcosm of larger diversities, is comprised of foreigners all 'in the same boat'. Hardy in turn finally renounces the novel; the gesture of the man who lies in the sun and pulls his cap over his eyes, which Hillis Miller has described as emblematic of Hardy's position, is part of a tactical withdrawal from reality, via the semi-reality of 'Wessex', and into a realm inhabited by the stunned spectres of desire. Hardy's ultimate decision to devote himself to poetry alone is of suggestive resonance in the context of this book, for it sends rippling impulses along the airy web of its argument: namely, that modernist fiction – to my mind, the peak to which fiction tended and from which it then declined – was founded on a dialectic of prose and poetry. Compared with Victorian fiction, modernist novels may seem simply poetic; in fact they are prose-poems, burdened with the unhappy consciousness of the chameleon, which can neither be poetry nor prose. The heavier weight of poetic elements and stresses required by modernism shattered the bases of Hardy's realistic fiction; the poetry displaced the fiction, and the characters of the fiction remained with Hardy as the insistent presences, the poignant absences, of his great poems. His diverse styles cancelled each other out.

The process of the genesis of modernism also underlies the difference between, say, Kierkegaard and Proust. That which is inconsistent in a novel like Kierkegaard's *Repetition* is due largely to the inappropriateness of the historical moment; it finds its appropriate form in Proust, who experiences the dissolution of the nineteenth-century belief in the wholeness of the individual, a belief that had confused Kierkegaard's pseudonymous aesthetics with the accents of the evangelist, for whom each man is one and responsible. Proust's moment is of course also the moment at which Lawrence's unrecognisable individual passes through allotropic states. These states are the lunar phases of the personality: it is typical of Lawrence's belief in the deep interdependency of the sexes that both his men and his women pass through stages like the moon. If personality is subject to modulation, then so is point of view. Hence there is a profound relationship between modernity and a sense of the relativity of perceptions. This relativity has less in common with agnosticism than with the knowledge that people are often 'beside themselves': with worry, on off-days, in ecstasy. Perception becomes transmigration within the set of possibilities open to, the rules of the game laid down for, the self. That is why, to my mind, the modern novel germinates from *Clarissa*: the epistolary novel illustrates relativity in action, from *Pamela* to Henry James's short story 'The Point of View' and beyond. This importance of 'point of view' indicates the nature of the relationship between modernism and the image of the double (see my essay on 'Doubles' in ch. 4), for the double only exists because the self is a 'shifter', and can invade the place of the other. The epistolary novel is of course not the only modernist form, but it seems to me to be the primal one. Its conscious stylistic fragmentation prefigures the stylistic variety of Musil, Pynchon and Proust. Its use of juxtaposition anticipates the method of setting up montages of monologues in the late Kafka. It is a precursor of the first-person narrator beset with existential solipsism. The variable style foregrounds the relationship between a writer's language and his imagination, between the unreal reality of language that is a keynote of French literary theory and the importance of 'character' to the English realist. The epistolary novel demonstrates that the novel conceived as a linguistic artefact is not necessarily opposed to the novel of character: in the epistolary novel, each character is a different language, and the novel has no hero, no privileged language. The stylistic fragmentation typical of modernist works is in its turn a concomitant of the development of democracy since the seventeenth century; one has to be relatively free and socially mobile to be able to imagine the thoughts of another person, to project oneself into his shoes. To this extent the apparent anarchism of the imagination is an agent of sober democracy. But the variety it engenders is not necessarily God's plenty, or life in its fullness. The modernist novel lives in fear of the void that underlies all the languages, the advertised selves and pseudo-selves, available to the individual. For the person one imagines – one's alternative self – is by virtue of his or her imaginary status no more than a pseudo-person.

Once the moment of fruitful tension between the knowable reality of the classic Victorian novel and the dematerialisation of the knowable community in the modernist novel – the novel of the big city – had passed, then the dialectic that had powered the great modernist novels collapsed. If modernism is still alive, it is not in Europe, which has left this moment in the remote past, and where realism and fantasy have negotiated a truce which allows them to cultivate their own academic gardens. The best Europe can manage is pseudo-modernism, as in Sarraute and Fowles. Sarraute's critique of the psychological novel from which her work descends undermines the bases of psychology by demonstrating the extent to which the stable ego has been fractured into 'tropisms', but it fails to draw the necessary conclusions and place the novelist herself in the critical dock. Instead, she sacrifices the narrator to save the skin of the novelist – like a more hard-bitten version of the late James. Thus her work constitutes a step back from that of Proust; she exempts herself from the *mise en abîme* of narrators. In Fowles, by way of contrast, the modernist superimposition of the sociological on the fantastic which renders *The French Lieutenant's Woman* so fascinating is also rather heavy-handed, for the profound difference between this and his other novels gives it the air of an exercise in an only partly mastered continental genre. It is the lack of mastery, however, that lends the work its freshness and preserves it from the triviality of more accomplished French *divertissements* in the same mode. But if the over-secure establishment of a 'tradition of modernism' has dissipated the sense of modernism by removing the experimental danger that accompanied it, the lack of such a tradition in the United States has enabled a few of the best of contemporary American novelists – Thomas Pynchon in particular – to experiment in a mode that is not merely post-Mallarméan and verbal, but existential too. True, Melville, Hawthorne and James had groped towards modernist methods, but all were pre-modernist, and in any case the differences between them combined with the sheer diversity of the States themselves to preclude any attempts to distil a unified tradition from their works, as Gide, the great middle-man, had distilled one from the various Symbolists. Modernism emerged out of the great Empires because they alone provided the individual with the means to dream of new worlds of the mind. The self-consciousness of the modernists reflected the self-doubts of these Empires the moment before their decline: self-consciousness may be said to fulfil a similar function in the recent American descendants of the modernists. The continuity between literary and scientific experiment at the turn of the century is most apparent perhaps in Musil and Freud – the novelist also being an inventor and mathematician, whilst the psychoanalyst was a great stylist – but it can also be seen in the genetic experiments to which Proust subjects nineteenth-century psychology. The individualism of the late nineteenth century is also mirrored in the exposed condition of the American individual, the teeth of whose ambitions have not been drawn by a welfare state. But there is a difference between the modernism of the beginning of the twentieth century and that of the nineteen sixties – which deliberately harked back to *art nouveau* – and it lies in the growing number of obstacles to prevent the individual from pursuing his experiment to its logical conclusion. The problem lies in the fact that literature itself has become a fully industrialised business, where experiment is senseless because mass-produced, instantly copied. And many a literary experimentalist is less an intrepid explorer than a man without a skin, preserved under glass in the academic hospital. Perhaps only Pynchon has been consistent and has recognised that the pursuit of experiment entails unremitting silence, exile and cunning.

The last sentence of the previous paragraph rehearses the famous Joycean prescription for artistic survival. Many critics have dubbed Joyce the presiding genius of the modern American novel; thus it may seem surprising that I have omitted him from this book. However, it seems to me that although Joyce has been canonised as the arch-experimentalist of the century, his experiments are more concerned to freeze and conclude thought than to stimulate and explore it. If both Joyce and Pynchon are masters of the quotation, they employ it to radically different ends: for Pynchon, the quotation is wreckage, frag-ment, waste, whereas for Joyce the act of quoting metonymically ingests the thing quoted, and the litany of quotations adds up to a scholastic summa. Where Pynchon is suggestive and fascinating, Joyce is exhaus-tive and exhausting. There is a fundamental difference between pas-tiche, parody and *style indirect libre* as practised by Musil, Proust and

Kafka (in Kafka it is the language of bureaucracy that is quoted) and that of Joyce. Throughout his life, Joyce is unwilling either to leave or to remain in a series of things: Ireland and Dublin, the family, marriage, normal sexuality, language. In an early story like 'A Little Cloud' one sees him fearful both of exile and of self-confinement in Dublin, of becoming either a Gallagher or a Little Chandler. In the end he is able to achieve self-respect only by renouncing his own language, and then discarding each style as he adopts it. In *Ulysses*, the fact that each section has its own style provides him with a continual escape clause by permitting him to have truck with a style on the condition that he be allowed to vacate it immediately after occupation. He inhabits a no-man's-land between language and music – expressionism and variations on a theme. But he does not abandon the individual voice for parody, as does the late Mann. Mann is aware that parody entails a certain love for the parodied object; it also presupposes a certain knowledge of that object. But Joyce's disgust with style and with existing literature is so great that he never spends sufficiently long at the feet of another author to need to resort to parody in order to escape him. Joyce was perhaps the only writer this century not to have suffered the anxiety of influence. Yet he needs the voice of the other just as a demon needs a body to possess, just as Proteus requires the shapes that are his momentary abodes. So he begins to write a variety of pseudo-parody, parody of the genre of parody; not parody of a particular object or person, not the kind of loving, appalled mimicry that has long been lavished on Wordsworth, but an approximate and half-hearted notation of something akin to a stylistic Zeitgeist. It is half-hearted because no particular style is the object of his animus; all can be adopted – almost all are – and all can be discarded equally casually. His parody is half-hearted inasmuch as most of its libido is fixated on its own technical virtuosity. What distinguishes this variety of parody from parody proper is that its object is not the famous but the anonymous; the typical writer of a past age, the poetaster of the popular magazine. The effect is perverse and depressing; masochistically, the author throws his reproductive talents away on texts that are not worth it. (He does not, like Pynchon, seek in them the solidarity of the preterite.) *Ulysses* is a long footnote to *Bouvard et Pecuchet*, with the paired characters assigned to different generations to secure the illusion of development. In Joyce, as in Hemingway, there seems to be a belief that modernity is simply a matter of avoiding sins of commission, of taking a traditionally realist text and mining it with gaps or with symbols: of sowing with potholes the otherwise smooth road of Natural-ist objectivism. Joyce neatly evades the difficulties attendant on the creation of a style and the evolution of a form of expression, for he claims to have all styles at his disposal (Here Comes Everybody), and never to need to choose between them. The separate styles thus become arbitrary, but they conceal the fact of their arbitrariness by allowing themselves to function as building-blocks in a narrative (this abuse of various styles is invalidated by Pynchon's 'V', in which it is shown that as a result of the adoption of multiple styles, narrative becomes the evanescent object of an allusion). Joyce will not concede that the same event can be revealed not to be the same at all through presenting it from different viewpoints, by means of different styles. The suppression of *Stephen Hero* is a repression of the validity of different styles: instead it is replaced with the more objective style of *A Portrait of the Artist*. This in turn gives way to the styles of *Ulysses* and of *Finnegans Wake*, which reveal Joyce's goal as the all-engulfing super-style, which will be all things to all men. Joyce pretends – like Barthes, incidentally – that one can quote from a culture without to some extent endorsing that culture. It is Pynchon's awareness that this is an impossibility, his joint love and hatred of the language he moves through, that renders him the most important living 'English' writer and enables him to conduct two-way forays across the frontiers of 'American' and 'English' English.

The following book is a collection of essays, some of them overtly related, some of them not. However, its author does not view the essay as the offspring of *belles lettres*. He follows Adorno in viewing it as the form in which it is most salutary and appropriate to conduct aesthetic investigations: it opposes both the monotony and self-righteousness of the pure theorist and the myopia of the positivist. These essays strive to develop theories in the context of particular analyses, testing the one against the other, lest theory become a modish or dateless slogan, and analysis mechanical.

1 Notes on the Novel

Stories that are not recounted from age to age are seen as fiction; they are read, not heard. The last teller of the true story transcribes it lest it be lost. He does so because people are refusing to credit it: similar events no longer occur, God no longer intervenes in daily life, there were Giants in *those* days. But even the act of pious recording partakes of the impiety it seeks to combat, for it presupposes that communion with God is an abnormal state that is unlikely to recur in the near future. The scribe is a man of little faith. General inability to believe the story – the Israelites' unwillingness to accept their sacred history – transforms history into a fiction. History becomes 'story' (as in the vocabulary of the Romantics) and children are instructed not to 'tell stories', i.e. not to lie. The fact that the written appears to be untrue (Plato was right to assert that writing weakens the memory) justifies conscious untruth in writing: the historian paradoxically prepares the way for the novelists. The first of these were the writers of the Apocrypha. The novel is an impossible history, for history has become impossible. It is powered by a negative Utopianism: it creates an image of an artificial reality, but not of a better one, as a prophet would. The Jews could ignore Christ because history had become for them a novel. And Utopia is the beginning of fiction and its end. The earliest novels are Utopias that end with a distribution of prizes. Modern novels are Dystopias, the sting in the tail of the earlier desire to leave this world for a better one. For whilst one was reading one lost track of the world and so was unable to return to it. One was trapped far away from it in dreaming isolation – like Emma Bovary. Sienkiewicz's abominable story about the Polish lighthouse-keeper who loses his job because he forgot about the ships whilst engrossed in *Pan Tadeusz* is an image of how the daydream of escape turns into a nightmare.

Children ask for a story before going to bed; hearing a story at bedtime associates the loss of one world with the birth of another. The bedtime story is an advance instalment on the next day. To read a story during

17

the day itself is to dissolve the boundaries between reality and fiction, to see reality as inextricably interwoven with fiction. One does not work during the day and then receive the transformed image of that day as payment with which to purchase the next day. One replaces work with fiction because the very notion of work has become a fiction; in the pre-stabilised harmony of a static society, which fears that a change would deprive it of more well-being than of chains, work becomes phantasmal, a legal fiction. Each mass-produced object, and person, is the ghost of another.

One writes fiction when the notion of comprehending society has become a fiction, when there are no more thrones from which to survey all corners of the land. Balzac did not begin his *Comédie Humaine* with the aim of picturing an entire society: its unity was hidden from him at first by the opacity of detail. Hence his system is imposed *a posteriori* and from the moment of its inception saps his work, as the novelist identifies with the power that is withheld from him and makes inflated claims about his ability to see everything. It is in the *a posteriori* nature of his system that there lies the key difference between him and Dante. Moreover, Dante puts actual acquaintances in the after-world that is an X-ray of this one – not phantoms of desire. They pursue opposite directions: for Dante, reality becomes phantasmal and transparent when viewed from the divine perspective; for Balzac, phantoms become reality for deluded humans. In Balzac, fiction is a compensatory, predatory appropriation of a world that is amenable to fiction because it is shot through with it: the social world is a panoply of lies made flesh.

One only identifies with the hero of a novel if one does not think of oneself: one's imaginary triumph is a reward for self-sacrifice. If one is so oppressed by one's experience that one follows the chimera conjured by a fleeting resemblance and strives to establish point-for-point correspondences between one's own life and that of the hero, thereby lifting one's meagre life to the level of Meaning – if one does this, one fails both as a reader and in reality. In the face of a real need for change, art's merely imaginary transmogrification of the world seems but a mockery. In such depressions we can only read poems: their greater degree of generalisation and of concretion prevents us from becoming disillusioned by discrepancies between our lives and those of the hero, for the speaker is everyone and no one, and the density of language that forces us to work restores our self-respect. The dissolution of the distinction between novel and poem is the great works of this century – in Lawrence, Conrad, Proust, Kafka, or Musil, for instance – reflects their solidarity with the suffering. The novels of the previous century had been a luxury, for their language had resisted memory, it had wasted with the largesse of a colonialist stumbling upon a seemingly boundless empire. Our novels are shorter, more functional, and even when they are longer, all the elements are used up in the often paranoid plot. Close readings of nineteenth-century novels are ludicrous (they have to leap endlessly back and forth between psychoanalysis and aesthetic appreciation): the guilty nineteenth-century individual seeks to hide himself in their dense thickets. The modern novel, by contrast, is cursed with self-knowledge: the knowledge that each 'he' is also an 'I'.

There are people who refer to themselves in the third person or by their own Christian names whenever they relate painful or embarrassing experiences; to disown one's own being is to permit narrative to come into being, as one's silent self identifies with the tolerant mocking voice of one's family. The third person is a tourniquet on infected experiences, a dreamlike displacement. By turning the disavowed experience into narrative, by outwitting the native silence of pain and embarrassment, one passes the experience on like a plague. Thus the novel is the dominant art-form of a society with a guilty conscience, as is also evident from the fact that it is commonly consumed in shameful solitude; pain drove the European nations to flee their own countries and become colonisers, and guilty conscience over the consequences of colonialism and industrialism dictated the narration in the third person, whose basic gesture is 'I am not responsible'. As always, 'he' is guilty. Writing weakens the memory, acts as an agent who helps one repress awareness of one's past crimes; it is no accident that in Kafka bureaucracy is identified with writing. Following 'the toilet assumption' described by Philip Slater in *The Pursuit of Loneliness*, the logorrhoea of the nineteenth century seeks to flush experience away. It locks it up in the pages and throws the key into the river of time.

Narrative in the present tense attempts to break down the complacency induced by the preterite, which implies that because B succeeded A, A was its cause; the present tense is attuned to an unpredictable reality. But the attempt fails: we hold the book in our hands and know that it has been completed, belongs to the past. Such devices reflect the author's yearning to recapture the excitement of episodic, serial composition, to introduce a greater immediacy into his relationship to a public he comes to fear is no longer there. Narrative in the present tense is Don Quixote tilting at the windmill of the book. The use of the present has been lauded by Barthes as a means of exploding the fixed orders and hierarchies implicit in the preterite. But he fails to perceive that the novel in the present tense has its repressive side too; it strives for a portentous pseudo-immediacy that itself keeps the reader in his place by preventing him from judging, by insisting that events are still open, that the text be swallowed whole. The novel reacts thus out of fear of rejection: it says: 'see, my time is your time'. Writing in the present tense displays an anxious false consciousness: it casts a sidelong envious glance at film, the art-form that knows only the present.

Film is breathless and unhalting because it is a race across the disintegrating ice of narrative continuity. Isolated images have the pathos of fragments or aphorisms, which cannot intervene in any debate, not even that of the story they mediate. Books of stills would be valid if films were novels and let us linger. But in film the traditional narrative meets its crisis. In film, the isolated and heterogeneous elements have to be steamrollered into a two-hour, exitless freeway because the audience is no longer believed to be interested enough to finish reading a story of its own accord. The alienations, disruptions, enforced mobility and endless television of the last few decades have cut the threads of continuous narrative. Whether the reader be Roland Barthes or a man educated by advertisments to require instant impact, he often tends not to finish the work but to see it as a symptom of an area from which he is excluded ('culture', or 'the past'), leaving him homeless in both past and present. Thus the absurd Structuralist talk of reality's absence becomes justifiable: to stay on the surface of a work, to see in it only abstract binary structures (the first phase of Structuralism) or an ineffable whirl of transformation (its second phase) is to be true to one's sense of alienation from it. Film violently compacts the elements of narrative in order to raise one's chances of getting to the end of a work. But even in film, which keeps alive the belief in one's ability to outlast the world, of which the work is a model, and so achieve an earthly resurrection, the separate elements fly apart in the unconscious. Thus one feels unease after even so apparently straightforward a film as *Klute*: the strength of Jane Fonda's acting undermines the male privilege inscribed in the title. For in a pluralist, opportunist era, the collaborative effort demanded by film usually results in incoherence.

Fiction is about how people become other people, as the increasing rate of change leads us to project the emotions we harboured for one person onto another, so that our images of 'real' people become contaminated with fantasy to an ever greater degree. In this sense, the description of nineteenth-century fiction as 'realistic' is accurate: reality is becoming so phantasmal as to be fictional, as Freud was to recognise when removing the clothes worn by our fantasy images of others to unmask their disparity from the (probably unattainable) real. People come to appear as after-images, living corpses (compare Poe), their being compulsively prolonged to buffer the shock of change. Fiction is closely related to the growth of the city. One constructs a life on the basis of a gesture at the opposite window to blot out one's subjective sense of emptiness in the face of phenomena one cannot name. People seen momentarily in a crowd are known yet unknown, and fiction silently names them: it erects a consolatory biography for the other and then dismisses it (and him, chained to it) as mere fiction, as 'non-existent'. Thus fiction also assuages one's sense of guilt at denying the other his humanity as one rushes past him in the street. As environments rapidly alter, history becomes 'story' (the history of Tom Jones is now his story), and when children 'tell stories' they lie; applied to children, the phrase underlines the inevitability and necessity of compulsive lying, which results from an inability to adjust to the abruptness of change. (It is also an ironic attempt to see whether or not the other knows one sufficiently well to distinguish one's reality from one's smoke-screen. This factor was surely at work in the formation of Thomas Mann's style.) History itself becomes a fiction – obviously so in the reconstructed pasts of *Nineteen Eighty-Four* and the novels of Pynchon. Thus in films it becomes possible to cast a person in a role and not know whether he or she is mis-cast or type-cast, for the illusoriness of our pictures of others makes it increasingly irrelevant whether or not the two match (the Bee Gees or utterly dissimilar 'look-alikes' can play the parts of the Beatles) – indeed, they erode all criteria for checking the degree of fit. Meanwhile, the increasing uniformity of the totality and its growing pressure on the individual wear away his features to render him interchangeable with others, inject him with the paranoid fear that crowds of doubles wait to replace him. People are coins whose faces share the same muddy, worn imprecision, and any one of them will fit the slot of the machine.

Novels in the present tense are likely to seem academic, in danger of arbitrariness. Since we are *here* and on the spot from which the narration is issuing, we feel that it would always have been possible to select a different detail from the immediate scene: or rather, we feel no need to select any object, for they are all still here. Narration in the present tense lacks the authority a story derives from the reader's knowledge that it is irrevocably past, transcribed unalterably in the Book of the Dead. It refuses to die. Thus its illusions are very modern ones; we act as if we were immortal. The present tense grants the reader the illusion of participation, of presence, and so renders even more bitter his actual absence. Its advent parallels that of the similarly structured post-war pseudo-democracies.

The novel arises when people have become so complex, fragmented and contradictory that they have to be written down to be remembered. The lepidopterist's pin transfixes them so as to be able to observe them at leisure and determine their principle of unity, 'what makes them tick'. Novels reassure us that we still have characters, that we have not become triads (ego, id and super-ego) or even swarming crowds of disconnected impulses. It fulfils this consolatory function in an age whose pressures often prevent the formation of a stable central ego, as Adorno has shown. The novelist is crucified on our behalf: he splits himself in order to create images of people as wholes. Only the Expressionist novelist, such as Musil, is able to confide in us the fact that he too is divided; and in the case of Musil, it is this division that prevents him from completing his novel. But from the traditional, realist novel we learn the fact of identity in order to pass the exam of life, the rules of which have become so rigid as to detach themselves from its actuality.

2 *Clarissa*, Dialectic and Unreadability

To discuss the novels of Samuel Richardson in terms of the tradition of dialectical thought may seem perverse. Nevertheless, it seems to me that both he and the German writers in this tradition exemplify more strongly than any others I know the dialectical problem of the relationship between the aesthetic and the didactic. I talk of 'dialectic' in general, rather than of particular dialecticians, because *Clarissa* does in fact contain two separate dialectics and thus links modern dialectic to traditional dialectic: it embodies an orthodox Hegelian dialectic, whereby the stages of Clarissa's suffering and martyrdom constitute a 'positive' dialectic, in which the negation of the negation leads to an affirmation and the manifestation of the Absolute: Clarissa becomes a saint; and it develops a 'negative' dialectic, such as has been advocated by Adorno, which sees suffering as purely wasteful, as it is in the case of Lovelace. In Hegel, as later in Marx, dialectic is predominantly optimistic and didactic; in Adorno, the damage suffered by the cherished ideals of enlightenment drives the dialectician towards the consolations of the aesthetic mode. Richardson is poised between the two. In this respect he anticipates the great modernists, Musil, Proust, Kierkegaard and Mann in particular, all of whom were torn between moralism and aestheticism. And his current topicality – stemming from his concern with feminism and with the problematic of 'writing' associated with Post-Structuralism – is itself an illustration of the dialectical reversal whereby an extremely unfashionable author can become a precursor of vital urgency.

Dialectic – dialogue within the self (as opposed to Socrates' dialogue with others) – arises out of the clash between the ethical and the aesthetic modes of perception. In *Clarissa* the novel is born as the opposites are personified allegorically as 'Clarissa' (The Didactic) and 'Lovelace' (The Aesthetic), and then allowed to commence a complex, dizzying interplay, which may seem like 'giving them their freedom to be real people', but is in fact a consequence of the vertiginous logic of dialectical thinking, which permits opposites to change places. The contradictori-

23

ness of dialectical thought stems from an awareness of the degree to which the mind is hamstrung by the schizophrenia that distinguishes opposites from each other: the classes, the sexes, fiction and reality, prose and poetry. Thus in *Das Kapital* Marx sought to create both a scientific economics and an artistic whole; thus Adorno extends the notion of science to include intuition. The fact that *Clarissa* was immensely popular in Europe cannot be unconnected with the European propensity for dialectical thought. Virtually no other English novel has had this wide resonance. In demanding how we are to choose between Lovelace and Clarissa, Balzac is posing a dialectical question. It was not one that bothered the nineteenth-century English novel overmuch, as it willed amnesia of Richardson and the eighteenth century, thus condemning itself to the awkwardness in handling ideas that mars the work of even the best of its novelists, George Eliot. Perhaps only a Leavisite wilfulness could deem *Middlemarch* the greatest English novel, and not *Clarissa*.

Richardson, like other dialectical and modernist writers, produces texts whose fascination lies in the way they refuse to fit any clearly defined frame of reference. One can read them each year like a Bible, or once only, as a mere verbal diversion. But if Johnson rightly remarked that Richardson had chosen the kernel of life and Fielding merely the shell, and if dialectic is still the dominant mode of Continental thought, this richness arises from a dialectic of openness and closure that renders his texts supremely readable and yet somehow unreadable. For dialectical texts accept every meaning we care to attribute to them and then allow these meanings to cancel each other out. They imbue us with contrary feelings of belonging and futility: we belong in the text, which in the modern world may be our only home, for the dialectical projection has taken us into account; but our presence is superfluous, we have nothing to add, for all has already been said. The authors of these works have such power over us because they are really crowds. The popular – the star – is perhaps that which is so enigmatic as to allow us to remake it – unknow it – in our own image: we adore it because it frees us to create whilst using its structures to control us, to preserve us from losing our way. But in adoring it we forget its aggressiveness. For the writer who resorts to enigma seems to use it to ensure that he is not forgotten: the crowd within him, the absorbed tradition, already tells him how little his individuality is worth, and he seeks to perpetuate it aggressively by 'giving us something to remember him by'. The Mona Lisa is the least forgotten painting of all time because we seek in vain to counter its provocation: a provocation inscribed not merely in the famous smile but in the image's obstinate suspension between a portrait and a religious painting: it mixes genres. Everyone gathers round the enigma that has given birth to literary criticism. This literature contains the seeds of the crowds it attracts; the panlogism attributed to dialectical thinkers and certainly apparent in Richardson is the word passed on in the endless crowd in an endless modern city street.

Clarissa is a dialectical novel: that is, it has the structure of dialectical argument, alternating between separation out and dizzying unification of elements. Frederic Jameson describes the dialectical change of gear thus:

> There is a breathlessness about this shift from the normal object-oriented activity of the mind to such dialectical self-consciousness – something of the sickening shudder we feel in an elevator's fall or in the sudden dip of an airliner. That recalls us to our bodies as much as this recalls us to our mental positions as thinkers and observers. The shock indeed is basic, and constitutive of the dialectic as such: without this transformational element, without this initial conscious transcendence of an older, more naive position, there can be no question of any genuinely dialectical coming to consciousness.[1]

This account is, of course, phenomenological, but serves us well in the stress it lays upon shock and the transcendence of the naive, which permit us to relate dialectical form with the novel's prevailing theme of suspicion and with the suddenness of its few cardinal actions. The account's limitation as a description both of dialectic in general and of the novel in particular lies in its overestimation of the power of shock; for the element of stasis in dialectic[2] lends the shock a spectral predictability that mutes its subversiveness. Richardson's reader experiences a similar shock whenever apparently opposed figures or actions emerge as being in league, as when Anna Howe suggests that Clarissa may be enamoured of Lovelace or when Lovelace himself fears that he may be an engine of James Harlowe's designs. Here we are jolted and suffer the dizziness implicit in such remarks as Einstein's observation that a man with phenomenal eyesight would be able to see the back of his own head. For at such moments the characters achieve the hallucinatory vision that permits them to occupy another's viewpoint. These moments are thus both intensely revealing and implausible. Revealing, for they stress the individual's unreliability and so demonstrate the need to place one's trust in the transcendental viewpoint of God, one of the book's primary themes. And yet implausible, for the individual viewpoint is all we are ever given at any one time (even Editor is one of the participants): having breached the normal order, these moments hang unrelated on the other side. (These moments can also occur virtually anywhere, thus erasing the normal/extraordinary distinction, but I will return to this later in my remarks on paranoia and the reader's participation). The undermining of individuality paradoxically also supports the view of one individual, Clarissa; though, to continue the paradox, her privilege stems from her willingness to dissolve individuality into the family, the traditional typology of martyrdom, and a plain style that is so transparent as to be invisible. Her glass-clear style is a chameleon: hence she is also Lovelace. His colours are frozen into a rainbow, whereas hers revolve so quickly as to create the whiteness of innocence. The dialectical shift is and is not a shock; the individual's freedom to speculate about events and motives in epistolary form both causes shocks and effects recovery from them by means of their traumatic reproduction. Speculation[3] anticipates every action so as to spatialise it, blurring it backwards and forwards so it becomes its own ghost.[4]

The dialectical text is what it is not and what it will be: the density of perceptions and sentences poised beyond the individual utterance threatens to invade it (hence Richardson frequently uses brackets to siphon them off.) Gopnik has produced an interesting examination of some of the multiple ironies that result. Nevertheless, his stressing of conscious, ironical echoes and of the recurrent patterns of isolated words leads him to ignore the maxims which glide through the text, and whose latent ironies may or may not cause them to blast themselves out of their contexts. Their abstraction from the reality above which they float represents a species of displacement which both allows us to apply them elsewhere in the book and to doubt the legitimacy of our doing so. In making us intervene whilst rendering intervention dangerous, they force us to share the characters' paranoia. When Clarissa writes, 'who knows not that difficulty gives poignancy to our enjoyments'[5], she is not thinking of Lovelace, yet this sentence parallels his enterprise with her own and so both supports and undermines her. The notion of irony deployed by Gopnik as a means of description seems less useful than that of dialectic: for the association of irony with sophistication (although Jameson identifies dialectic with lack of naïvety, Adorno, following Benjamin, has allowed for a non-sophisticated dialectic) expresses unwittingly the modern fascination with Lovelace that frequently causes readings of the work as a series of surreal and bravura set-pieces interspersed with some dull moralising, a fascination that eliminates the very tension upon whose energy it is fixated. It seems that the variations are less usefully seen as ironies than as *Aufhebungen*: syntheses, acts of preservation and cancelling out. Hence the dialectical text represents a process, enacts a history: 'it does not take up a standpoint in advance', as Adorno notes.[6] The abruptness of its end is a dialectical antidote to its apparently endlessly ricocheting prolixity or panlogism: it has the unexpectedness of self-critical silence in mid-phrase.

Dialectic stems from isolation, be it that of the Utopian or that of the exile (Marx and Adorno were both). This isolation is oppositional, for the dialectical writer is powerless to execute this thoughts[7]: his position is that of a child within the family. This child is adolescent, on the threshold of power and yet still impotent: for him, tolerance is repressive. In Richardson, dialectical thought is the form of expression of youth, which lacks the fathers' privilege of dogmatic statement and stammers between Classicist stasis (approbation of the given world) and Romantic rebellion, as it does in Hegel. The dialectical leap is a means of holding together the totality of European life in the face of nationalism's inroads, but the shock wherewith thought meets the other testifies to the irreversibility of the trend. Thus Richardson both borrowed from the French – this is one reason for his success in France – and denied the debt, as if in anticipation of the Romantic idea that separate languages embody different universes: thus what can be borrowed is only external, inessential. This may also explain Coleridge's duplicity regarding his plagiarisms of Schlegel and Kant. The dialectical thinker takes the place of any possible opponent because the fathers sit internalised in his breast; this is the source of Clarissa's Puritan self-scrutiny. As a result of this, he may be accused of panlogism[8] or cunning in executing the ruses of reason, as his positive-negative tropism mimics pacing up and down in the stripped prison of consciousness. One may be pacing out the prison on another's behalf or pacing it in desperation oneself, the former being Lovelace's and the latter Clarissa's dialectics respectively: this is the duality of dialectic as described by Adorno.[9] Dialectic represents the will's attempt to transcend the moment into which it fears all history is freezing. To see oneself as another sees one is to create that other and so break into a new time and defeat isolation. This escape – often via allusion such as Lovelace's (Adorno's texts are also highly allusive) – introjects the other and so reduces the self to the level of helpless play. For Lovelace's stratagems are not simply means of securing Clarissa, since he delights in them for their own sakes; though on the level of rationalisation, he interposes the plots between himself and her in order to hold her at a

distance from which he can idealise her, from which aesthetic contemplation will lend appositeness to the omnipresent language of art; whilst
on yet another level, he does so because the divine principle will not
permit him to enter her charmed circle (except for one moment – the
crux of the book, shrouded in darkness like the Crucifixion). His
consistent delay is both lascivious lingering and expressive of a desire to
escape from his own actions, as is the suppression by him of any
description of the rape. Paradoxically, Richardson's personal intention
of condemning Lovelace is contradicted by his validation of Lovelace's
image of her – it is Lovelace who first sees her as a saint, ascending to
angels whilst a pit yawns below himself – whilst his inability to outlive
her for long suggests some deeper inter-dependence. If Clarissa is
spirited away by Death the lover, Morden (who comes to see her at her
death and whose name signifies *mors*) is Death encountering Lovelace.
Part of the book's dialectic is that it leaves Clarissa's fate clear and
Lovelace's cloudy: were he simply to be condemned and damned,
Clarissa's hope that he might be forgiven would be merely vain wishful
thinking, perhaps even the result of unconquered inner love, and would
in any case dislocate mercy from justice. Another reason for Richardson's hesitation here is that whereas for Clarissa death is a continuation
of life (so that earthly life's other name is death, carnality) and hence
imaginable on the basis of previous experience (this explains the duality
of her allegorical letter about going to her father's house), for Lovelace as
energy, death is the antithesis of life, so that which succeeds it remains
without image. Whereas Clarissa's last words and gestures are depicted
in exhaustive detail, crucial bits are missing from the account of
Lovelace's end: he mutters to himself before crying 'LET THIS
EXPIATE!'[10] The prolix voyeurism of the novel is balanced here by its
reticence and air of mystery: texts end when they reach the uncrossable
limit at which silence becomes more important than words.

Yet this silence is present throughout the work as well as the empty
space one has to fill out by using one's imagination, correlating the
various accounts. Thus the knowledge that there are plots leads one very
often to suspect one where there is none: if attention is the waking prayer
of the soul, it is also paranoia. The reader both participates in the
devising of such plots and often doubts whether actual plots should be
defined as such, since for the majority of the time Lovelace already has
Clarissa at his mercy. Much stress has been laid in modernist art on the
necessity for the reader to participate in the creation of the work.[11] One of
the most pregnant instances of this is the point in Musil's *Der Mann ohne
Eigenschaften* at which Clarissa writes to Ulrich 'Wann verstehst du einen

Mensch? Du musst ihn mitmachen!' ('When do you understand a person? When you help make him!')[12] Clarissa's proximity to insanity lets us see how close such participation is to delusion, for the participation modern texts require cannot be likened to the pre-Romantic reader's participation by applying a set of generic expectations to the text, and this is because the genres that would lessen the risk of interpretation have been destroyed by the Romantics and by the artist's need to escape from mass-produced clichés. The work that makes its reader work, that elicits his participation, is the one whose theme is the paranoia that results from this absence of given structures. Such works differ from those of the nineteenth century in that they feel too weak to stand alone (hence the emergence of so many movements at the turn of the century: the *Gesamtkunstwerk* is an army of all the arts massed in opposition to society). Paranoia connects everything, for the plot is felt to be all embracing: since everything is connected, since lines run everywhere across the surface of events so as to form a black cloud around them by linking them all, the reader can draw his own lines too: one more line will not darken the cloud appreciably. Pynchon's *The Crying of Lot 49* is a brilliant examination of the extent to which the construction of a plot to reality becomes paranoid when the reader of signatures of abandoned things is isolated[13]: and who is more isolated than a reader with such an immense book as *Clarissa*? Having stumbled into the modernist problematic, Richardson sought to extricate himself from the consequences of allowing the reader – with his baggage of prejudice and predilection – to forge the text's significance. In order to do this, he strengthened the editorial devices in the second and third editions, but in fact he simply augmented the confusion by superimposing yet one more voice on what can strictly be called the Babel already present. (Gopnik's assumption the the use of the Editor solves the novel's problems[14] presupposed the existence of a text fully spatialised and distilled down into a moral proverb; part of the Editor's inadequacy is due to his use of references rather than quotations whenever he seeks to discredit Lovelace, as a result of which he seems prone to adduce as dogmatic evidence texts he simultaneously suppresses, as if in fear of what they actually say.)

For the Baroque – by whose visual images Richardson was deeply influenced, whilst its plays contain the iconography of Rakes and Martyrs he was to deploy[15] – life's primary imperative was *memento mori*. Clarissa arranges for her future coffin to be transported to her room and it has been inscribed with edifying maxims in accordance with her wishes. Similarly, dialectic is *memento mori*, seeing the skull (totality, ideology) below the skin of every utterance: like a usurper contemplating the king. For dialectic and the Baroque, the dying thought re-emerges as a phoenix several pages later, thus illustrating the changeability of reality and the author's protean adequacy to its transformations.[16] The text dissolves and reforms as in reverie. Such a text is bound to be paratactic (parataxis accompanies the breakdown of the subject into several characters: thus dialectic's rise accompanies that of the novel.) In Richardson's work, the order and alternation of letters is often so arbitrary that we never know exactly why we are reading Lovelace at one point and Clarissa at another, since the epistolary form as he conceives it does not encompass any predictable pattern of exchange and alternation. The editor's contrivance often declares itself as he intervenes to justify curtailing letters on the grounds that the same events have been narrated elsewhere. Richardson withholds Clarissa's original correspondence with Lovelace so as to render more complete the novel's conceptual dualism: Clarissa faces Anna Howe and Lovelace faces Belford, so the two protagonists stand back to back like duellists who never fire a shot. The editor's organising meta-language is too closely allied with Clarissa to be entirely believable: he sees her past actions in the light of what she has become through self-mortification and so refuses to discern the minx-like self-righteousness of her first appearance, for if she could change, could not Lovelace also have done so? This possibility threatens the dualism between ethics and aesthetics which Richardson seeks to establish by means of the book that simultaneously questions it. Such swirling mythical darkness surrounds the two sides that the reader can leap from one to the other in an act of interpretive participation and yet not know upon which of them he stands.[17] If Clarissa's deliberate morality is unequivocally good, how are we to dispense with the suspicion that conscious moral resolve is not the sole determinant of actions, for love is not a voluntary passion? If morality is basically will, is it not also pride, so that Clarissa's readiness for death at the close resembles the will's dissipation once pride is shaken? (One might say the same of the Baroque after the humanist hopes of the Renaissance). And is Lovelace (loveless – a word describing both passive state and action) only metaphorically or actually Satan? The result of all these interactions is, as in all dialectic, a language that unmasks itself as *de trop* and unreliable. The same occurs in Boehme's writings, which influenced Hegel as well as Richardson[18], where the multiple definitions of the process of creation cause a blurred exposure and drive the visible towards the invisible. Dialectic is silence's revenge upon language (hence in Adorno its alliance with music): the silence of other people that forces one to take their place, of the dead upon whose bodies the tyrant

cannot rest.[19] It is also the past's revenge on the Enlightenment's
assumption that one could step out of the succession of crimes and follies
and into an ideal world – the Enlightenment wanted a clean break whose
impossibility was demonstrated by the compensatory emergence of
dialectic. The contradictory parables of the Gospels – ambiguous because their context is withheld – mirror the silence after the death of God:
dialectic tries to resurrect the dead to discover the truth.

The seriousness of *Clarissa*'s concern with religious truth is not simply
dependent upon its allegorical elements, which continually question the
felicity of calling it 'the first realistic novel', but is apparent in the
hallucinatory intensity of its language, which gives one the feeling that
the most important of issues is being discussed. Richardson's long
sentences rest occasionally on isolated words (usually Anglo-Saxon
roots, spat out vehemently, which provide one basis for the imperious
italicising he carried out in later editions), as if the dialectical complex-
ities have produced a temporary faint or 'Aufhebung'. Here the suicidal
spatiality repressed by the dialectic's movement momentarily becomes
apparent. The isolated word is a cipher of fixation: very often in
dialectical texts, sentences are not causally connected but circle obsessively round a single word, registering the unreliability of language by
their incapacity to define it. Similarly, the wave-like shuttling of definitions of key words studied by Gopnik corresponds to two impossibilities:
the impossibility of revolution (neologism) and the impossibility of stasis
(transparency). The element of revolution is the children's desire for
power to determine their own fate: Lovelace is male and active and split
from a family, so he represents this desire in its most fulfilled form. The
element of stasis has often been noticed. Mark Kinkead-Weekes writes of
'the curious effect of stasis'[20], Coleridge compares reading Richardson to
being in an over-heated sick-room[21], and – in a lesser-known example –
Miss Elspeth Nachtigall observes that 'the depiction of the Harlowe
family ... remains static, like a painting'[22]. Miss Nachtigall considers
this a flaw in the novel's realism, but since her own study has demonstrated that the image of Clarissa surrounded by admiring crowds is in
part a surrealistic transposition of the experience of Marguerite de
Valois into a non-aristocratic sphere, it is evident that the novel is far
from simply realistic. Rather, the stasis freezes the world for rejection: it
meets dialectically with the quest for revolution it opposes. The development that determines the fates of Lovelace and Clarissa is not just a
re-orchestration 'to give the characters another chance, as part of their
freedom to determine themselves'[23], but is also predetermined as the
allegorical opposition between Good and Evil. In the allegorical dimen-

sion, the work is superfluous (this is why the Romantics disliked allegory: art became reality's handmaiden), a footnote to the Bible that arrives at its destination in the author's preface; in this sense, it is the ancestor of all melodramas, which are similarly predetermined. But the allegory also contains 'non-allegorical' elements, as Benjamin observes when he modifies the Romantic theory of allegory to encompass the moment of opaque existence that accompanies the moment of signification.[24] So, on another level, in a secular, open-ended world in which truths still remain to be mapped, the novel is autonomous and independent. When Clarissa deceives Lovelace in a note referring to an intended journey to her father's house, he reads it realistically as anticipating an earthly journey. His realistic reading is criticised, but so is the mendacity that accompanies the disguise of meaning: Clarissa regrets the necessity of deceiving thus. Since her real reference is to her Heavenly Father, her end is both a Platonic return to the place of emanation and a new, unexpected development – death.

As a result of this duality, one is frequently unsure how to read the text. Dialectical texts alternate between evoking complete acceptance and total rejection in their readers: accepted as true, they may be rejected as pointless. For Adorno, this lack of a point is its main justification: it escapes the ideological demand for usefulness, for sentences that will be death sentences. The dialectician seems to be at home in universal alienation (perhaps a universal alienation of property). Lukács describes Adorno as having taken up residence in a Grand Hotel at the edge of the Abyss.[25] The image has a polemical intent, but it betrays some sympathy: next to the *haut bourgeois* comfort there is a gulf. And this gulf is a real one: Adorno writes of 'das Schwindelerregende' (the sense of vertigo) as the central characteristic of dialectic.[26] Like Baudelaire's Pascal, he takes his Abyss with him when he travels: the endless travel is the source of the dematerialisation (*can* there be a dialectical materialism?) that removes reality from the range of the acquisitive grasp. The dialectician uses everything at his disposal in the same way as a trapped man scours his mind in search of an exit: thought lives from moment to threatened moment. This sense of perpetual threat relates to the growth of the city. Richardson disliked city crowds intensely, and Benjamin has written of how the shocks in Baudelaire's poetry mimic the passer-by's experience in the flowing city crowd. Here one should remember the deeply dialectical nature of Baudelaire's Satanism. In similar fashion, Richardson's patented method of 'writing to the moment' corresponds to the atomistic mode of thought of a man oppressed by the city who seeks to roll its multifariousness into a ball –

The Great Wen – and stand outside it. Phrases like 'it is difficult to go outside ourselves to pass a judgement against ourselves; and, yet, oftentimes, to pass a *just* judgement, we ought'[27] or 'for the blood of me, I cannot but think that soothing a man's weakness is increasing it'[28] recur throughout the book and each, in its paradoxicality, is a microcosm of the book's indecipherable, unreadable problematic. The combination of such mirror-shaped sentences into a list – beads told on the rosary of obsession – is baroque: each line is separate and detachable so as to permit the writer to remain continually ready for the end of the world, ready to end a writing of whose validity – in this transitional period – he is still unsure, so his temerity withholds final commitments to it. He is wary of being caught munching the fruit of Good and Evil in the Garden of Art's Autonomy. The position of the writer at his desk, frequently with a skull before him, is immobile and so imitates the readiness for death all mortals must cultivate; his words pass to others only indirectly, like the speech of the dead. This is the link between the various modes of enclosure through which Clarissa passes (the series of rooms that culminates in a prison and a coffin) and her passion for writing. Dialectic is the over-development of one faculty at the expense of all others: the faculty of writing. Croce sees dialectic as the result of impoverished experience; Adorno agrees, but adds that all thought is damaged in a damaged society.[29] With great prescience, Richardson anticipated the modern dilemma resulting from the over-specialisation required by technological society, and like Adorno later, was aware that this social situation approximates a stasis in which people are isolated monads given over to paranoia and narcissism.[30] (Freud defines narcissism as a paranoid neurosis.)[31] In one of its moods the modern form of dialectic that privileges movement is paranoia[32]: this is Derrida's hypostatisation of change[33], which sees through every thought to the thought behind it so that the lack of any Ultimate Signified becomes a frenetic denial of the possibility of thought's death (since the over-specialised thinker identifies himself solely with thought) and so reinforces the logocentrism it attacks, as well as reflecting the bottomless consumerism of desire among advertisements: tantalising displacements. Richardson is conscious, however, that this endless movement is also the trapped stammer of compulsive repetition: writing is all one can do when one is trapped. Hence *Clarissa* is, apart from *King Lear*, perhaps the most painful book in the English language. Both are about the unkindness of kind brought about by the transformation of the family constellation by the children's sudden adulthood. Both move from a terrifying paradoxical interaction to an abrupt break, after which – as in melodrama – a purged and unearthly silence and dualism establish themselves. In *Lear*, this break is the storm; in *Clarissa*, the rape. One writes because one has no chance to speak. Interrupted by her mother in the work's early stages, Clarissa remarks that 'sobs [were] my only language'[34] and her truth is communicated to the world only posthumously.

Dialectical thought tries to capture a future that seems impossible in order to render the present bearable: it is the consolatory sophistry of pain. It is bound to the experience of nightmare and dilemma. It diagnoses the contradictions of the present, but since its own contradictoriness reproduces the shape of those contradictions, it infects itself with the combated disease in the hope of thereby inoculating itself against it. It is a physician trying to heal himself. Hence one's difficulties in interpreting its intention. The author tries to escape personal intentionality by dissolving self into the reality that insistently recycles him back into the trap of the self. *Clarissa* divided Europe into pro-Clarissa and Pro-Lovelace factions, but it also divided Richardson. The text's multiple exposure precludes the fixing of a definitive edition. Appalled by the extent to which readers found Lovelace sympathetic – which was such that even Lady Bradshaigh urged him to conclude the novel with the sterotyped reclamation of the rake – Richardson re-worked his text by adding moralising passages and italicising key words (even though the latter procedure had already been parodied in the letters of the pedantic young clergyman Elias Brand, who italicises to underline points for readers he insults by considering simple). One cannot elevate any one edition as essential, as does Mark Kinkead-Weekes; for Mr Weekes continues by arguing inconsistently (thus unwittingly indicating the need for a dialectical consideration) that Richardson muddied the texture of his original design and yet remained a fully conscious artist [35]. No one draft is solely valid because the work is potentially endless yet arrested (this fragmentariness—yet-completeness renders it crucial in the genesis of Romanticism): not just in the sense that it is prolix and Richardson was self-confessedly a poor pruner, but also because any one of the numerous characters' versions could be expanded or contracted at will. Each is a germ of a larger growth: this is another reason for the reader's participation. And here emerges the problem of chronological sequence. Not only do letters abound in cross-references, but later ones often appear before earlier ones, continuing a particular thread before backtracking to 'meanwhile. . .'. The dialectical text is one whose editing is in many respects virtually arbitrary. *Clarissa* verges on a shuffle-page novel. Editing was a severe problem for Adorno too, partly because the dialectic takes one to and fro between 'fact' and 'whimsy' and each appears dubious in the light of the other. The editing problem could have engulfed the *Aesthetische Theorie*. [36] Richardson's editorial devices mirror the insuperable problems of didacticism in fiction, for he both desires to teach and believes that only a constructed (falsified? hence the theme of forgery) reality will teach what he requires. But the moment he constructs a reality, he joins the ranks of the artists he aligns with Lovelace, at the same time as he uses Lovelace's allusive self-alignment with artists to place him in a typology of the deforming, overweening imagination that includes Julius Caesar and Milton's Satan. He is aware that the bombast of Lovelace's language stems from unfulfilled desire, yet – as Eaves and Kimpel have shown – its impertinent life is closer to Richardson's own spontaneous idiom than is Clarissa's scrupulous notation. Even before the Romantics, art here becomes its own critique. Thus Adorno's words about modern music could easily be applied to Richardson: 'that which remains in existence only through heroic effort could just as easily not be there'.[37] One can correlate this with a remark like the following by John Butt: 'When Richardson published his first novel, "Pamela", in 1740, he was already fifty-one years old, an advanced age for a man to enter upon a new career, let alone devise "a new species of writing"'.[38] 'Entering upon a new career' is the self-transcendence of dialectic. And Elspeth Nachtigall has noticed that the majority of Puritan writers began their careers late in life, as if needing first to overcome a belief in writing's vanity (or to have something solid to fall back on); writing could be seen as a double luxury, since all merit lay in the Bible and the imperative to work proscribed frivolity. [39] Dialectic is a form of thought that, by apparently encompassing the totality, squeezes outside it and becomes imperceptible to it; it says the unsayable. [40] Richardson identifies Clarissa's transparent style with virtue[41], and such a style, being pellucid, is invisible: woman must be inconspicuous. Her early death is an allegory of the fate of the plain and innocent style: the style is unseen like the presence of the dead. The same applies to the aphorism: a text composed of aphorisms, such as is typical of Adorno, lacks the redundancy necessary to being remembered. The unbroken intensity of the aphoristic text is a monument to the author's belief, based on a present feeling of alienation, in his future annihilation. The aphorism replaces annihilated personal experience and is an instrument in its destruction. (The annihilated earlier life is the one forsaken for a new career: thus Adorno abandoned composition for a homeless passage between philosophy, sociology, musicology and literary criticism). The aphorism's life is posthumous, like Clarissa's, for only when it has been entombed in a page, removed from conversation, do we appreciate it,

meditate on it, for the intensity of its demand has been muffled. The text
that transmit it betrays it.

The area in which dialectic is played out is that of irrational dilemma.
Jameson remarks that dialectic replaces causality with analogy[42]. This
movement of analogy is one of substitution; if one element can replace
another, it is because of society's growing uniformity, as a result of which
the individual's existence seems to him to be irrational. Where everything is connected by paranoia, causality and teleology collapse, or
rather, reveal their inherent spatiality: space replaces time. One stays
with the family all one's life long, as it spreads nightmarishly to become
'The Great Family of Man'. How can one say that Clarissa's relatives are
fulfilling Lovelace's plans when they oppose them? The mixture of noble
and bourgeois elements in her family creates the irrational image of all
society boiled down into one inescapable place: the family's plans to rise
from its bourgeois status by securing a peerage for James have been
ruffled by grandfather's decision to bestow some of the requisite estates
on Clarissa, but it reacts to threat with the inveteracy of a feudal clan
defending its honour, and the references to *Romeo and Juliet* reinforce the
sense of timelessness: the family seems to be as deeply rooted as the
Capulets. [43] This particular reference spreads the family backwards into
a mythical time, and in any case it already mythically focuses the
elements of its own time as if for a forest fire. Its relationships are both
normal and surreal. The father wields absolute power, yet his absolutism
is questioned by the split between justice and mercy that accords the
faculty of affection to the mother alone; and this power is diminished still
further by: his illness; the sketchiness of his infrequent appearances; the
household's dependence on a James Harlowe driven by ambition and
envy of Lovelace; and the mother's superior social status (she is a
viscount's daughter). Clarissa terms Solmes an 'upstart man' 'for he was
not born to the immense riches he is possessed of' [44], and in the face of
these aristocratic sentiments in the mouth of the 'bourgeois' Clarissa, the
sociologist's distinction between aristocrat and bourgeois and the Marxist's assignment to each of his respective ideology both collapse[45].
Elspeth Nachtigall has isolated one of the sources of this irrationality in
the dislocation of the *Memoires* of Marguerite de Valois from an aristocratic milieu. Marguerite suffers months-long imprisonment, the envy of
companions, false accusations and intrigues; she experiences prophetic
dreams and people crowd to glimpse her wherever she appears. All these
experiences match Clarissa's. 'Since in this world the "normality" of the
other world had the effect of the extraordinary, Richardson's books had
an unheard-novelty'; 'here one discerns the reason why the image of the

bourgeoisie "discovered" by Richardson was not a realistic one".[46]

Similarly contradictory signals accompany Lovelace's appearances. He is 'not an infidel',[47] yet he is also the Devil.[48] He can wear an untroubled countenance whilst inwardly in torment.[49] (This may be Richardson's envious rationalisation of sinners' success). If he is a 'pathological liar', he lies in order to be perpetually out of reach of an understanding he envisages as purely hostile.[50] Belford writes of his 'false bravery, endeavouring to carry off ludicrously the subject that most affect thee'.[51] Spoiled in childhood, he has become tender to any hurt and uses his imperial self-stylisation to ward off a meaningless present in a manner that represents a perfectly realistic response to its threat. His attraction to Clarissa can, in its helpless submission to her pull, be seen as an attempt to recover the intensity of the mother's love for the young child (this is why she must be above him in his dream and why he is as helpless to rape her at first as is a child). Romantic love, as Philip Slater has described it, is always backward-looking and transgressive and is founded on the belief that there is only one woman in the world of any account: the mother.[52, 53] If Clarissa is drawn to him unconsciously, it is because for both of them 'writing to the moment' corresponds to vulnerability: the moment is a very thin ledge. One recalls that Richardson himself preferred to issue commands to the men in his workshop by means of slips of paper. Lovelace's duality is such that at one moment he seems darkly impenetrable and at another merely witty and human.[54] He is in Hell–but so is everyone else on earth. Even as he is placed in the infernal company of Mowbray, Tourville and Belford, in all of whom physical deformity is symptomatic of inner depravity, he is isolated from it by his sheer attractiveness. On one level, this reflects the Biblical paradox whereby Lucifer comes clothed as an angel of light. On another, it contradicts the easy dualism of juridical morality. The smoothness of his manners is the brazenness of a shield. 'I suppose all mankind to be plagued by its contrary'.[55] Writing of his first love (Richardson represses these events just as he represses cause in general) he remarks that he was 'frighted by my own boldness'[56]: he is perpetually staging his own Faustian show and watching it from the wings–in this concern with his own dead and living image, he anticipates Mailer.

The ambiguity of Richardson's relation to Lovelace, which is part of the riveting and disturbing mixture of secretiveness and exhibitionism in his own character, begins as early as the author's preface. He starts by talking of Clarissa. 'To have been impeccable must have left nothing for the divine grace and a purified state to do, and carried our ideas of her from a woman to an angel. As such she is often esteemed by the man whose heart was so corrupt that he could hardly believe human nature capable of the purity which, on every trial or temptation, shone out in herself.'[57] This passage is riddled with subterranean contradictions. That Lovelace esteems her an angel may be a sign of his corruption, yet for everyone else she is an example too: and how can 'human nature' be capable of this purity when it is the product of 'divine grace'? Richardson's hint that unaided human nature is capable of such purity half tempts one to align him with the infidels. The first sentence stresses Clarissa's human frailty; the second, by maintaining that her probity shone forth 'on every trial or temptation', retracts any suggestion of mortal weakness. He attempts to dissociate his own image of Clarissa from Lovelace's but the development of the novel is such that Lovelace's view of her achieves the status of prophecy, ambiguous second-sight. For, by the novel's close, she is decked with the panoply, if not the name, of a saint.

This combination of Protestant Calvinist and Catholic elements suggests that what Raymond Williams would term the 'structure of feeling' of an undivided Christendom retained power over the imagination long after its disintegration into feuding camps: and the violence of their opposition expressed a fear of inner similarity when used force to rip its own identity from identity with the other. A similar view underlies Szarota's controversial term for German Baroque drama, 'saekularisiertes Maertyrerdrama' (secularised martyr-drama).[58] Thus although, in Protestant fashion, Clarissa is not shown being assumed into Heaven, this is counterbalanced by Lovelace's Baroque dream, in which the chiaroscuro of total dualism imitates a Baroque Ascension. The reader would simply side with Clarissa in her view of Lovelace's world if we only had her letters: without Lovelace's correspondence, the book would simply duplicate *Pamela*. In Lovelace's letters, Richardson builds into his novel the parody lavished on *Pamela* by Fielding, and this coup cuts two ways as a criticism of the parodist and as mockery of its grotesque object. Dialectic is repairing one's errors: one's first book cannot be dialectical. (If one's first *published* book is, this is because one has suppressed the unpublished one(s).) Once the reader has read Lovelace's letters, he has lost his innocence: this is why the book cannot open with *his* letters. Richardson retains the illusion of his heroine's hermetic purity by suppressing the letters from Lovelace that *she* reads. But in compensation for this, the reader outlives the book, for to cut oneself off from half of life is to die, as do the main characters. Lovelace remarks to Hickman that 'though the lady will tell the *truth*, and nothing *but* the truth, yet, perhaps, she will not tell you the *whole* truth'.[59] In Lovelace, knowledge of the totality is identified with the range open to comedy, which, by relying on disjunction and incongruity as well as chameleon mimicry, represents movement. This is also the Devil's principle: comedy's mobility is that of the Devil who comes the moment his name is uttered and who appears at the beginning of the Book of Job as one who spends his time walking up and down upon the face of the earth. And there is no record of Christ having laughed. Lovelace is mid-way between the comic (because defeated) Devil of the Middle Ages and Dostoevsky's possessed. Sophists such as Lovelace (and, one could add, Heidegger) look closely at words (often coining new ones[60]), like Shylock, who is a typological descendant of the defeated Devil who seeks to ensnare his enemy by means of the letter of the law. It is perhaps no accident that Shylock should be a Jew, since dialectic is a minority's means of self-defence, resolving conflicts in the imaginary realm whilst one's opponents hold real power. When considering Lovelace's resemblance to the restless Devil, *simia dei*, one should remember Philip Slater's argument that an intensely mobile society is one in which experiences and places are homogenised[61]: whence Lovelace's ennui and the uniformity women have for the seducer: whence also the form of criticism prevalent in the highly homogenised United States, against which Mark Kinkead-Weekes rails, which incorporates various fictions into the body of an overarching myth. Lovelace's alarming and uncanny quality is evident when he argues that one extreme produces another[62] and so devises the common modern justification of his conduct. Dialectic is often unnerving in that apparent chop-logic enables one to arrive at ideas that have no obvious relation to oneself (it is possible that dialectic is less self-consciousness than mystified self-consciousness), or to the present, but which later seem like prophetic short-circuits in time. The dialectical diagnosis can seem empty at the time of utterance, but later resembles a magnet attracting future history: a trap baited to catch it. Thus there arises Adorno's status as a precursor (the same can be said of Richardson), together with the dual response of rejection followed by acceptance noted by the Polish writer Stefan Morawski describing his reaction to *Philosophie der neuen Musik*: 'at the time I treated this notion with reserve as an idiosyncratic extension of *a priori* Hegelian schemes concerning 'the end of art'; today it is one of the most vital issues of the actual artistic situation.'[63] This leap through time seems demonic and is the source of Adorno's interest in the demonic principles behind phenomena, as well as of Mailer's attraction to mystery. Lovelace's interception of letters and ability to disguise himself or mimic others

gives him an omnipresence and prescience that seem demonic to Anna
Howe: 'I never had any faith in the stories that go current among country
girls, of spectres, familiars and demons; yet I see not any other way to
account for this wretch's successful villainy, and for his means of working
up his specious delusions, but by supposing (if he be not the devil
himself) that he has a familiar constantly at his elbow'.[64] Her suspicions
are tormentingly true and false: true, for he acts on behalf of evil; false,
because he is simply human. Yet even here we cannot be sure. He makes
a similar mocking suggestion to Belford: 'who says that, sleeping and
waking, I have not fine helps from some *body*, some *spirit* rather...?'[65],
and this remark is both comic and horrifying, for he has a soul that real
truck with Satan could destroy. His shadowy circling round the edges of
Anna's and Clarissa's letters, as they seek to deduce the source of his
apparently supernatural knowledge, gives him the air of a spirit (known
only by repute) or a ghost glimpsed at the edge of the retina. His dual
nature as an angel with horns corresponds to the way Richardson uses
reported speech: the combination of epistolary monologue with recounted dialogue both reveals reality and covers it with a film of
interpretation. We hear both the reported voices and the voice doing the
reporting and they frequently jam each other. Reported speech is an
allegory to which the key has been lost: we have to work to decipher it yet
we cannot verify the accuracy of our decoding. Masked in this fashion,
even faithful accounts become tinged with falsity. Here are some
examples of passages that require in consequence a double reading. 'In
these three... he declares: "that neither his own honour, nor the honour
of his family... permit him to bear these confirmed indignities"'; 'In my
answer, I absolutely declare, as I tell him I have often done, "that he is to
expect no favour from me against the approbation of my friends..."';
'To this, in his last, among other things, he replies, "that if I am actually
determined to break off all correspondence with him, he must conclude
that it is with a view to become the wife of a man whom no woman of
honour and fortune can think tolerable..."'.[66] [In all these quotations,
the ellipses are my own.] In all three cases the opening of inverted
commas by Clarissa signals a direct quotation from the correspondence,
but in order to read the passages as such, we have to alter the personal
pronouns: the necessity of changing Clarissa's words infuses a subtle
doubt into the others and is paradigmatic for the double reading the
novel demands. In order to be true to its spirit, one is forced to be false to
it. How this double effect arises can be seen from the following extract
from Eaves's and Kimpel's excellent biography.

In Hill's version, Clarissa's sister, Arabella, when she looks on Lovelace as her suitor, praises his manly beauty:

'*Let me see!* she cried, (and danced up to the Looking-glass –) In truth I have not a *quite bad* Face neither! Many Ladies had done Mischief, with inferior force of features for it! – Her *Eyes*, at least, she could not think were much amiss (and truly I had never seen 'em shine so brilliantly!) – Nothing here perhaps too flamingly transporting; and yet nothing neither to find fault with – *Is* there, Clary.'

In the earliest published version, this passage reads:

'But then, stepping to the glass, she complimented herself, "That she was very *well*: That there were many in women deemed passable, who were inferior to herself: That she was always thought comely; and, let her tell me, that comeliness having not so much to lose as beauty had, would hold, when that would evaporate and fly off: – Nay, for that matter," (and again she turn'd to the glass), "her features were not irregular; her eyes not at all amiss". And I remember they were more than usually brilliant at that time. – "Nothing, in short, to be found fault with, tho' nothing very engaging, she doubted – Was there, Clary?" '[67]

Here rewriting transforms the original text by stepping back from it, placing a veil of paraphrase before it, so the original text remains intact behind the published version. Its silence *within* the published text gives us room to interpret the events the later text elliptically relates. Where revisions are as total as they are here, the author is writing against his past self: revision is negation of the style that is so close to Lovelace's: the style of the hunter who pounces on phrases. And yet, paradoxically, Richardson's desire to render his heroine more elegant gives her style of narration the air of a protracted yawn of boredom that characterises Lovelace's accounts of others' words: the second version lacks the animation of the first one, replacing direct quotation with a mixture of quotation and paraphrase that implicates Clarissa in the speaking of Arabella's words, as if they were uttering them in syncopatedly drawling chorus, thus complicating the first version's polemical dualism.

Lovelace's forgeries testify to his instability and his resulting capacity to be possessed; for a long time, actors were thought to be without souls. Richardson exhibits a deep intuition into the psychology of forgery (perhaps his own wish to be acknowledged as an innovator, a wish that led him to suppress any mention of indebtedness to others, is allied to the forger's mentality) by having Lovelace compose new letters from frag-

ments of old epistles, so that the sense of *déjà vu* reaches us like the tell-tale
odour of flesh rotting. Tom Keating's Palmer forgeries were similar
mosaics of quotations, and forgery in general seems to be linked to a
craving for revenge (Lovelace revenges himself on the feminist Anna
Howe by appropriating her voice; Van Meegeren revenges himself upon
the artistic community that refused him recognition). The forgery has
the obscene horror of the living dead because its parts are the mutilated
constituents of a larger whole, and they scream silently to reveal their
origin: Van Meegeren's Vermeer forgeries send shivers down one's
spine. The forger is a man who has blunted all feeling and has only
technique left. Clarissa remarks to Lovelace: 'what sensibilities must
thou have suppressed!'[68] The seducer is no longer a person but a
mechanism for ruining girls, thus there arises the recurrent metaphor of
the machine or engine. Forgery is the Devil's work, comically self-
conscious (as also in Welles's film *Fake*) and tragically impotent. As
comedy, it criticises the dogma of the inviolability of private property.
This comic element relates it to the put-on, of which Mailer writes
brilliantly in a way that links Lovelace's acting passion with his promiscuity. He writes of Monroe:

> she is also a first artist of the put-on – she dramatises one cardinal
> peculiarity of existence in this century – the lie, when well-embodied,
> seems to offer more purchase upon existence than the truth. The
> factoid sinks deeper roots than the fact. The oncoming desire to
> inhabit the interior of the put-on and so know one's own relation to a
> role (in a way that others cannot) will affect a whole generation in the
> Sixties. They will rush into the shifting mirrors of the put-on – it is the
> natural accompaniment to sexual promiscuity.[69]

Lovelace may just be putting Clarissa on: there is a syncopated
bounce to many of his threats that betrays skipping glee at deception.
Mailer would say that he anticipates the Sixties: dialectic is the stance of
the precursor.[70] And perhaps of the affluent.

Lovelace is caught in the contradiction represented by romantic love
in a male-dominated society. This is also a contradiction that affects the
libertine aristocrat in his affluence: without the inducement to marry for
money or social advancement, he can only be held by a woman in whom
he invests transcendental significance. He is as abstract as paper money,
and his experience reflects its advent. The combination of adoration and
desire to dominate links his old habits as a seducer with his new ones as a
courtly knight: his response to Clarissa is such that she cannot be simply

another woman, yet he is in part imprisoned by force of habit. Opposed areas – the higher and the lower, heaven and earth – are contaminated to produce the explosion in the psyche that is dialectic. Sophistry bridges the contradiction: 'how often have I known opposition . . . create love?'[71] Sophistry is the insane after-life of a language incarcerated in the space of silence. Since a solution to his dilemma is inaccessible, he resorts to plotting and acting, which tend towards an end from which they perpetually distance him. This ambivalence of plotting is finely summarised in his image of her as 'spinning only a cobweb'[72]: Lovelace perceives only the insubstantiality of the cobweb, forgetting that it can also catch flies. His mockery rebounds ironically upon him. The inmates of the brothel, especially Polly and Sally, enjoin upon him the necessity of subduing Clarissa, but even when the whole household surrounds her, she is able to paralyse all her opponents, like Circe among the swine: such is the ritual power of virginity. Here she represents reason as primitive tribes might experience it: reason as magic. Similarly, the division of her days into periods allocated to various edifying activities has a ritualistic aspect. She is reason whilst the brothel is stalked by the beasts of lust associated in medieval thought with idolatry. To emphasise this animality, Richardson often has Lovelace call the girls 'toads'[73]: at another point, they are 'the maiden monkeys'.[74] Lovelace alienates mind from body in these grotesque descriptions, but so does Clarissa in her ethereality; the way tears crumple and dehumanise a face often makes it hard to sense the pain behind the grotesque (Lovelace's reaction[75]), but Lovelace's attractiveness effects a similar separation of inner and outer so as to mask his feelings (whence Clarissa's reaction – 'le "coeur" du pervers est donc insondable'[76]). The grotesque, like the mask, is surface detached from expressivity; so is beauty. Sophistry stems from a similar detachment: it is alienated thought that prefers to weave nets to catch the wind, like an animal fasting while it is ill, refusing to take in any new sensation. Hence the book's stasis, its nightmarish treading of water. Lovelace is in love but 'loveless' too, for romantic love is fixation upon the absent. For him, 'love, that deserves the name, never was under the domination of prudence, or of any reasoning power.'[77] Love is defined as 'lessness' or negativity, and therein lies the case with which it turns into sadism.

Clarissa separates ideal from genital love: in this sense she *is* in love with death[78] – but since this separation is normal in women[79], her attitude is as much 'normality' as 'neurotic prudery'! After the rape, she states that Lovelace has sinned 'beyond the possibility of forgiveness'[80]; she means this as implying that *she* cannot forgive him, but Richardson

in his moralism and Lovelace in his fatalism would also see this as
putting him beyond the reach of divine mercy. His fatalism is a refusal to
judge actions; he can be aware that what seems trifling to him may not be
so to Clarissa, but since this dialectical thought results from distance
from himself, he is unable to draw from it conclusions about his own
conduct.[81] If women separate ideal from genital love, they are readier to
leave this life than men, and less likely to seek an ideal here; for
Richardson, women have an after-life and men have none. The phallus is
dual – erect and a means of combination and metaphor, or limp and
detached, and it is possible that these two properties represent a certain
male schizophrenia in Richardson's eyes, which would correspond to the
way Lovelace frequently baffles onlookers by projecting both at once,
adopting two tones simultaneously. He is courteous and aggressive,
playful and ruthless, vain and appealing.[82] This duality is that of the
figure who relates only to internalised archetypes even when moving
among crowds, the lonely genius or isolated individual discovered by the
eighteenth century.[83] Lovelace is the ancestor of the Gothic hero-villain:
the ruined castle this figure inhabits is emblematic of the personal
neglect and of the synthesis of nature and culture envisaged by Hegel
and Hoelderlin. In Hoelderlin's words:

Doch die ewige Sonne goss

Ihr verjuengendes Licht ueber das aelternde
Riesenbild, und umher gruente lebendiger
Efeu; freundliche Waelder
Rauschten ueber die Burg herab.[84]

Clarissa's dilemma balances Lovelace's and is fused with it. The
following passage by R. S. Brissenden catches the tension well:

Lovelace's function in the allegorical scheme of the novel is complicated and even contradictory. At one level, he represents the ultimate
logical extension of the eminently reasonable assumptions by which
Clarissa can justify her opposition to her family. He has the intelligence and honesty to see through the Harlowes' pretentious hypocrisy.
But Clarissa, when she is with him, supports her family and refuses to
admit to him that they were in the wrong. She thus places herself in the
ironic position of supporting the very attitudes and beliefs which, in
the early part of the novel, she has herself been attacking, and which
have in effect driven her into Lovelace's arms.[85]

Clarissa's dilemma is extremely complicated and leads to her successive rejections of various different courses of action. As in dialectic,
where the motion of thought towards praxis turns back on itself, there is
no right way of acting. When her mother instructs her to break off the
correspondence with Lovelace, she replies 'be pleased, madam, only to
advise me how to break it off with safety to my brother and uncles.'[86] She
envisages the worst. When her mother says 'The law will protect us,
child! Offended magistracy will assert itself' she replies 'But, madam,
may not some dreadful mischief first happen? The law asserts not itself
till it *is* offended.'[87] Law, being for the generality, does not safeguard the
individual. Clarissa is right to believe this: Lovelace will not be hindered
by the preventive fear of punishment, for his indulgent childhood has
screened him from the law. Even as her view is cowed and paranoid, it is
realistic. Yet she is also wrong, for his threats are simply instruments in
his plot to gain her with which he would readily dispense were an
altercation between himself and her brother likely to alienate her from
him. The sole escape from 'dilemma is the blanking out of consciousness
under pressure, but the escape itself generates a new problem: Clarissa is
described as leaving with Lovelace before we or she knows why, and this
manner of representation evokes her loss of consciousness (which may
also be the moment at which censored desire speaks).

Throughout the book, rifts run between love and duty; earthly and
heavenly honour; love and liking; earthly and heavenly love; and
reasoning will and emotion. Such is the irrational complexity of these
criss-crossing oppositions that Fiedler can identify Lovelace with reason
and Clarissa with sentiment, whereas Eaves and Kimpel comment that
one could stand this opposition on its head – in fact, the opposition
performs a double somersault.[88] Perhaps the dominant and determining
rift runs between interiority and exteriority. During the first volume,
Clarissa writes: 'The world, as I have often thought, ill-natured as it is
said to be, is generally more just in characters (speaking by what it *feels*)
than is usually apprehended: and those who complain most of its
censoriousness should look inwardly for the occasion oftener than they
do.'[89] She can speak thus of Solmes without applying her precept to
herself, *because* she does not apply it to herself. Expression itself thus
becomes a form of blindness or guilt, for which the readjustments of
dialectic subconsciously compensate. Words contradict looks: 'I
thought, by the glass before me, I saw the *mother* in her softened eye cast
towards me: but her words confirmed not the hoped-for tenderness.'[90]
'Mock me not with outward gestures of respect. The heart, Clary, is what

I want.'[91] Thus the word 'mother' loses its meaning. Words contradict
looks because writing is speaking when no observer is present, akin to
speaking to a person in the mirror, as Clarissa does here. The writer's
invisibility to others renders him or her akin to a spirit: hence Clarissa's
passion for an after-life, in which she will continue to be invisible to those
on earth. But invisibility is also criminality – sought by Lovelace so as
the more effectively to prosecute his designs, but also sought by Clarisssa
through her opposition to her family. The precondition for committing a
crime is imagining oneself invisible (which is why the night is the haven
of criminality), for by transgressing one crosses boundaries between
matter and spirit, life and death, speech and silence: a letter is silent
speech. Hermes is the god of thieves and a messenger, and he wears a
helmet of invisibility (so in Mann's *Bekenntnisse des Hochstaplers Felix Krull*
(Confessions of the Confidence Man Felix Krull) the invisibility of the
writer recounting his criminal exploits is part of that criminality as well
as an offshoot of the examination of the Hermes myth[92]). Thus Clarissa's
writing represents a desire to stand outside society that ironically
mirrors Lovelace's, as Brissenden notes. She seeks it in order to be safe.
Clarissa's contradictoriness, her marginal and disordering status, is well
perceived by Max Byrd:

> We see her special, subconscious connection with unreason strikingly
> in her hold over Lovelace's imagination: she charms, she bewitches,
> and she drives him, he claims, to the insanity of rape. . . . At some
> disturbing level, I think, the opposition begins to dissolve. Clarissa's
> and Mrs. Sincair's hysterical entrapment in the same prison-like
> brothel and the sexual connotations of their deaths actually suggests
> an identification between them.[93]

Because the contradictions lie half inaccessibly in the area between the
conscious and the unconscious, the critic is led to make connections he
simultaneously suspends, as if in fear of writing rubbish, as if he were
writing dialectically: 'I think', 'suggest' and 'he claims' enable him to
register the air of unspoken dimensions in *Clarissa* which one perceives
blinking, unsure of their presence. Clarissa is ambiguous because in her
is focused the Puritan's suspicion of woman as Eve, the principle of
Law's subversion, that led him to name girls after virtues in order to
neutralise their threat by reconnecting them to the moral system.

Out of the duality of projection upon a pre-existing reality that elicits
that projection and so confirms its validity, Richardson develops the
dialectic of the heroine's relation to the villain.[94] The villain is a figure

who consistently succeeds, and as such he provokes our envy. Young and healthy, he cannot be pitied, for nothing has driven him to his villainy: his background, which would elucidate his nature, is either suppressed or sketched cursorily, which is why we read so much more of Clarissa's family than of Lovelace's. The work of art is the process whereby this notion of success as criminality is re-defined to encompass the villain's negativity so as to turn it against him: 'success' becomes 'success against the villain'. Since this can only occur through incorporation of the villain, the victory causes the hero's (or heroine's) loss of self; by the close, innocence is forfeited. Clarissa's inability to escape Lovelace results in part from his nature as her half-separated projection; it is true that there are other, more tangible reasons, but Richardson's dialectical prose tends partially to dematerialise objects and events and rematerialise them as tantalising mist between the lines. By assimilating the positive/negative opposition to a sexual war and to the psychological differences traditionally ascribed to the sexes (passive/active), Richardson attains a depth inaccessible to works that simply oppose a *hero* to the villain. The hero/villain opposition is melodramatic and dilettantish, for it concerns only half of humanity. Richardson, however, evokes a tragedy at the basis of all human relationships. When the villain justifies himself to the hero, we see his words as specious and do not regret his death, for the hero represents another man who can take his place and so heal the breach in humanity's ranks; but whenever Lovelace justifies himself to Clarissa, we waver between condemnation and a feeling that the disparity lies in the existence of two sexual languages, so that condemnation would simply reflect misunderstanding.[95] For Lovelace is identified with the text: he sees himself as an artist, and the text does not end until he dies. The middle term that transforms 'success as evil' into 'success as good' is the villain's foreignness (Lovelace is often abroad, and the work's basis in Clarissa's family lends him the mantle of the homeless, reinforced by his having only aunts and uncles) as an alien element within the system: his allusions indicate his commitment to otherness, and his unhoused state renders him equivalent to the stage-managing principle of circulation that sustains the narrative. The moment of Lovelace's destruction occurs when the categories of success and failure intertwine: this moment is the long eerie stasis that follows the rape. Here we realise that those who are most intent upon success are the greatest failures, so that the villain's external success reveals itself as failure (and hence identical with the heroine's failure to vanquish him). The text's last-minute hesitation and suspension of values is the infiltration of language by silence in Lovelace's dying minutes, which fold back into the centre of the work at which Clarissa's language breaks down after the rape, having taken Lovelace's with it, since his customary description of all his actions stops at the rape; this folding back is a reprise, musical like all dialectic. The link between centre and end is personification: at the centre of the book, Lovelace has momentarily become Evil; at its end, Morden personifies Death. In both cases, the point at which the name becomes an allegory of a man's function (Loveless – mors or murder, with its equivocation between Death as every man's due and assassination that makes Lovelace more a victim than a scourged sinner) fuses outer and inner into stasis. Language loses its arbitrariness and expresses essences, and the sliding independence of name and meaning that has sustained the work's incessant, struggling attempt to unite the two is able to rest: the spinning top falls to the ground. As in a frozen frame in a film, the moment at which the name denotes an essence turns the man so named into an emblem, with the wooden, allegorical pathos of the absent remembered movement.

On reaching the end of *Clarissa*, we feel a need to re-read it, for the book comprises a series of re-readings of a very few actions, and they have accumulated into the indecipherable palimpsest of the final page. The work differentiates itself from melodrama by its willingness to return to the moment of confrontation between heroine and villain evinced by its protraction of that moment, as if obsessively blowing it up or slowing the film to perceive what actually happened. Yet it remains allied to melodrama by virtue of its dualism and its willingness to subordinate art to another area: religion. It resembles Poe's 'The Purloined Letter'[96] (though in Poe, art is subordinated to magical science) in the way the middle and end of the work mirror and duplicate each other. When Dupin says in the middle of the story 'when you have signed it, I will hand you the letter', one's lack of knowledge of how he acquired it invests him with a demonic air: because he and the minister, the villain, are both poets and ingenious enemies, because both repeat the same trick with the letter and both *wait* with it (Dupin does not take it to the police, they come to him – as they do to criminals), there is a hint of possible identity, for true knowledge is obtainable only for the abnormal; but the reader escapes from this moment in which identity threatens to dissolve, in which language verges upon demasking itself by playing on the ambiguity of the word 'identity', by closing his ears to the siren-song that menaces his progress through the text. Nevertheless, at the end this evasion leaves one dissatisfied (and this is the reason for Edmund Wilson's dissatisfaction with detective stories, whose endings he saw as anti-climactic[97]). If the ending is inadequate, it is because of the text's potential endlessness which is contained in a paradoxical cipher in the moment of possible unity between the protagonists that would end the text in its middle (one speaks of a 'happy ending' for writing is pain, negativity) by demonstrating the endlessness and flexibility of all characters; the impossibility of using the categories 'heroine' and 'villain'; and thus, of using language at all. The text's end, its climax, is situated in the middle of the story, where it is buried so deeply as to be virtually inaccessible; it is concealed there as the text's secret, scandal and treasure. The scandal is represented dialectically, in two forms: the ipecacuanha plot, which is a happy end that closes the narrative by reducing opposition to silence (Lovelace's feigned illness draws Clarissa nearer to him); and the rape, which is the tragic end, and similarly destroys language. One could apply to Richardson Barthes's words on Sade:

le secret est donc en fait un voyage dans les entrailles de la terre [thus the rape is the devastation of Mother Earth and of the mother whose fantasy image underlies romantic love: the rape is when the lover imprisoned by such love takes revenge], il existe toujours, dans l'espace sadien, un 'secret', où le libertin emmène certaines de ses victimes, loin de tout regard, même complice, où il est irréversiblement seul avec son objet ... dans un monde profondément pénétré de parole, il accomplit un paradoxe rare: celui d'un act muet.[98]

The need to return to the centre of the work grounds the necessity of criticism, which seeks to recover the self at the point at which it was most fully lost and absorbed. For Richardson, each re-reading and re-interpretation approximates to the re-reading that will occur at the Last Judgement; the inadequacy of criticism's every reconstruction measures the distance of such final truth.

3 The Nineteenth Century

FOUR GERMANS: HOFFMANN, KLEIST, GOETHE AND BÜCHNER

1. *E. T. A. Hoffmann: 'Die Elixiere des Teufels'*

Criticism of *Die Elixiere des Teufels* (The Devil's Elixirs) usually assumes that the events recounted and suggested by the novel are susceptible of paraphrase. This assumption serves to repress the real difficulties experienced by the reader in the course of a reading. Such positivistic bias denies the extent to which the narrative itself is uncanny. In the notes that follow I will strive to be faithful to that experience of disorientation, for it is this that makes Hoffmann so modern.

Relatively early on in *Die Elixiere des Teufels*, before the plot has convoluted itself into its almost unbelievable complications, there occurs a scene in which the monk Medardus – commissioned to carry a message to Rome for his monastery – sees a man perched on the edge of an abyss, dressed like himself. He tries to warn the man of his danger – and in doing so, topples him into the abyss. The man is Count Victorin, a libertine who had hoped his monkish disguise would enable him to approach Euphemie, his lover, under the very eyes of her husband. In killing him, Medardus unwittingly assumes the role – and personality – of Victorin, and his subsequent seduction of Euphemie inaugurates his transgressive career. Yet at the same time, Victorin is simply a parallel figure to Medardus, whose worldliness – or, strictly speaking, carnality – has already declared him unfit to wear the monastic cowl. When Medardus sees Victorin at the edge of the precipice one has the eerie feeling that he is really viewing himself, disembodied and re-embodied. It is thus significant that from this stage onwards the story will be more and more densely populated by monks who are and are not Medardus: Valentin; Hermogen, who like him dons the habit to smother tempta-tion; and the insane monk who slips in and out of the role of his

Doppelgänger. One has the feeling that one is following the same story in different parallel and mutually interwoven versions – a series of reincarnations nightmarishly compressed into the space of a single life, overlapping, superimposed to create a blur. Chilling repetitions augment this feeling: Euphemie suggests that Medardus murder her husband the count in exactly the same way as he killed Victorin – though in fact she knows nothing of Victorin's death. It is as if she has unconsciously divined the secret within him, or, worse: as if reality involves an endless repetition of the same infernal cycle of events.

The reader's suspicion that no event is 'itself', that each event – and each person – is the same one seen from another vantage point, intuits the presence of a multiple universe, which anticipates the realities of relativity theory. That the reader feels this way also suggests an extreme self-consciousness in the manner in which variants are juxtaposed by the narration. The problem of choice and authority is central to the book; the monk Medardus is the space in which a violent dialectic oscillates between the dictates of divine authority and private sensual drives. The two are of course linked, otherwise the dialectical struggle would not take place; the blessed saint Rosalie is also the Aurelia of Medardus's dreams. This problem of choice has its equivalent in the shuffling of variants, no single one of which is dominant. Hoffmann stands at a crossroads between feudalism and individualism. This situation is reflected in the modes of his narration.

On the one hand, as in feudal and medieval reality, there is only the one story to tell, which imposes itself upon the author as a preordained external authority; however often the author may forsake Medardus and seek to exercise his freedom in the creation of individual characters, they always prove to be either after-images of Medardus, or to be related to the themes of his life; turn away from Medardus and one sees a Victorin or a mad monk, both of whom are also images of Medardus; as in medieval reality, there exists no reality of the individual over and above that of the species; all men are images of each other.

On the other hand, Hoffmann parodies the belief that all men are alike, by carrying its aesthetic consequences to the point of grotesque absurdity. The external authority imposed upon the narrator, who can no more escape it than Jonah can evade the will of God, is the 'fremde Macht' (foreign power) that is sometimes said to govern the characters, and this power is a mystification of the force of the narration itself.

The validity of the single, exemplary story has been shattered by Hoffmann's decision to place the narrative in the hands of a monk who admits to hallucinations and who writes in the first person. (Here there comes into play Hoffmann's consummate ability to depict figures who seem akin to projections of the central character's obsessions, and yet are also real demons. Hoffmann, like Germany at the beginning of the nineteenth century, occupies the boundary line between realism and fantasy, religion and de-mythologisation. One thus has to ask whether the book's title is intended literally or metaphorically.) This narration in the first person is ambiguous. The 'I' is highly labile and anyone (Euphemie, the narrator, Reinhold) can employ it in order to relate stories within the overall story; thus the self is admitted to be subject to disintegration; the narrator hands over his 'I' to a projection, which – animated by the 'I' – carries on speaking. Thus the 'I' need not be restricted to any one person, and can achieve an almost medieval impersonality, as the novel gravitates towards a juxtaposition of state-ments. These statements are grouped around an absent centre, an absent pre-textual event; this is the result of the inevitable agnosticism of the voice that says 'I' and is unable to know everything. Even so, impelled by intuition (an inkling of its own identity with the narrator of the book, who also knows the end?), the 'I' plunges feverishly on to a goal it is sure must be there.

Hoffmann's self-consciousness concerning his narration can be seen in two features. One is his compulsive use of adjectives. The adjective crystallises an aura of shock around each object. It is also a sign that no person or thing is quite what it seems. For a noun requires an adjective only when it is non-identical with itself, or when language has become so conventionally deadened that names cease to correspond to objects. The noun has to be galvanised by the adjective. The obsessive, one-to-one pairing of adjective and noun may be long-winded, but it also corres-ponds to Hoffmann's awareness of the implicit multi-sidedness of an event. The adjectives show the noun from another angle: cubistically, they juxtapose a view from above or below with the normal nominal frontal view.

Another such feature is the eventual arrival of a point at which the entire fiction threatens to dissolve into a dream. When a judge informs Medardus of the existence of a second Medardus, who has already confessed to 'his' (?) crimes, and when Medardus then gives a second, revised account of his encounter with the deranged monk who stood at the foot of his bed, but narrates it as if he were himself in the place of that monk, rummaging through the possessions of his 'real' supine self – then the narrative comes to seem either impossible or purely fantastic. One begins to feel that there is only the illusion of narrative, which enters the fifth dimension of the impossible, Escher-like object. Thus we become aware of the fact that the narrative itself is a construction; only this awareness (which violently ejects us from the experience of reading onto the plane of reflection upon the theoretical conditions of all fiction) can preserve us from losing our minds in the face of the conundrums of this particular text. As Marx notes, one thinks of the maker of a tool only when the tool itself fails to function; thus when one responds to this episode by recognising the connection between the making of a fiction and Medardus's beleagured, compulsive lying (the lie is threadbare and transparent, so he intervenes *as the narrator* to save himself within the narrative by transforming that narrative into a total fantasy, in which everything is permitted), one is responding to the crisis of narrative registered by Hoffmann. The crisis is of course the solipsist dilemma of the early nineteenth-century Romantics: if idealism and realism are one, for reality is shaped by the imagination, can there by any reality outside my own head? any story to relate? or can there only be a musical shuffling of motifs and themes (one recalls Hoffmann's musicianly ambitions) – writing as non-conceptual as music is condemned to be? Is it not possible that Hoffman's real symphonies are his novels?

2. *Heinrich von Kleist: 'Die Marquise von O.'*

In the main, Kleist's stories are neither 'stories' nor 'anecdotes' – they are what the Germans term '*Novellen*'. In the late nineteenth century, an aesthetic code was established for the *Novelle* which lent it some of the rigidity and unreachability of sonata form: the Ideal *Novelle* lay beyond the mortal writer's grasp. But this was simply because it had already been written; for the mathematical rigour prescribed to the form by theoreticians was a petrified after-image of Kleist's dazzling achievement. His prose pursues an almost inhuman rigour, and the achievement could not be duplicated. Kafka's *In the Penal Colony* can stand as an emblem of Kleist's relationship to writing: he identified with the infernal mental machine that scored his life with its fevered writing. There are two reasons why Kleist identified himself with the machine, with the ruthless structural logic of dialectic. Firstly, he wished to explore, to see where it would take him; this reflects the unpredictable, hectic course of his wanderings through Europe. Secondly, he wished to remain anchored to a (portable) point of departure: even as he traverses exotic realms, he remains locked in the atmosphere of his native Prussia (he will admit, for instance, that 'Die Marquise von O.' originated in a Northern context and was then transposed to a Southern one); his sentences round their clauses with a clicking of heels, and their frenzied imitations of legal protocol identify in vain with the cold ethos of his own military family, in whose eyes his predilection for writing was the mark of a renegade. Thus his thirst for paradox is itself prompted by a contradictory longing both to rebel and to be considered a good son – to his family and to Prussia. But the law of dialectic to which Kleist is subject is not simply an expression of his idiosyncratic experience. As Adorno remarks:

> This law is not a cognitive law, however. It is real. Unquestionably, one who submits to the dialectical discipline has to pay dearly in the qualitative variety of experience. Still, in the administered world the impoverishment of experience by dialectics, which outrages healthy opinion, proves appropriate to the abstract monotony of that world. Its agony in the world's agony raised to a concept.[1]

Kleist is the first to stand Hegel's dialectic upon its feet, planting one on each side of the opening abyss.

I have said that Kleist's 'stories' are 'in the main' contradictory beings – neither stories nor anecdotes. They are not stories, for the length of the story would dissipate the dialectical tension upon which his work is founded – as eventually happens in 'Michael Kohlhaas'. On the other hand, the anecdote is too brief; its demonstration of the unknowability of the paradoxical world is too off-hand to be fully serious. Kleist's masterpieces seem to me to be 'Das Erdbeben in Chili', 'Die Verlobung in San Domingo', 'Der Findling' and 'Der Zweikampf'. This leaves 'Die Marquise von O.', a work which defies my classification inasmuch as it is in fact an anecdote blown up into story dimensions. The result is, I think, not only a failure, but a peculiarly un-Kleistian one: the volcanic truth-seeking impulse that erupts in 'Michael Kohlhaas' and makes of that story an honourable failure is lacking here. It is mildly disturbing to note that 'Die Marquise von O.' is his best known story. For it seems that by accepting this story above all, the public has contrived to continue to deny Kleist the recognition he so craved, and never received, in his own lifetime: it values him for his least 'Kleistian', least passionate, and most mannered work. So mannered is it that it could be filmed by Rohmer, the most limpidly arch of directors, in a fashion that although distorted (and his film includes one inexcusable alteration: the rape of the Marquise is removed from the scene of the fire and transformed into a conventional boudoir seduction scene) is not totally false to the spirit of the original. But quite what is the difference between this story and Kleist's other 'Erzählungen'? Perhaps I should now indicate more closely what I have in mind.

From the very outset, the atmosphere of this story creates a feeling that it has come from 'the school of Kleist' rather than from Kleist himself. The title, the subtitle and the very first sentence combine to evoke a suspicion that this story is not going to unfold with his customary violent innocence, is not going to bristle with the spikes of an awesome Gothic construction.

Firstly, the title. The use of an initial instead of a name is contrary to Kleist's usual practice. Instead of drawing all circumstances into the open, it sets the tone of a knowing, euphemistic concealment. It plays the social game, respects the conventions of eighteenth-century titillation.

The parlour game is continued in the subtitle: Kleist informs us that this true event has been transposed from the North to the South. Why this transposition? Kleist's work in general recognises the need to distance his shocking material, to remove it from a conventional framework in order to allow the flower of paradox to bloom instantly but not incredibly. Anything can happen in the alien, exotic hothouses of 'Das Erdbeben in Chili' or 'Die Verlobung in San Domingo'; in these stories the exotic setting is really a dream X-ray of the present, earthly life seen for the first time in all its violent contrasts by a reporter from Mars. But in 'Die Marquise von O.', Kleist is unable to move his narrative outside Europe or outside the present, for it would thus forfeit the logic that informs it, the logic of a comedy of repressive manners. And its feel remains very Prussian. Instead, he shifts the locale to the South. In doing so, however, he succumbs to a banal prejudice, and seems himself to be indulging in repression: 'verlegt' (transposed) is very close to 'verlegen' (embarrassed); one recalls the frequency of blushes in his work. Is it not likely that in reality Kleist is embarrassed by the suggestion that such scandalous doings can occur in the heroic North (see the lionisation of the Germans in his notorious play *Die Hermannschlacht*) and so removes them to the conveniently 'fiery South'? Moreover, his close empathy with public prejudice is apparent in the retention of the Russian hero-villain: for it is part of the German psychopathology to project an image of the Russian as a libidinous wild-man. Kleist allows this image to stand, instead of unmasking it as the prejudice it really is. But his story-line thus becomes compromised: one may well ask what Russian troops are doing 'in the South'.

Thirdly, there is the opening sentence:

In M . . . , einer bedeutenden Stadt im oberen Italien, liess die verwitwete Marquise von O . . . , eine Dame von vortrefflichem Ruf, und Mutter von mehreren wohlerzogenen Kinder, durch die Zeitungen bekannt machen: dass sie, ohne ihr Wissen, in andere Umstände gekommen sei, dass der Vater zu dem Kinde, das sie gebären würde, sich melden sollte; und dass sie, aus Familienrücksichten, entschlossen wäre, ihn zu heiraten.

[In M . . . , a sizeable town in Upper Italy, the widowed Marquess of O . . . , a lady of excellent reputation and the mother of several well-bred children, let it be announced in the gazettes: that, without her knowledge, she had entered into a changed condition, that the father of the child she was to bear should present himself, and that for reasons of family she had determined to marry him.]

To the casual eye, this opening may indeed seem typically 'Kleistian': the paradoxicality, the stuttering parallel clauses, the use of indirect speech to achieve greater rapidity (the rapidity of a speedy annihilation at chess), the air of scandal and impassive legal transcription; all are familiar. But there is a crucial difference. For the paradox of this sentence is founded upon titillation; not, as in Kleist's greatest stories, upon the catastrophe that initiates a relentless passage through ever more fearsome events until the truth about the contradictions within society is brought to light. Truth here is not metaphysical but inherent in a particular, exceptional case. The use of initials instead of names is deliberately tantalising. The title uncannily foreshadows that of 'L'Histoire d'O.', and although the two stories differ in almost every respect – Kleist's has a dashing purity whilst the French story is unpleasantly studied pornography – in both cases the letter 'O' is associated with a woman who has already been sexualised (the Marquise is a widow), the 'O' of the woman who has been penetrated, 'Woman-as-Hole' (though for Kleist she is also a gap in the world, a gap to be filled). The euphemistic tantalisation of the reader (and the Marquise) inaugurated by the title continues in the dash that separates 'Hier' and 'traf er . . . Anstalten' (Here – he took . . . measures [my ellipsis]) and that represents the moment of the rape; it assumes almost farcical proportions in the image of the Count holding a dripping hosepipe, and in the parody of the Immaculate Conception. Thus the opening is less a paradox than a riddle. Kleist's knowing manner here contravenes his usual practice; his theme – the unrecognisability and fragility of the ambiguous world – is trivialised by the implication that reality is not inscrutable *per se*, but only for the Marquise (or the reader), who does not hold the key to the riddle. It lies in the hands of the narrator, who hides it behind his back but lets us know it is there. When, near the close of the story, Kleist writes of the 'gebrechliche Einrichtung der Welt' (the fragile arrangement of the world), it has the aura of a quotation from one of his other works; it is not justified by its context, which collapses under its weight. For the theme of the story has not been the difficulty of acting (except symptomatically and impulsively) in a world of crushing paradoxicality, but rather the unreliability of dualistic codes of manners. In 'Die Marquise von O.' Kleist has written a fable of enlightenment, a new version of 'Beauty and the Beast' – not the flaring documentary indictment of universal contradiction that is 'Das Erdbeben in Chili', perhaps his masterpiece. And it is perhaps this that makes the work so congenial to our age. It says that the id can be domesticated, and implies that our lives are played out to the tune of a chamber music. In a century that has easily outstripped the catastrophes envisaged by Kleist's other 'Novellen', the preference for this work surely smacks of wishful thinking, of complacent nostalgia.

3. *Goethe: 'Die Wahlverwandtschaften' and 'Wilhelm Meisters Lehrjahre'*

Goethe winces when he describes figures: he surrounds them with adjectives embodying an eighteenth-century propriety to show that they, like such stilted adjectives, can only fester now the French Revolution has occurred. He shrinks back at the touch of their rotting flesh. They are trees that ought to have been deracinated by the Revolution, bobbing along as they do in the floodwaters of Kleist's prose. These texts are the living dead of the eighteenth century. Phosphorescent, they glow in the dusklight of the forgotten provinces, phantom limbs of the dead body politic. Thus in *Die Wahlverwandtschaften* (*Elective Affinities*) he creates a form on the boundary of the novel and the novella so as to emphasise the galling irony of the lack of freedom felt by characters after the Revolution; only the fact of the Revolution has shown them they are enslaved, but it has no power to liberate them. Goethe takes the conception of a novella and imprisons his characters in it, locating their gaol on the empty plain of the novel ̇so that they can see from their windows the free space denied them. They cannot develop independent life, as can the inhabitants of a novel. The necessity that binds them lacks the positive attributes of Fate and is instead aligned with matter and the inorganic chemicals to which they are likened. Submitted to symmetry, they lose the name of human. With perverse virtuosity, Goethe seeks to demonstrate the impossibility of the novel from within the confines of the novel form; it is impossible because freedom is a catastrophe. Like all great modern poets, Goethe can write great prose but is incapable of writing great fiction; the self-consciousness of his language diverts attention from the characters and leaves them to freeze. Once the character has frozen, it can be adopted as the object of a quasi-scientific experiment; this is why poetic novelists often tend to be men who have undergone a scientific training, such as Musil or Pynchon or Goethe himself, who was doggedly intent upon refuting the optics of Newton. The characters are static like allegories or fetishes. *Die Wahlver-wandtschaften* presents characters locked inside aphorisms that permit them no development; there is a Poe-like, constrained air of people trapped inside their own portraits. The aphorisms of which the late Goethe is so fond are closed systems without waste; as is his book; as are the relationships it describes; within it, endogamy and exogamy fuse. If, like Faust, all people are divided, then the two pairs are images of two schizophrenic lovers; this undercurrent of insanity, held at bay by the mathematical patterning that is the schizophrenic's favourite device, may be the reason why the novel is so disturbing.

Early in his career, Goethe is said to have wavered between poetry and painting. This equivocation would seem absurd were it not for the fact that many writers in early nineteenth-century Germany presented the painter as a hero of their novels. They did so partly in order to achieve a distance between themselves and the image of the artist at the centre of their works (writers do not yet enter the paradoxical abyss of writing about writers, as Proust and Mann will do later) – thereby ultimately distinguishing between fiction and autobiography even as they brought them closer together. Another reason was the existence of a tradition of greatness in German painting that could act as a spur and a lodestone to a largely underdeveloped literature. Moreover, the painted image provided a *lingua franca* that mediated between the various mutually alien German dialects and so justified the Romantic artist's claim to represent his national culture. Finally, the image represented that mysterious potentiality that so fascinated the Romantics; it embodied the self-sufficiency of the moment. The otherness of the image is a symptom of the nagging wound of the separation of the arts at which the Romantics constantly pick away. And this separation is a symbol of the disintegration of society into hostile classes and trades; in writing of the painter, the Romantic seeks to achieve a synthesis of the arts that will pave the way to a resolution of the conflicts within society. This is particularly obvious in Büchner's *Lenz*, where Lenz both praises the Old German masters and seeks to speak for the oppressed, those whose lives have been reified. The late Goethe, however, is no longer drawn to the painter-hero; an anti-Romantic, he prefers to show writers and men of the theatre. That is – as in *Dichtung und Wahrheit* – his possession of social power lends him the self-confidence he requires to present himself as the ideal.

Wilhelm Meisters Lehrjahre (Wilhelm Meister's Apprenticeship) moves from an apparent chaos and openness to a resolved classical symmetry. The fact that Wilhelm is 'Meister' (master, foreman) already shows that he really has nothing to learn and balances nicely between according to youth a Romantic privilege and repeating the Classical statement of the necessity of discipline. The deep irony of the work lies in the way the Romantic, mysterious figures (Mignon, the Harpist) that enlist the sympathies both of Goethe and of ourselves (the gestural language of Mignon in particular is of Kafkaesque suggestiveness) are finally revealed to be clearly explicable in terms of the Italian society from which they originate; Goethe starts with Romantic presuppositions and then reveals their inadequacy, as the promise of genuine otherness is broken. Here one sees the significance of the melodramatic elements in the work; of, for instance, the use of coincidence to separate Wilhelm from Marianne. For melodrama is Fate subjected to parody and stripped of all claims to metaphysical dignity. The melodrama becomes rancid and dissonant. Masochistically, Goethe uses melodrama to deny freedom both to himself as narrator and to his characters; one's apparent acts of liberty were really stage-managed by an Euripidean God. As in Romantic works, the image of authority – of the castle inhabited by the troupe of actors – is mystified, but since Goethe himself lives in the castle, he represses his rage at authority by half identifying with it; thanks to his self-dramatisation he is both inside the castle as himself, and outside it as his projected persona. For he has the worst of both worlds (whence his obsession with hermaphroditism): he can identify neither with the administrator nor with the artist.

The form of *Die Wahlverwandtschaften* is contrasting and complementary: it begins with classical symmetry, and then allows this symmetry to break open to reveal irrationality. The text passes from the solid house above ground, the two symmetrical couples, and the civilised belief in cultivating one's own garden, to: the shifting mirror of the lake, asymmetry among the characters, and the religious fanaticism that accompanies the funeral of Ottilie. Goethe accelerates the ending bewilderingly because he does not wish to witness the débâcle of his Utopia of unity in diversity, whose combinations finally turn perverse: simple arithmetic taught by de Sade. Even the scientific enlightenment becomes sinister:

people are forced to interact like chemicals to determine whether or not their coupling will demonstrate the universality of a theorem, but the experiment destroys them. Goethe delays the inevitable, seeks to hold Romanticism at bay, and then capitulates suicidally when there is no longer any hope; the ending is even more Romantic and bizarre than the novels of the Romantics themselves. It began with a geometrical simp-lification and near petrification of relationships; it ends with its schema evacuated, and red-hot lava flowing. Disturbing is the unresolved, Romantic necrophilia that draws it to a dead Classicism (and that attracts the early Benjamin to it as one of the living dead of literary history; it is as if Benjamin could see in its non-recognition a suggestion that his own fame would be posthumous); unsold first editions were still available at the turn of this century. The scientific metaphor incubates unreason (it is itself irrational, for it does not quite fit the nature of the case; no third element is engendered in life, as it is in the experiment). The contemporaneity with Mary Shelley is hardly accidental; Goethe's position is that of Frankenstein, seeking to galvanise corpses (characters from Voltaire) into a semblance of life. The Classicist and the Romantic elements cancel each other out and leave only a bitter void. The value of symmetry is questioned; it does not simply give pleasure through balance, as Mirabeau asserted, but also serves to destroy the individual. And the Romantic Tragedy of Fate is criticised by stripping it of its historical fancy dress and by reducing the outstanding individual to the level of those who surround him, if not lower – for Eduard is further diminished by the unconsciousness with which he acts. He is no proud rock affronting the waves of historical necessity but a regressive adult making love to a child.

Goethe described this novel as a wound ('eine Wunde'), but he also considered it his best work. It was written at great speed, like a night-mare he wished to depart as soon as possible. In the midst of his pain he steps back from society to speak in aphorisms, like a disgruntled oracle. Aphorisms differ from proverbs inasmuch as they are fundamentally abstract; they lack imagery. The aphorism is a compromised form, the statement of an individual that nevertheless aspires to the generally binding status of a proverb. But proverbs come in pairs ('many hands make light work'; 'too many cooks spoil the broth'), and their authors are anonymous; they are without the individualism of the aphorism. Aphor-isms are bitter and incoherent, for they are formulated by people who are too deeply entwined in a courtly or centralised culture to be able to attack it systematically, but are also insufficiently favoured and so feel driven to become mysterious, in the hope that this will bring them power. In fact, it simply impels them towards madness. Aphorisms are the mode of expression of the discontented courtier seeking to found his own faction. As Goethe feels himself moving into the outskirts of a German culture increasingly dominated by the Romantics, he resorts to aphorisms, criticisms that halt after a line, lest their unfashionability bring down brimstone upon the critic. For his world-view has run aground; the fish out of water is becoming a skeleton.

4. *Georg Büchner: 'Lenz' and the Medusa's Head*

In a lecture delivered in Zürich on the subject of "Schädelverven' (the nerves of the cranium), Büchner stated that 'alles, was ist, ist um seiner selbst willen' (everthing that exists does so in and for itself); in a letter written in July 1835, he remarks that man cannot improve upon the work of nature, that God has created all things at they should be. It is from this sense of the self-sufficiency of the object that there arises the paratactic style of *Lenz*. Every item in a description exists in and for itself; the landscape in which these objects loom up is massive and discontinuous. But because everything in nature is sufficient unto itself, there can be no teleology or desire among objects. This is the position of the scientist, which precludes anthropomorphism. It is also the source of the overwhelming sense of isolation felt by the dramatist Lenz as he walks through the mountains; he feels no connection with the scene, he regrets that he cannot walk upside down. Büchner's anti-teleology is as ambiguous as any teleology. Confronted with nature, man feels empty and purposeless, and there is no more reason for him to do one thing than to do another. And other people are similarly massive and unreachable; in Lenz's eyes, the inhabitants of the valley in which he seeks refuge from his own unmanning fear are themselves elemental beings, creatures from another world, who experience an uncanny sympathy with underground reality, can detect hidden springs, and so on. Anti-teleology leads to a petrification of the individual, just as teleology causes him to evaporate in time. The tendency towards petrification – a response to one's inner petrifying fear – is expressed in the inevitability with which Büchner selects details, and above all in Lenz's wish that he could be a 'Medusa's Head' and so freeze a fine scene with two girls in a landscape and summon passers-by to come and view it. Yet the actual petrification of a figure (its passage into death) horrifies him, perhaps because he feels that he, the would-be Medusa's Head, shares some of the responsibility for that death; thus he strives in vain to bring a dead girl back to life, and blasphemes wildly upon his failure. In the eyes of the Medusa, each moment exists in and for itself: a film by Büchner would be a succession of frozen frames (something akin to the work of Werner Herzog). Lenz's desire to petrify life (to revenge himself upon it for his own petrification?), together with his belief in the elemental characters of mountain dwellers, makes it worth while comparing him (and, of course, Büchner) with Wordsworth. There is in both the same empathy with stones, the same tendency to classify people and things together, the same anti-eroticism founded upon an antipathy to teleology (Wordsworth's verse never seems to go anywhere, and in a Lucy poem like 'Strange fits of passion' even the horse he rides grinds to a halt).

But there is another sense in which Lenz (and Büchner) resemble Wordsworth. There is a letter by Büchner in which he describes the Vosges, the scene of *Lenz*, as a mountain chain he loves as one loves a mother. Viewed psychoanalytically, the mountains of *Lenz* are both 'bad breasts' and father figures. One recalls Wordsworth's fear of the moving mountain in the stolen boat episode of *The Prelude*. The mountains enclose and protect, but they also destroy one if one disobeys; they are thus part of the paternal imagery that structures the course of *Lenz*. Residing with the pastor Oberlin, Lenz is near a man he will constantly hear addressed as 'father', and will probably address him as such himself; Oberlin becomes a substitute father, the true father of 'the family romance' (for Oberlin was not simply a humble withdrawn pastor, as he appears to be in the story: he was a renowned figure, and thus the ideal father for the famous dramatist Lenz). In entering the valley, Lenz is behaving like a prodigal son – but, as in a myth, his beginning and his end are one: he is both the prodigal son returning to his spiritual father, and the same son in flight from his physical parent. When Oberlin himself travels beyond the edge of the valley whilst Lenz remains within it, Lenz appears as a child who is not permitted to stray too far from home. Yet on one level of the story's various significances he is also destroyed by fear of the father he has fled, who wants him to assume a bourgeois career. In placing Lenz among mountains that tower above him like parents, Büchner asserts that the pattern of his life is already fixed, petrified.

This pattern is one of a terrible, devastating feeling of emptiness, punctuated by moments of vision, which leave him drained and so precipitate in him the emptiness he so fears. He is both at one with the mountain folk he sees around him and exists radically apart; there is a contrast between their peace, the peace of the embodied landscape, and Lenz's hunted state of mind, but there is also an identity between his sinister hollowness and their silence. For the quiet in the valley is almost lunar, and people are said to speak softly lest they disturb it. Thus the valley becomes like an irascible parent, in whose vicinity the children walk on tiptoe.

Lenz both is and is not Büchner. Büchner can say that God has made the world as it ought to be, whilst Lenz tells Oberlin that if he were God he would save the world, he would not be able to endure the spectacle of its pain. And yet the anti-Idealist aesthetic Büchner attributes to Lenz is identical with his own, as expressed in a letter from 1835 in defence of *Dantons Tod*: he too seeks to present the reality of the down-trodden, as Lenz himself had done in his play *Der Hofmeister*, in which the private tutor finally demonstrates his awareness of his social impotence by castrating himself. Büchner's anti-Idealism directs the artist to speak for the oppressed and their plight. But for Büchner himself this imperative was always accompanied by the problem of the relationship between himself and the inarticulate: how can he voice their sufferings without resorting to words, and yet how can he identify with their sufferings, convulsions and spasms without himself succumbing to inarticulacy? In *Dantons Tod* he strove to bridge the gap between himself and the oppressed partly by means of bombast, and partly by supporting Danton, whose lurid language is more congenial to the people than the mincing diction of Robespierre and Saint Just. In *Woyzeck*, he attempted to bridge it by means of a folk stylisation, a loose balladic structure. But in neither case was he able to present a figure akin to himself. He achieves this in *Lenz*, which thus becomes his most interesting and intricate work. How does he manage to do so?

The most important factor in his success was the pre-existence of Oberlin's own account of this period in Lenz's life. *Lenz* does not simply proceed along dazzling chains of associative dialogue, as do Büchner's plays, but works out a structure too, one which Büchner, a post-Romantic, adopts without identifying with it. He moves through it, through Oberlin's text, as if through a foreign country. His own voice arises out of Oberlin's and in opposition to it, as he deepens and intensifies the original account by involving us in what is happening within Lenz – rather than, like Oberlin, holding him at an appalled distance. Oberlin provides the material for one of the greatest of case-histories, but it is Büchner who writes that history. He identifies himself both with Oberlin, the observer (here his medical training comes into play), and with Lenz, the hag-ridden writer. His story is thus an Expressionist case-study: the protagonists are both real men and represent aspects of his own mind. Thus it is significant that he makes no reference within the story to the fact that Oberlin also writes: this is because Oberlin's role as writer is assumed by Büchner himself. This omission – one of the many small transmutations whereby he transforms a pedestrian narrative into perhaps the finest short story ever written – also serves to sharpen the contrast between the inhabitants of the valley, who only speak, and Lenz, who is a writer. It magnifies, and so justifies, his sense of total isolation.

Büchner's magnificent story ends with an account of how Lenz is placed in a straitjacket and led away by several men whose task it is to ensure that he does not do violence to himself; 'so lebte er hin' (so he lived on) are the last words. These words have at times been interpreted as so perfunctory as to indicate that *Lenz* is a fragment. This view is hardly tenable. Here, at the point at which Büchner, the sober narrator, and Lenz, the schizophrenic, appear to be furthest apart, they are one; Büchner shares his indifference, and both forgets about Lenz and identifies with him by passing into his soul and looking out at the world with his subject's blank eyes. And, as Paul Celan has hinted in his allusive address on receiving the Büchner-prize, entitled 'Der Meridian', the 'hin' with which the sentence ends has the casual depth of true greatness: for 'hin' means 'lost' or 'away'. As Lenz passes out of our sight, he is already lost, petrified, dead. The men who accompany him are his mourners.

THE ILLUSTRATED NOVEL:
THOUGHTS ON THE NOVELS OF DICKENS

In the late nineteenth century, the illustrated novel mediates between the popular narrative of the past recounted by an individual, and the popular narrative of the future, which will be presented by a group: between novel and film, individualist and collectivist forms of art. In the context of this transition it is particularly instructive to consider the position occupied by the author-illustrator. Having done this I will pass on to discuss the aesthetics of the illustrated novel in general.

The first example I have chosen is Lewis Carroll. The weakness of Carroll's illustrations to the 'Alice' books is evidence of a basic decision in favour of writing, but his obsession with the visual arts evident also from his excellent photographs (perhaps this photographic gift shows an admission of the primacy of the real within the visual sphere, thus accounting for the weakness of his fantastic drawings) is the irrational gap in an apparently purely word-obsessed work that renders it so disturbing to many children and adults; the gap indicates the dual personality Carroll is known to have possessed, and through it Tenniel squeezed to achieve his powerful illustrations. Tenniel's illustrations disturb us because they are so good and thus upset the balance between Carroll-writer and Carroll-imagemaker; the vestigial organ turns into a tail and wags the dog. The unity of two conceptions is the source of the book's mythical status; and when I call it 'mythical' I have in mind its capacity to overwhelm us. When the same argument is presented in dual form, it subverts our capacity to counter – the free subject is subjugated to the arraigning collectivity and forfeits his selfhood. We place such illustrated books in the sphere of childhood (all children's books are by definition illustrated), hoping thereby to neutralise them, but also secretly paying homage to their power to steal our individuality; they can reduce us to helplessness, just as they did when we were children and lacked the typologies necessary to blunt the impact of isolated works. The word-image combination that overwhelms the reader transmits the author's own childhood feeling of helplessness in the face of the older generation's towering authority. The reader conceived as a child is the barely literate proletatian, the 'twelve year old mind' so beloved of Hollywood.

My second example of an author-illustrator is Thackeray. His stated preference for drawing over writing can be seen to be the cause of the externality of *Vanity Fair*, its lack of a hero. In this context, Kubrick's decision to film a novel by Thackeray (though he chose *Barry Lyndon* rather than *Vanity Fair*) becomes quite an acute one; for Thackeray's objectivism befits the behaviourism of the camera. But at the same time, a moralist within Thackeray struggles with his dispassionately observing self, and this moralist seeks to impose values upon the apparently reified material and doll-like people. There is a conflict between a writerly desire for judgement and a painterly wish simply to record. The former prosecutes a narrative and is thus concerned with time, with the causes and effects of actions that call for criticism or approbation; the latter simply delights in the motionless momentary scene, in the fetish-character of each protagonist. Thus there emerges the ambiguous mixture of satire and humour that characterises his work.

In illustrated novels, the image is the authority that vouches for the words and vice versa; as authority it protects the imagination from the consequences of its absolute freedom. Thus the images that make stories more accessible to children and to the working class actually prevent them from using their imagination, tactically withdraw the freedom they appear to offer. In fact, literature uses images to stop the gaps and moments of weakness that threaten the spell-binding triumph of linguistic reason. Film narrative comes into being when the gaps can no longer be stopped, when the level of the image is granted equal authority by the *fin de siècle* doubt in the efficacy of language, the power of reason. The silent film with intertitles is the illustrated book as the working class experience it, and as those who criticise reason know it to be: the importance of the images magnified by lengthy contemplation, the words that cannot order irrational reality shrunk into mummified tokens.

Image and word fit together in books that reduce us to the helplessness of childhood by demanding of us a dual response. This duality can be found in all significant authors of the modern, post-Baudelairean era. It is native to all modern art that makes total demands (and offers to give 'a world' in return) and it can be isolated even in the unlikely subject of Dickens. Thus it is sometimes stated that a contradiction exists between his sentimentality and his cruel wit; in fact there is none. Dickens – the Cagliostro and dwarf-king of the English novel – simply selects those elements that will have a sure-fire effect upon his audience. He delights in exercising evident power over it during public readings, and quickens his own death with repeated performances of his *tour de force*, the death of Nancy. He subjugates the audience in a manner that anticipates Wagner. Thus it is no accident that Dickens's novels are the only ones in 'the great tradition' that cannot be prised out of the husk of their illustrations; they calculatingly overwhelm us like the works of author-illustrators. Orwell's remark that Dickens's books are abominably built but are topped off by marvellous gargoyles can be re-phrased and re-interpreted; the gargoyles are the sudden arresting flourishes fired at an audience already hypnotised by mechanical repetitions (one such baroque touch is the rotten wart on the forehead of the mill in Chapter III of *Our Mutual Friend*). The unexpectedness of the fanciful detail drops accusingly on the inattentive reader-pupil. Dickens soothes the public with melodramatic devices that make them feel at one with, or even superior to, the author, and then the Symbolist poet in him disrupts their security. He can render the squirming misery of put-upon children with such exactitude because he occupies the best of all vantage-points to observe them, that of the arbitrary schoolmaster. Even so, his repetitions are not just tactics to induce hypnosis in his pupils before violently firing off a piece of chalk at the one whose eyes are seen to droop; they are also signs that he is passing through the depressive doldrums of his own imagination. This experience of the doldrums gives him his real empathy with children; they are the periods when he shares their helplessness.

In Dickens, the reader enticed out of the text by the illustration (during the periods of the author's doldrums the reader is only too happy to defect) is then punished by the text for his faithlessness. Text and image are Scylla and Charybdis. The reader feels the suction of the whirlpool as he nears the image; the tempted eye travels to and fro between text and image, and the image spins round in the mind like a boat at the top of the maelstrom before the single sentence it illustrates sucks it down into its occasion. (This is the feeling of vertigo characteristic of the modern.) Thus the text finally swallows the image up – and the reader who looks back to it during the course of later reading experiences it as mere driftwood circling aimlessly outside the purposeful current of the narrative. Retrospectively, the image appears to be the representative of a different, unwritten text, for its portrayal of the characters usually diverges from our own mental image of them. Thus the illustration seems like a discarded variant, part of an alternative narrative coursing along unofficial channels underneath the authoritative final version. (It plays its part in the genesis of the aesthetics of the permutable text.) Whilst reading the dismal final pages of *Our Mutual Friend*, which betray art in the name of hypocritical optimism (the danger signal is Dickens's stated pride in his own accomplished resolution of the story), one recalls with regret the non-existence of this other text. Two-facedly, the text enlists the image to create a diversion that distracts the reader and so renders him incapable of judging the text (together, word and image evoke myth; the image is a still from the Hollywood film whose ideology Dickens already anticipates as he sells his rights to his book). Once the diversion has done its work, the text assassinates its partner, leaving his immobile corpse in a backwater as the narrative itself flows on. Yet when one's reading is over and one has been disgusted by the unctuousness of the required happy ending, one longs for that backwater; for the compromised narrative has led to a weir.

Near the beginning of Chapter VII of *Our Mutual Friend* one encounters the following two passages in close proximity: 'Stumping with fresh vigour, he goes in at the dark greasy entry, pushes a little greasy dark reluctant side-door, and follows the door into the little dark greasy shop'; and then, later: 'The face looking up is a sallow face with weak eyes, surmounted by a tangle of reddish-dusty hair. The owner of the face has no cravat on'. Here one sees something characteristic of Dickens; features are reiterated, the writing is almost embarrassingly complacent in its indigent resort to stock epithets (though this is also expressive of Dickens's intuitive sympathy with the destitute, his respect for the rhythm of consumption of the semi-literate), and then a tourniquet is placed on the dribbling of epithets and the spent power of language is girt up anew. Dickens's novels are non-identical with themselves (that is why they attract illustrations – concrete ciphers of that non-identity); their dual nature precipitates them into stylistic lurchings and into a passion for objects that are similarly riven, compromised. Thus the grease of the first sentence migrates everywhere (like the dust or river slime that pervade the novel), and every object is viewed through a unifying smeared lens; and yet in the second sentence, a man is merely the owner of his face, which does not express him. The impossibility of self-expression is one source of the duality of Dickens's style, for the hard mask of grimacing wit will not permit emotion to seep through it and feigns instead a spine-chilling derisiveness, whilst the emotions, unexpressed, become maudlin and vague and break through the flippancy in quick bursts of bad melodramatic dialogue. The Dickensian stock epithet is akin to the Wagnerian leitmotif; both are repeated obsessively because to cease to assert one's identity would be to pass into the belly of the machine that breaks John Harmon down into Julius Handford and then into John Rokesmith and that administers money to the character as an unguent to alter it for the worse. Tautologous repetition of one's one identity with oneself becomes the last bulwark against irrevocable loss of self, for the stock epithet or 'characteristic' tic is the grotesque form individuality assumes – sticking helplessly in its groove, outwearing its single tune – before it is eradicated. The rhythm of departure from oneself and subsequent return that is the rhythm of the seasons and of folk art is interrupted by the advent of capitalist industry. There are no seasons in the uniform horror of Dickens's London, whose pervading smog screens off all remembrance of an order founded upon anything other than man's exploitation by man, and Dickens himself perpetuates this exploitation by enslaving his audience. The false ending he appends to *Our Mutual Friend* is a sign of the breakdown of his own identity, as he ceases to be an artist. His characters, like himself, see-saw back and forth between mania and depression, gush and image-like fixity. This duality is typical of figures who are invisible (in the modern crowd, all men are invisible men): figures like John Harmon or Dickens himself, frantically striving to establish his own visibility as an author by reading out loud before a public. He is aware that the famous author has to be seen, has to become an icon, just as the text that wishes to woo both the upper and the lower classes must contain both images and words. These invisible figures have been de-materialised, 'idealised', and could never be securely 'en-graved', for they have never lived and so they can never die. The text is non-identical, breaks open at points to admit illustrations and then fills the breach to repel them. The duality of image and text in Dickens is that of body and soul, exacerbated by the abuse of the body and the ignorance of the soul promoted by industrial working conditions.

The conclusive sign of man's non-identity is the existence of a woman with equal rights. As women attain these rights in the late nineteenth century, men become increasingly non-identical. When seeking to depict positive female characters Dickens frequently has to resort to cloying euphemism. Euphemism is a sophistic attempt to repress the image of a thing by superimposing a positive mental image upon a basically negative one so as to induce a visual blur; it is language divorced from *things*, related only to itself, setting up within itself a malign dialectic whose whirlings are intended to distract the reader from reality (that is, to prevent him from imagining the scene and grasping its falsity). In *Our Mutual Friend*, Jenny Wren and Bella Wilfer (what names!) both use euphemistic baby-talk when addressing their parents. The euphemistic speaker, like the euphemistic writer, blindly equates fantasy and reality; he sees no contradiction or dialectic between them. Euphemism assumes a saccharine reconciliation of good and evil, with the good predominant of course: thus Jenny Wren's drunken father is described by her as 'my child', and as in sickly freakishness she names him other than he is, Dickens hypocritically suggests that fantasy can hold its own with an evil reality by repressing awareness of its true nature. In fact, the fantasy is the consequence of the sentimental helplessness of the fantasist. Dickens believes that fantasy can provide an alternative language to the idiom of Utilitarianism, but at the same time he emasculates it by subordinating it to the demands of a (more or less) realistic fiction. The result is pseudo-fantasy, akin to the apparent privileging of the ideologically 'female' that actually imposes upon women the existing stereotypes. The pert yet submissive bride (Bella Wilfer) is a totally unreal synthesis of disparate elements into a numbing unity. Nineteenth-century programme music acts in a similar manner inasmuch as it elides the conflicts between the arts by melting them into a sticky homogeneity – the music that mimics a cuckoo or a storm claims to be something other than music, to have concrete referents. Unsure of itself it bolsters itself up with language, just as in Dickens realism embezzles funds from fantasy, and just as the written word lives on the credit it draws from the illustration.

The linking of author and illustrator is a merger of bankrupts: a
pseudo-solution to problems that are not treated head-on until the
advent of modernism.

II

The illustrated novel and the novel published in serial form appear at the
same time. The individual episodes of the serial novel have to possess a
certain degree of autonomy, their closure prefiguring the overall postponed closure. But because this relative autonomy exists, there is also
the danger of a loss of continuity; that is why the plot of the Victorian
novel is often so ramshackle. The illustration re-establishes continuity.
It provides a mnemonic device, a metonymic image of the character who
acts in the narrative, and so serves to refamiliarise the reader with the
story instantaneously. However, it also helps to destroy the element of
story and so takes the first step towards the eventual destruction of
narrative in modernism. It does so by causing the reader to concentrate
on character and relationships as entities that are fixed. The primary
example is of course Dickens. In order for the image to present a
metonymic précis of the story, that story must be one in which the
characters are unchanging and can be fixed as icons. No character can be
allowed to develop or to shed his mode of behaviour. Moreover, the
illustrator's way of seeing influences that of the novelist; the result is the
expressionist externality of the cartoonist, which has its prose equivalent
in Dickens's compulsive simultaneous exaggeration and flattening. As
Patrick Swinden notes, 'Dickens' characters ... are fit only to be looked
at. What it would be like to look at the world *through* Mrs Gamp or Miss
Havisham or Mrs Clenham is unthinkable.'[1] Moreover, the fact that
Dickens's characters exist only in a certain setting, surrounded by
objects that reflect energy onto them like the play of a fire before a
watching face, indicates the depth of the symbiosis between his stories
and their illustrations; the character is conceived, but the umbilical cord
of his original environment is never cut. He is trapped in it: one reason
for the recurrent Dickens motif of the prison. The figure who appears in
this way is the inhabitant of a drawing, a single generalised moment.
When they leave their settings the characters suffer intense disorientation, like Little Dorrit in Italy. In some respects Dickens can be said to be
less a caricaturist than a self-caricaturist: his own language is as
grotesque and as laden with repetition as that of his characters. In this
context, the illustrations provide windows in the wall of the stylisation;

they create a sort of relief, as if the author wished to demonstrate by their means that he is less self-enclosed than he seems, that he is able to co-operate with others and admit another artist into his world.

In his study of *Victorian Novelists and Their Illustrators*, John Harvey states that the serial novel required illustrations to function as eye-catching advertisements for the text, but that 'another factor, however, was the essentially visual character of the comedy'.[2] An important ellipsis underlies Harvey's useful generalisation. The comedy may indeed have been of a primarily visual nature, but should the serialised novel be equated with comedy *tout court*? Harvey makes the identification unconsciously; and although the case of Dickens underlines the validity of the identification, it should be accompanied by more reflection. For the comedy of Dickens is not simply a matter of traditional farce. It is also a response to the deliberate degradation of the human character into the machine of the industrial age, part of which was the reduction of the writer to a cog in the serial's machine. In identifying himself with this machine, in retaining the serial mode of production that brought him the success of *Pickwick*, Dickens thought he was identifying with the audience; in fact, he was adapting to the planned centralised circulation of capitalism. One recalls that it was the degradation of the human into the mechanical that was interpreted by Bergson as representing the essentially comic; it is really the black comedy of industrialising capitalism. Dickens presents the effects of the reduction of the real characters of Jane Austen – the real humanity briefly perceived during early Romanticism, which resounds, as Adorno notes, through the historically privileged moment of the music of Beethoven – in the conditions of urbanisation and a centralising economy. The people spawned by this historical process are what Orwell terms Dickens himself: gigantic dwarves. Dickens's work is symptomatic of the feeling that the new developments had amputated the human character. All that remains is the relentlessly self-repeating machine, its ghost exorcised. Thus the comedy of the illustrated novel is fundamentally bitter; as the illustration abbreviates personality into 'character', so the novel is degraded in order to represent a more marketable product: the ancestor of the modern pseudo-book.

The illustrations to a text constitute a reading of that text. The attitude of this implicit reader is meant to show us how to read the text. Yet the need to provide such a reading implies an authorial fear of the real distance from the reader (perhaps Dickens's fear that his habitual externality exiles him from the body of mankind?). It is as if Dickens realised very early that he would lose the immense readership of *Pickwick*; as if one side of his personality consented to develop far beyond

Pickwick on the sole condition that the works that outstripped it would be condemned to appear in the same format. The retention of the illustrated format indicates both an Utopian will to oneness with the public, and a nightmarish feeling of entrapment in the same behaviour. Thus in the course of Dickens's development a gap begins to open up between text and image – a gap that finally expressed itself in the acrimonious break with Browne and in the decision to permit Marcus Stone and Luke Fildes to illustrate *Our Mutual Friend* and *Edwin Drood*, although both artists represented a newer, more naturalistic style of drawing, which had been attacked by. Dickens himself. Here the novelist and the illustrator cease to be partners; rather, the illustration serves as a popularising agent, a means of maintaining the increasingly tenuous links with the public. But as Dickens moves into the final phase of his development, there are losses as well as gains, and the resulting disorientation is reflected in the uncertain relationship between text and image. The loss of bearings expresses itself in the increasingly uneasy mixture of realism and fantasy in these late works, producing what I have termed – perhaps unkindly – the 'pseudo-fantasy' of *Our Mutual Friend*. Here Dickens is seen grafting onto his hard-nosed comedy a certain seriousness and intended social diagnosis. He is no longer content with his earlier fantastic metaphors for reality, of which the schoolroom, the workhouse and the prison are the most effective. He moves away from a metaphorical presentation of society to a more realistic one. But as he does so he remains the tragically self-divided clown who wishes to play Hamlet, a precursor in many respects of the flawed career of Chaplin. The illustrations worn by his novels tinkle to the very last like the bells that betray a jester; they mock his aspirations towards social statement. They repeat and parody the text, licensed to do so by Dickens himself, who degrades his best spontaneous turns of phrase with self-serving repetition – the toll paid to the machine that pays by the line – wearing out the crisp contours of their first mintage.

III

The word 'serial' is ambiguous: it can designate either an advanced musical practice or a soap opera in sections. This duality renders it one of the points at which the complicity of 'high' and 'low' culture is revealed; such ambiguous words are the 'primal words' upon which Freud has meditated (e.g. 'to cleave' means both to bifurcate and to cling to). The works of Dickens are similarly ambiguous. Such works and words are conductors of the contradictions within society and the mind.

The notion of the serial is post-Romantic. With the advent of Romanticism the parts of a work, of a society, of a life, become detachable from the whole. The self has to break up, dissolve into its constituent parts (ego, id, super-ego), before those parts can become sufficiently discontinuous to be arranged in a series. The first and fundamental break is caused by the Romantic invention of the Double, who is the inhabitant of a society in which the democratically proclaimed rights of the individual, the fruit of the French revolution, conflict with the necessity of social institutions, which contradict freedom; the disparity splits the self, and by the time of modernism the splits had become so numerous and profound as to generate a multiple personality; in modernism the individual can oppose society all the more effectively because he is himself a society and so need never depart from his own interiority. This multiple selfhood is adumbrated in Hoffmann. The compulsive repetitions in his *Devil's Elixirs* create a field in which the same event is seen from the viewpoint of different observers; and these observers are all 'one person' at different points in the space-time continuum. There emerges a difficulty in choosing which person to be – as in modern 'role' sociology – which is also a difficulty in choosing what to write. The text becomes a series of self-caricatures (for it has no integral selfhood), so it is no suprise that Hoffmann should have been fascinated by the image of the Double, in the face of which one's being (and writing) becomes grotesque; by the repetition of the alienated self, the first product of the mass-production line. No one variant can be finally eliminated, just as no person can be left behind by Medardus: he leaves them and they rematerialise. The narrator thus becomes aware that his own work, like the life of Medardus (both are recounted in the first person), is a series of repetitions. Character is formed by compulsive repetition. The self-consciousness this engenders forces the writer to alternate between deliberate innovation (in an attempt to outwit repetition) and writing any old how, knowing that he cannot step over his own shadow. The result is a mixture of high art and masochistic trash, such as is found in Hoffmann, and later, in Dickens. And the continuity between the high and the low can be seen in the way Dickens and Melville both pass from the popular serial (in Dickens, this means his work is actually serialised; in Melville, that it is composed of detachable parts) *without realising what has happened*: both feel themselves still to be true to themselves, but both are aghast at the alacrity with which audiences melt away.

The post-Romantic serialised text is ambiguous. The serial is made up of detachable parts, is published in successive issues of newspapers and journals, and the interval between issues allows the author to gauge which elements do and do not 'work' as far as the public is concerned. The narrative can then be overhauled and a more enticing element inserted. The process involves both a degree of collective participation in the making of the text (participation above all by the collective uncon-scious), and the trickery of the demagogue who says *vox populi, vox dei* but whose sole god is his own Absolute Ego. The length of time over which the serial appears also enhances the effect of realism. It makes reading like living; the serial is the novel borne down by the ball and chain of the reality principle. A certain sympathy between the 'low' serial and the 'high' novel is evident in the fact that both are post-teleological: neither knows where it is going. A long-term goal is sacrificed to a series of short-term goals. Each represses the knowledge of the inevitability of the end that is the knowledge of death. Instead of an ending there is the shock of interruption, the pseudo-end. The popular serial obeys the dictates of the collective unconscious, which is of course to a large degree 'the political unconscious'; the unpopular serial, the non-serialised serial, follows the winding paths of the unconscious of its own author, like the improvised novels of Melville. Both are afflicted by a crisis of the linear – by a desire to deny death, since death has ceased to represent a further stage in the linear progress of a life that is prolonged into, or inverted by, an after-life. Each is made up of a series of insertions and repetitions the main purpose of which is to postpone the end. Another name for the insertion is of course the disgression, the anti-formal guiding principle of countless Romantic works. The digressive work is often picaresque and composed in the first person. The narrative 'I' cannot guess what lies beyond the horizon, so each experience beckons with the trauma and thrill of the Baudelairean 'nouveau'. This blindness to what comes next is a reaction both to the unforeseeable course of a history that has been dislocated by technological change and to the increasing compartmentalisation of society: all men slave at thair sepa-rate machines, their conversation crushed by the intervening din. Whence the obsessive isolation of Dickens's figures; like schoolmasters – his archetypal subjects – they gesticulate in the vacuum of their separa-tion from adult society. The triumph of the narrative over the serial, which is celebrated when it is published as a book and reveals its rhyming plot, is a Pyrrhic victory, for the novel bears the scars of its gestation and its plot is a bedraggled self-parody.

It is rare for novels to be serialised nowadays. This is partly because the popularising illustrated component of the serial has now detached itself from the novel and assumed separate televised life. The brief conjunction of text and image broke down when it was revealed to be a marriage of convenience, a stepping-stone in the process of self-education. This self-improvement was of course deeply characteristic of the nineteenth century; the illustrations allowed the illiterate to enter the text and stood as signs of the possibility of bettering oneself. But in the end the Gospel according to Samuel Smiles proved an Apocrypha. Those who were able to enter the text by means of the image, passing on into the higher world of literacy, closed the doors of the image behind themselves to preserve the relative exclusivity of their recent elevation. Those who wished to read denied the existence of the useless appendix, the organ of sight, the wondering, non-knowing look. They carried on into a blank world of novels without illustrations. Meanwhile, the others were left only with the mystified, unenlightening image-streams of the films. The serial reader is a Romantic and the last episode is the stuff of his dreams during the interval before the next part. But his Romantic impatience finally bred a desire for instant gratification, and so there emerged on the one hand the single-volume novel open to total immediate ingestion, and on the other, television, where the programme glides on automatically to the next item and leaves no pauses for dreaming. For if it did, the dream would reveal itself in its true colour – black – as a nightmare, part of our increasingly frightening history. The link between the individual and the collectivity has been shattered; an absolute gulf yawns between the book, the art of the individual, and the television programme, the art of the collectivity. Of course, in the process all these words – 'art', 'individual', 'collectivity' – become fearsome self-caricatures. In the light of subsequent developments, the serialised and illustrated novels of Dickens seem to have been the expression of a vanished expectation, the broken Utopian hope of an art for all men. The hope was fading even as Dickens himself was writing his way into the fog of *Our Mutual Friend*. Inhabitants of a culture whose unified, baseless rhetoric gives no individual person ground on which to stand, we have lost our Great Expectations.

READING SIGNS: HAWTHORNE AND THE CHARACTERS OF ALLEGORY

It is generally agreed that Hawthorne is an allegorist; indeed, he says as much himself in his remarks on the untranslated 'French writer' Aubepine that introduce *Rappacini's Daughter*. But what kind of an

allegorist is he? Is it possible to practise allegory following the Romantic
upheaval, which had condemned allegory on the grounds that the signs
it employs are merely arbitrary? Is allegory compatible with novelistic
realism, and if not, does the genre of the romance provide an atmosphere
ambiguous enough to sustain the two tendencies? And are there two
concepts of allegory, as A. D. Nuttall maintains, or even seven types
thereof, as Empson and the Cabbalists would doubtless argue? I will try
to intimate some answers through an examination of *The Scarlet Letter*,
The Marble Faun, and an assortment of the tales.

Let me begin by saying that irrespective of how many types or
concepts of allegory there may be, the allegorical impulse is clearly
manifest in two different ways in the two media that constitute the
mainstream of allegorical art. For there are allegorical paintings, and
there are allegorical texts, and the two are closely related in one era of the
history of art in particular, that of expressionism. The two art-forms may
seem to preclude one another: the allegorical painting will feature a
figure, often a saint, identifiable (connected with a conceptual system
beyond the sensual moment of the picture-space) only on the basis of the
single object he or she holds, such as Catherine's wheel, Lucy's eyes on a
platter, and so on; the allegorical text will present figures bearing the
names of virtues and vices, who have no sensuous being and are
arranged like counters to designate various mental events. The fascination of Hawthorne's work lies in the way in which he confronts and fuses
these two aspects of allegory. In his work, allegory as image and allegory
as writing interact. Benjamin has described how, in the period of the
Baroque, the written strives to become an image, a hieroglyph, and sees
this urge as characteristic of allegory.[1] His words could have been
written with *The Scarlet Letter* in mind. The link between the
psychomachia of the written allegory, which projects aspects of the mind
in the form of personifications, and the painting of the figure equipped
with an emblematic clue to its identity, is the fact that the allegorical
image is an image that is a mystified part of the self that views it. Or
rather, it is that self in the form of otherness: possessed by Rage, the
person becomes Rage itself. Allegorical psychology studies the modes of
human possession; whence Hawthorne's fascination by obsessions that
resemble possession by demons. And yet the people so possessed remain
people. Hester Prynne is both the personification of a state of mind
(Shame, Defiance and Remorse: the mixed mood gives her a nature more
complex than that of the figures of traditional allegory, so bestowing on
her an illusive realism) and the bearer of an emblem that requires
decipherment (and which because of her relative complexity resists

decoding), the letter 'A'. In *The Marble Faun*, Donatello's ears and Hilda's doves perform a similar function. Thus Hawthorne's characters are both people and emblems in tableaux.

Hawthorne's figures are 'characters' inasmuch as they partake of the atmosphere of a realistic or historical novel; 'images' insofar as they are ciphers in an allegory. Nuttall writes of allegory:

> Dr. Johnson says, 'Fame tells a tale, and Victory hovers over a general or perches on a standard; but Fame and Victory do no more.' But the effect of this is to stop allegory in its tracks, to 'de-metaphysicise' it and to relegate it to the same sphere of static personification. Similarly, Lewis, writing about Statius, says, 'Mars is "discovered raging" when the curtain rises and before he has any reason to rage. Naturally; for when *War* is not raging he does not exist. It is his *esse* to rage.' Yet how is the task of describing the inner world to be carried forward if we are not to see that the virtues and the vices do *to one another*?'[2]

The case of Hawthorne prompts one to ask whether anything is in train in his works – a question that also arises in connection with the self-oblivious, discontinuous nature of his narrative – and also whether a temporal event can be an allegorical one. The opposition between temporality and stasis suggested by Nuttall renders the problem of transformation a peculiarly acute one for Hawthorne. One can see if and how he resolves the problem in *The Marble Faun*, which was entitled *Transformation* in its first English printing.

The narrative of *The Marble Faun* occupies two levels. One is the level of total stasis, a level on which nothing happens in a text that consequently has to be padded out with leisurely reflections from Hawthorne's tourist notebook. This is the level on which Hilda, Miriam and Kenyon exist. To revert to the terms of the passage by Nuttall, none of them do anything to each other, for all are fixated on their own transformed images, which are manifest to them in the form of their own art-works. Their activity as artists reveals only the fixed nature of their characters. Here the only event is an oblique reflex of the main event of the novel, which is the murder by Miriam and Donatello of her shadowy persecutor. This oblique event is Hilda's recognition of her friend's true nature; the fact that she had not perceived Miriam's character before only indicates the depth of her self-absorption. (Hilda's lack of knowledge of Miriam is compounded by the author's confusion of the two, both of whom he compares to the portrait of Beatrice Cenci. They can both be likened to the same painting because the painter's model is not identical with the role he ascribes her on the canvas, and this non-identity is a recurrent theme in the novel. In this context, Hilda would be the model who is represented in the painting of Beatrice Cenci; Miriam, Beatrice Cenci herself.) But on another level, something really does happen in the novel: Donatello is initiated into humanity, and forfeits his faun-like gaiety. Hawthorne neatly evades the difficulty of showing how one state of mind is affected by another: on the one hand, by making his allegorical figures the seats of several emotions, whose alternation passes for development; and on the other, by depicting Donatello as less than human. Thus Donatello's gaiety does not symbolise Innocence or Joy. For as far as Hawthorne is concerned, there is no such thing as human Innocence; Donatello's innocence makes of him a frisky animal, a skipping faithful hound. His crime is a precondition of his birth into humanity; here, as in *The Scarlet Letter*, the image of the Garden of Eden and the notion of the fortunate fall are strongly present. He enters the human world as Remorse, and only then, as he becomes human and allegorical at one and the same time, can he enter the element of Miriam, who then becomes capable of loving him. Crime and Remorse make a fitting pair – though of course only Remorse, only Donatello, can sit in gaol. His crime separates him from the circle of Nature's dance and banishes him to the tower. For Hawthorne, individuation is the fruit of crime. And this pattern of stasis on one level of the story and transformation on another mimics the method of *The Scarlet Letter*, in which Pearl occupies the amoral position of Donatello, and the other figures are frozen in allegorical poses. It is only through allowing one figure to exist outside the allegorical schema that the allegorical text is able to proceed and to mesh its static allegorical personifications with its temporal allegory of the development of consciousness. Pearl and Donatello are the ghosts who turn the tables of Hawthorne's narrative. But because his novels are weighted in favour of the allegorical characters, who are in the majority, they are prone to sink under ponderous ornamentation and whimsical arabesque. The fiction congeals because the stream of realism trickles so thinly through the allegorical fields. And this is why Hawthorne is so much the inferior of Richardson, in whom allegory and realism are in constantly provocative tension, and neither achieves dominance. It is because the allegorical code is predominant that one can read *The Marble Faun* in its first version, without the Postscript, and feel no urge to know any more about the characters: they have been sufficiently fully 'placed' as allegorical images for us not to wish for any further realistic details. They have been fixed in the present moment of a painting. Those readers who pressed Hawthorne for more details were clutching at the straws of the realistic sub-text in the work in order to try to stand it on its feet as realistic fiction, rather than leaving it in the air, surrounded by a blank, like a portrait on a wall.

Allegory is a peculiarly seventeenth-century form of realism; it is in Bunyan, whose influence is so apparent in *The Celestial Railroad*, that the two meet. And yet realism had developed in a different manner between the time of *Pilgrim's Progress* and that of Hawthorne. In order to steer the novel closer to its seventeenth-century origin, Hawthorne takes the moralism of Gothic romance and lowers its temperature in order to make it appear more realistic, giving the Gothic an air of sobriety in which its morals recall the proverbs of Bunyan's folk-art. However, it is his weakest and most perfunctory works which subordinate characters completely to their allegorical function in the manner of Bunyan. This is the case in 'The Man of Adamant', which is predetermined by its title. In this short tale, Richard Digby retreats into the words to escape the sinful world; here the petrification of his heart finds expression in the petrification of his body by the lime in the water that drips from the roof of his cave. More interesting is a tale which takes up the theme of the marble heart that is one of Hawthorne's constant preoccupations, *Ethan Brand*. Significantly enough, the title is semi-allegorical. 'Brand' alludes ludes to the flames into which Ethan steps. Are these the flames of hell, of a self-consuming monomania, or simply of the actual kiln he enters? Can this brand be plucked from the burning? As usual when Hawthorne is at his most intriguing and induces the reader to join in the effort of interpretation, one has to say: all of them and none of them and perhaps (and here the characteristic frustration Hawthorne evokes may come into play) something beyond them all.

Allegory is a method of interpretation closely associated with Biblical hermeneutics. Consequently it is interesting that both these tales mention the Bible as the prototype of the unreadable text; to attempt an unequivocal reading is to destroy oneself. Thus, as the forest darkened around Richard Digby, he 'made continual mistakes in what he read, converting all that was gracious and merciful, to denunciations of vengeance and unutterable woe, on every created being but himself'.[3] Similarly, Ethan Brand is consumed by his attempt to unravel the significance of the words 'the unpardonable sin'. Puritan allegory is the realism of a world in which all totalities have been fragmented and in which democracy has infiltrated, and been poisoned by, religion; for each man has been allowed to invest the Word with meanings dictated by his own private experience, and to inflate the incidents of his life into universal symbols. For Hawthorne, this means that three types of book are consistently misread. Firstly, there is the Bible, misread by Richard Digby, Ethan Brand, and the early Puritan communities of New England. Secondly, there is the Book of Nature. *The Great Stone Face* is about the persistence of the misreading of nature; and even the privileged Ernest, who perceives the difference between the great stone face in the mountain and the faces of those ostensibly great men who are supposed to be like it, is himself unable to recognise it as his own face. The comet in the sky is misread in *The Scarlet Letter*, and Hawthorne's own sense of impotence in the face of Nature is apparent in the decayed neo-classical language with which he refers to it (he talks of 'the sylvan banquet' and 'the floral tribe'). The phosphorescent nature of this language recalls that of Goethe's *Die Wahlverwandtschaften*. Finally, the book of the artist himself is misread. And here one notes that Hawthorne's work, like the Bible, is as it were deliberately confused in order to make it harder of access, in order to punish all those who have no ears to hear. This is apparent from Kenneth Dauber's excellent analysis of *Rappacini's Daughter*.

> Though the one title serves for the whole, though the two stories are told within a single narrative frame, yet there are discontinuities, odd dislocations that suggest a co-presence of tales that retain their individuality. The tales reside on the same printed spot, as it were, but follow independent logics. As Aubepine narrates, he emphasises now one, now the other, now both simultaneously. But it is as if each story is complete from the start, and Aubepine, shifting back and forth, is keeping them both going, preventing them from receding into the narrative surface they both inhabit.[4]

I think this dual motion can be perceived at times even on the level of a single sentence, such as this one in 'Ethan Brand':

> And it seemed to little Joe – a timorous and imaginative child – that the silent forest was holding its breath, until some fearful thing should happen.[5]

Here Hawthorne is both a Post-Romantic, inclined to project feelings onto nature, and an American, outside the known and largely subjugated landscape of European Romanticism, who sees nature as harshly other. On the one hand, the forest does seem to hold its breath in fearful sympathy with the human scene; on the other, Joe is timorous and imaginative – the worldly Puritan in Hawthorne mocks the avid Puritan reader of the signs of nature – and so his artistic character puts him in a position in which he misreads the facts. Hawthorne's stilted style enacts an extreme self-consciousness about the degree of his own uniqueness, and also a grim inclination to belittle it (as in 'Alice Doane's Appeal', where his narrator quotes with casual mockery from a tale of his own devising and suppression).

For Hawthorne, language is neither diaphanous nor opaque, but a black veil. *The Scarlet Letter* is so successful because the partial, fragmentary nature of the letter-sign demands and frustrates the effort of interpretation and thereby foregrounds the uncommitted metaphysical whimsicality of Hawthorne's style. It is whimsical because it experiences neither the despair of exclusion from meaning nor the happiness of initiation; its flashes of desperation come from its fear that because it is lukewarm it will be 'spat out', as the Bible warns that the Laodiceans will be. It is lukewarm because it is only by withholding meanings, only by suppressing what follows the letter 'A', that it can graduate from the level of language to that of the hieroglyph, from the world of language and change to the desired fixed state of a painting. The will to stasis – and the concomitant fascination by processes of petrification – generates a fascinating, uneasy compromise between linearity and stillness. Hawthorne's prose advances an uneasy dialectic of events and their neutralisation. A voice will ring out, but the disruptive immediacy of the act will then curdle into a description that transforms the voice into history. If Hawthorne writes of American history, it is to show how soon events lose their momentum and become national emblems and myths. The process is akin to the one whereby people are suckled into their portraits in Poe – except that Hawthorne eliminates the drama of the struggle between the transcriber and that which he transcribes, which at first resists mortification. In *The Scarlet Letter*, John Wilson is compared to a portrait. 'The voice which had called her attention was that of the reverend and famous John Wilson, the eldest clergyman of Boston, a great scholar like most of his contemporaries in the profession, and withal a man of kind and genial spirit. This last attribute, however, has been less carefully developed than his intellectual gifts, and was, in truth, rather a matter of shame and self-congratulation with him. There he stood, with a border of grizzled locks beneath his skullcap, while his grey eyes, accustomed to the shaded light of his study, were winking, like those of Hester's infant, in the unadulterated sunshine. He looked like the darkly engraved portraits which we see prefixed to old volumes of sermons; and had no more right than one of those portraits would have, to step forth, as he now did, and meddle with a question of human guilt, passion and anguish.'[6] The passage is intriguing: the Puritan past is made present in a form stamped with its own preterition, the sign of its present absence. The necromancy of the romance seems 'to bring history to life', but this life is then revealed to be an hallucination above a tomb, as the book reminds us of the fact that it is only a book by alluding to other books in which John Wilson is present only as an unspeaking image, forbidden to come forth from oblivion (forbidden to step out of history and into this novel). Wilson is apparently humanly present, but then we realise that he cannot be present directly, for all knowledge of the past is mediate. At first the novel claims superiority to the strict writer of history, and then surrenders to history by discovering that its imagination is dependent on the dusty book of sermons. As is his habit, Hawthorne presents a person or object, and then muffles their presence by pointing away from them to the context that reveals their significance, to the emblem they bear. The repression of the uncategorised event is a puritanical repression of the spontaneous.

In Hawthorne's world, every disruption dialectically provokes its own repression. Every action is the occasion of an equal and opposite reaction, whence the air of hindrance and deadlock in his prose. Hester Prynne will on the one hand step outside the Puritan system; but on the other she declines ever to depart from the Puritan settlement. The deadlock between possibilities appears even in microscopic features of the narrative, such as the opposition between 'red' and 'scarlet' in this passage in *The Scarlet Letter*, which is also part of the opposition between seeing and naming:

> 'It were well', muttered the most iron-visaged of the old dames, 'if we stripped Madam Hester's rich gown off her dainty shoulders; and as for the red letter, which she hath stitched so curiously, I'll bestow a rag of mine own rheumatic flannel, to make a fitter one!'
>
> 'O, peace, neighbours, peace!' whispered their youngest companion; 'do not let her hear you! Not a stitch in that embroidered letter, but she has felt it in her heart.'
>
> The grim beadle now made a gesture with his staff.
>
> Make way, good people, make way, in the King's name!' cried he. 'Open a passage; and, I promise ye, Mistress Prynne shall be set where man, woman and child may have a fair sight of her brave apparel, from this time till an hour past meridian. A blessing on the righteous colony of the Massachusetts, where iniquity is dragged out into the sunshine! Come along, Madam Hester, and show your scarlet letter in the market place!'[7]

'Red' is what the colour seems to the eye: it is a neutral denotation of colour. But 'scarlet' is red inserted into the context of moral language and culture; of the idiom which speaks of 'scarlet sins' (by calling them 'scarlet' it renders them a deformation of natural red) and also, of course, of 'scarlet women'. Hawthorne's novel alternates between the judgement, the acknowledgement of the rights of culture, embodied in the word 'scarlet', and the symbolist reverberations of 'red': the red of life, of blood, of shame, of passion, of the flames of Hell. The red object that flares out against its background is an obsessive motif in Hawthorne's work: it is the eye of the furnace in *The Snow Image* and *Ethan Brand*, the flame that engulfs the witch, the fire of the artist's thought in *The Devil in Manuscript*. In all these cases, the way in which flame stands out identifies self-assertion with self-destruction. It is characteristic of Hawthorne to present his story as pre-existing the narrative process that manifests it in the world; this justifies his self-consciousness about the appropriateness of any translation from the context in which it is embedded into the a-contextuality, the arena of free play that is the novel. The scarlet letter ostentatiously prefigures *The Scarlet Letter*; *Wakefield* is a meditation on the anecdote contained in its opening paragraph, and hence on the relationship between the verbal, public, iconic story and the story written in isolation, which could in theory stretch to infinity; in *Main Street* the artist ineffectually rehearses a past that has no need of his mediation; in *Alice Doane's Appeal*, the telling of a story to a few girls involves the suppression of the author's own written story, from which it quotes. This story juts out of the authorial pentimento like a ruin. The letter 'A' in *The Scarlet Letter* is also a ruin, the beginning of something that is not completed – the alphabet – and the inauguration of language, which makes possible the many stories of which this is but one.

The text or the events which appear in a partial, ruined form call forth the allegorical method of reading the signatures of all things. The allegorical image is a ruin, a fragment, a dream-trace; the Romantic predilection for ruins and dreams stems from the fact that both are characterised by the partial nature of their images. The rest is hidden. 'Allegories are to the realm of thoughts what ruins are to the realm of things.'[8] It is appropriate that after the appearance of the world of ruins, Rome, in *The Marble Faun*, Hawthorne should move on to his last, incomplete romances. Thus, it can be seen that Romanticism is less critical of allegory than of one of allegory's ossified forms. Although the Romantics generally praise symbols and deprecate allegories, in actuality the Romantic criticism of the allegory is simply the nether side of the Romantic practice of allegory. Both are aspects of the experience of the fragmentary, the incomplete. The allegory is its negative aspect, the pain of incompletion; the symbol is the part elevated to the level of the germ of a new whole, the mystical moment that appears to subsume a totality into itself rather than allude to the perpetual absence of totality. In fact it is not the Romantics *per se*, but the idealistic Romantics, who criticise allegory; it has the bitter taste of realism as it reminds one of the world the art-work excludes and of the pain of exclusion in general. In this sense, allegory is a form of realism, symbolism an idealistic dream of plenitude.

The Romantics criticised the allegorical image on the grounds of its arbitrariness. In their works however the image remains arbitrary, but it is the arbitrariness of the object lost in its environment, which the poet picks out as a sympathetic echo of his own isolation and alienation. It is the object that catches the eye of the drifting *flaneur* in the city: Baudelaire's 'Le Cygne', the appearance of which is hardly an accident in a poem that declares 'tout pour moi devient allegorie'. 'Pour moi' – its allegorical character is ascribed to it by the viewer. But the space outside the image to which it refers is no longer a carefully constructed cosmogony but a void. The Romantic allegory differs from classical allegory in that the cultural dispossession of its beholder prevents him from assigning any one significance to it. This unhoused state may result from a dislocation in space, such as that of the homeless American tourists in *The Marble Faun*, or that spatial dislocation may itself be an allegory of the human metaphysical disinheritance. In any case, it is from this standing apart that there stems what Yvor Winters has called Hawthorne's 'formula of alternative possibilities'. Thus Donatello may or may not have the ears of a faun; the spectre that visits Miriam in the catacombs 'might have been merely a beggar', 'or, as was perhaps a more plausible theory, he might be a thief of the city', 'or, he might have been a lunatic'[9]; similarly, Miriam in her turn might have been 'the daughter and heiress of a great Jewish banker', a German princess, 'the offspring of a South American planter', or 'the lady of an English nobleman'[10]. The method that works through alternative, semi-realised possibilities represents the post-Romantic's compromise between speaking and silence. As a writer, he must continue to 'speak'; but since he is a *writer*, an exile from an oral culture, and since his books are only read, or more likely skimmed by an eye subliminally impatient for the uncharted acres of the print beyond this text, he cannot speak authoritatively. In fact, he cannot speak at all; Hawthorne's fascination by painting is part of his fear that his book is merely an image, a fetish, unread. 'The death of the author' in recent literary theory is less his total annihilation than his persistence as a ghost, between presence and absence. The same applies to his allegorical text. The various possibilities it proposes both tell stories and do not tell them. They strive to embrace all the other books beyond the reach of the text, to create a narrative generative grammar, and so remove the threat to the moment of Hawthorne's own text. Hence it can be seen that the self-consciousness of the post-Romantic writer is simultaneously a consciousness of the existence of other books and of the literary market on which he lacks success. When one considers the degree to which Hawthorne's stories anticipate those of Proust, of Musil, of Robbe-Grillet, of Fowles, by weaving a cat's cradle of airy possibilities, it becomes hard to understand why Gabriel Josipovici should write of a 'logic of compulsion'[11] in his works; nor is it easy to see upon whom the compulsion is exerted. For many readers, it is the fact that Hawthorne is not 'compelling' that renders him irretrievably minor. Surely Josipovici's description is more aptly applied to Poe? For Hawthorne's world is one of possibility and its frustration; every image frustrates its observer. This is why *The Marble Faun* is so interested in painters' models, those infinitely pregnant examples of the non-identity of image and meaning: this body belongs to the painter's lover, and yet here it is – as Hawthorne notes with disgust – masquerading as the Madonna. Every model is an ambiguous cipher and can figure in various dramas. Both Miriam and Hilda can be said to resemble Guido's painting of Beatrice Cenci. Their unity within the one figure is a sign of their unity within Hawthorne himself. They represent two aspects of his artistic practice: Miriam states that the painter is opposed to Nature, shuts out the light, and creates unconscious, expressionist images; Hilda on the other hand copies images of the past, just as Hawthorne uncodes the scarlet letter, enabling these images to breathe through her. Hilda copies Guido's painting without having it before her, just as Kenyon sculpts Hilda's hand in her absence, just as Hawthorne mimics the absent past, that very past he perceives to be absent from America. Hilda and Miriam, impressionism and expressionism, are one in Hawthorne: the image sinks into the person in such a way that its later expression by that person is as impersonal as the printing out of the figure in a wax seal.

Hawthorne's world of frustrated possibility is one of frustrated romance. His flat characters lack the pre-individualistic lucency of the romance. They feel trapped in their two-dimensionality. This flatness however is less a failure to achieve realism than an indictment of the wishful thinking of the realistic novel; for Hawthorne, there are no real people in fiction because there are no such people in reality. Real people, like real books, are divided, not unified.

In Hawthorne, the romance and the realistic novel suffer mutual contamination. All forms of society are proposed and criticised by the formula of alternative possibilities. Neither the closed, collective, pre-individualistic world of romance, nor the individualistic one of the novel is acceptable. The dual nature of this criticism entails a delicate balance that slides all too easily into torpid paralysis, the 'intense inane' pilloried by Yvor Winters. Thus, Hawthorne is most successful when the problem of interpretation, the simultaneous necessity and impossibility of choosing between the possibilities, forms the explicit heart of the story. This is the case in *The Scarlet Letter*, it is also the case in the story of *Young Goodman Brown*.[12] The last page of this story isolates in a separate sentence-paragraph the question around which the whole narrative pivots: 'Had Goodman Brown fallen asleep in the forest and only dreamed a wild dream of a witch meeting?' The story brilliantly exploits the Puritan propensity for naming persons after virtues to create a structure precisely poised between allegory and realism. Faith is the name of Young Goodman Brown's wife; but in losing Faith by stepping into the forest he loses his faith in humanity, and from the day of his return views with suspicion all the other 'Goodmen' around him, all of whom seem to have been unmasked as evil by their appearance at the coven in the woods. The horrible possibility that all the persons Goodman Brown has respected since youth, lending them a reverence that has preserved him from sin, are themselves malefactors imbues him with the paranoia of the isolated individual that is to be thematic in American literature, a paranoia that dogs the alternative possibilities of the final pages of *The Crying of Lot 49*. Is the name 'Faith' as misleading as that of Beatrice in *Rappacini's Daughter*, or as Gervayse Hasting's face in *The Christmas Banquet*? Appearance and meaning are disjunctive, as they are in the relationship between the painter's model and his subject. *Young Goodman Brown* repeats the theme of 'Wakefield', but more effectively: one step outside the known community can transform one (the transformation is Hawthorne's constant theme) into 'the Outcast of the Universe'. What Young Goodman Brown sees in the forest may be a private hallucination (realist code), an allegory of the loss of faith (allegorical code), or a study of the workings of the Devil (religious code). The various contradictory possibilities that arise in the course of the reading flow from two tributaries: the doubling made possible by the implicitly generalising faculty of language, which can term both father and son 'Goodman Brown', and the doubling possible for the Devil, who hath power to assume a pleasing shape. The Devil – or devils – may appropriate the corporeal forms of real people in order to deceive Goodman Brown (one may ask, as contemporary reviewers did when writing of Hogg's *Confessions of a Justified Sinner*, why such exclusive attention should be lavished upon him – though Hawthorne would doubtless answer that this is because, allegorically, Young Goodman Brown is all men). Or perhaps language itself is culpable, sophistic even when truth-telling? For when the Devil informs Young Goodman Brown that his father too served the Devil, does this simply mean that his father also sinned, as do all men, or does it imply an additional turpitude commensurate with that of the son? The ambiguity lies in the fact that the world as a whole is sinful, whilst also containing sinners and Goodmen. Hawthorne is aware that we read people both as characters and as allegories. As characters, they exist in and for themselves, outside the domain of language. But they also occupy positions in a structure of relationships, and in this context one says of them that they are more this and less that, more honest than this man but less so than another and so on. 'He stands for honesty' in our mind's eye. We identify 'him' with a single quality. However, whenever we try to see people in both perspectives, they become ambiguous, neither speaking nor silent. It is this half-light at noon in which Hawthorne's world stands, baffling our sight.

4 The Text Against Itself

THE DIALECTICS OF ENLIGHTENMENT: *ELECTIVE AFFINITIES* AND *WOMEN IN LOVE*

The fewer the number of characters in a novel, the more the novel gravitates towards myth. Thus the drastic reduction in cast-list effected by the modernist novel was one of the factors in its engagement with myth – as in Mann, Kafka or Joyce – with the anthropological rather than the social. Myth occurs when the compact assembly of different generations that constitutes the individual is allowed to speak with one or two (rather than a pentecostal multitude of) voices. Perhaps the last great anti-mythical work is Proust's *A la recherche du temps perdu*; he separates out the discrete strands of heritage and blood that have knit together into a single individuality. He depicts individual traits as having been handed on from other generations and then transposed into a different key; part of Proust's deep concern with music lies in his reading of genetics as musical variation, with the same characteristics re-scored for a different voice, as when qualities of the female line of the Guermantes re-incarnate themselves in Charlus, or as when the latter's homosexuality slides like a possessing spirit into the body of Saint Loup – at the genetically pre-ordained time. Analytic isolation of the individual into his separate components presupposes consideration of an entire family. But as the family breaks down under pressure from the Expressionist critique of the fathers, as heritage becomes a fearful fate in the work of the Naturalists, and as urbanisation and the increasing sophistication of modes of transport enable the children to leave their parents behind, the awareness of re-orchestrated continuities marshalled by Proust as the basis of his de-mythologisation of the individual becomes unattainable. There appear authors for whom the only family is the nuclear family, and it provides insufficient evidence of the variety of possibilities inscribed within the individual to enable him to know where

88

he comes from or where he is likely to go (what aspects of past lives he will re-enact). Instead of tracing the permutations of features in a potentially endless history, authors imprison them in a single character. Thus the family as prison is the fundamental image in *Metamorphosis*. The nightmare of this prison-life is being chained to a person who is one's opposite (Kafka has to be weak because his father is strong); this shadow continually insists on the partiality of one's being (it is the double, an obsession in stories of the modernist period, from *The Secret Sharer* to the figure of Narcissus). It blocks one's ability to change by maintaining that the only alternative to being as one is to be utterly other – there are no gradations between people. Either/or; Philistine or Artist. This limited universe is governed by parallelism and death. The parallelism issues from the simplifying polarisation of society seen by Marx as the consequence of industrialism, and it also serves as a subliminal dress-rehearsal for the First World War. The parallelisms deployed by art represent a species of merely rudimentary order that reflects the crisis of the notion of order in general; they evince an experimental self-consciousness with regard to the status of narrative. *Women in Love* gains its exemplary position through the strength of the tension within it between realistic chaos and the binary order seen by Lévi-Strauss as characteristic of mythical thought. To compare it with Goethe's *Elective Affinities* is more than an exercise in arbitrariness; strict parallelism is common to both works, both mingle Utopian and Dystopian features, Goethe's novel first gained real critical favour in and around the period of the First World War (above all thanks to Benjamin and Gundolf), and Lawrence's close involvement with German culture may even include a slight debt here. It may be significant that one Lawrence commentator has written of this novel:

> the symmetry, pattern and balance that are so pervasive in the novel tend to remind us, however unexpectedly, of the classical art of the eighteenth century. And this impression is confirmed and made explicit by certain specific passages in the book. The opening scene, in which Gudrun and Ursula sit together stitching and drawing and discussing marriage distinctly recalls Jane Austen.[1]

Jane Austen was of course a contemporary of Goethe. The commentator continues:

> if the novel begins by intimating a concern with the decorous balancing of opposites, it ends by completely invalidating such expectations.[2]

But in this respect too it resembles Goethe's novel, whose enforced initial order incubates the anarchy of the close. The common ground is increased by Paul Stöcklin's remark of the narrator of *Elective Affinities* that there is 'something English in his manner.'[3] Both novels were at the time of their appearance widely considered either immoral or a-moral. Both combine symbolic and realistic techniques, intense passion and ironic distance. For their two authors, both works were syntheses and dead ends.

The castle inhabited by Eduard and Charlotte, the two prime protagonists of *Die Wahlverwandtschaften*, is ambiguous; it is the site of the ideal eighteenth-century enlightened community that cultivates its own garden and is determined that its every action be exemplary; based on proverb and itself the occasion of a maxim. But it is also the isolated chateau on the dark side of the eighteenth-century imagination, the place where the Marquis de Sade stages his experimental arrangements of tormented humanity. Instead of the exemplary there is the safe indulgence of lust far from the public eye. Goethe nicely catches the equivocation between the two tendencies in the scientific metaphor that gives the novel its title; the similarity between humans and minerals can either demonstrate the harmony of a universe whose laws embrace every link in the great chain of being, or it can deprive humans of all volition and relegate them to the level of stones. Thus the narrator emerges as a mixture of de Sade and a dispassionate scientific observer.

This combination of the Sadistic and the Utopian is native to both *Elective Affinities* and *Women in Love*. The strict limitation of the number of *dramatis personae* is part of the engagement with the short story in both works; Goethe conceived his work as a novelle which then overran its bounds[4], whilst *Women in Love* juxtaposes vignettes that have a large measure of autonomy. (Its encompassing and critique of the short story is part of its critique of Gudrun, alias Katherine Mansfield). This outgrowing is in both cases extremely interesting – a sign both of the work waxing out of control and spilling over into areas of the author's unconscious[5], and of the Utopian desire metonymically to inflate the restricted into the representative. Both features result from the authors' sense of isolation from society by factors that are too complex to be disentangled here but which include, in Goethe's case, the death of Schiller, and in Lawrence's, the fact of war. One often creates one's own isolation so as to be able to work uninterruptedly; Lawrence habitually wrote in long, uncorrected bursts, and '*Elective Affinities* is completely unlike most of Goethe's other creations inasmuch as he worked on it in one breath, gaily and unhesitantly, under the sign of necessity.'[6] It is striking that both men considered these works their best. Although the degree of representativeness that can be accorded the protagonists of *Women in Love* has been questioned, they become representative through subsuming into themselves the fundamental available alternatives. It is I think this subsumption of a whole series of polarities – with the tutor-polarity Birkin ('art' and 'relationships') versus Gerald ('industrial depersonalisation') – that gives the work its mythical dimension. (Lawrence is using 'typical figures'. Compare Goethe's use of similar figures: 'not an artistic principle alone, but a motif of fateful being is grasped by means of this typicality. This fateful mode of being, which encloses living natures in a single complex of guilt and punishment, is developed throughout the work by the poet'.[7]) Lawrence generalises his characters in the mythical dimension to enable them to move on three planes: the personal, the social and the anthropologically archetypical. The superiority of *Women in Love* to his other novels lies in the delicate balance between the three, which later tips over into the fundamentally archetypical (as in a title like *Aaron's Rod*). The development of the book is not a widening of perspectives but a deepening; this leads to a multiple exposure of the same parallelism, which superimposes discoveries made in the course of the writing itself upon the fixed design to create a blur that contains both real figures and a mythical, pre-individualised indeterminacy. The new is unmasked as the old reborn – the basis for an embittered conservatism (this also applies to the end of Goethe's novel); one aspect of this conservatism is the novel's final solidarity, as it kills Gerald, with Lawrence's renunciation of the genuinely new, as represented by the bisexuality which was one of Birkin's characteristics in the cancelled 'Prologue'. The book closes with the explicitly mythical, sloughs off social discourse in the name of the archetypical, for which all is always the same (on reaching an archetype a novel must end, for it has violated its own code); thus Lawrence's characters leave for Germany, the place of origin of the Saxon language that provides the basis of working-class dialect and of Lawrence's own style, and the death of Gerald is predicted within the novel itself by Birkin's meditations on the totem and on the snowy end that awaits the northern races (the predictable end is a feature of myth; a myth is a story whose ending is known beforehand by the audience, as was the case with Greek tragedy); it further accords with the final winter of existence predicted by Norse mythology. Goethe's novel similarly reverts from an eighteenth-century rationalism and symmetry to the assertion of the presence of concealed powers – a finally grimacing religiosity.

One aspect of Lawrence's concern with myth is his interest in the visual; a work composed largely of exchanges between two people is one that renders easy its own visualisation – the plastic elements have been simplified for the mind's eye. But the concentration on pairs interacting at particular moments also pulls away from visualisation, as one becomes semi-subliminally aware that the pairs are aspects of one invisible personality. The theme is touched on when Birkin remarks to Ursula: 'I don't *want* to see you. I've seen plenty of women, I'm sick and weary of seeing them. I want a woman I don't see.' Birkin is conscious that people are as invisible as they are visible – and Lawrence strives to evoke the intangible area by means of the questionable vocabulary of mysticism, a vocabulary that is deliberately allowed to be questionable by the Lawrence whose self-criticism permits him to place in Birkin ('place') a character very similar to himself. In so doing, he grants the invisible equal status with the visible, for it is in relation to oneself that one is most clearly aware of the invisible – one's invisibility to others as shown by misunderstanding, one's actual invisibility to oneself, the novelist's invisibility in the face of his readers – and by inserting 'himself' in the novel, Lawrence stresses the dual nature of invisibility: freedom from others, and inability to connect with them. He projects 'himself-as-Birkin' into the novel so as to escape solipsism – a solipsism that is Birkin's temptation – and thus ceases to be Birkin. (Nevertheless, Birkin too shows the germs of a novelist: he states to Mrs Crich that most people don't exist, and this is the novelist's view, since his characters are embodiments of non-existence, whilst 'real' people are merely quarries for fictional material.) Having visualised himself in his misunderstood form, Lawrence can adopt the fruitful invisibility that is the prelude to writing, which will permit him to find the people who will understand him, beyond the constricting circle of his misinterpreters, and to cease misunderstanding himself and others, as he does whenever he speaks what ought to be written. 'For the man who no longer has a home, writing becomes his sole domicile.'[8] Writing is the only place in which the restlessly wandering Lawrence rests. But because he has a body, however diminutive, and because he is also a painter, 'in the end the writer is not even allowed to inhabit his writing.'[9] The wrestling scene between Gerald and Birkin contains the following sentences: 'Birkin was more a presence than a visible object; Gerald was aware of him completely, but not really visually. Whereas Gerald himself was concrete and noticeable, a piece of pure final substance.' Birkin's invisibility here stems from his proximity to Lawrence: the writer is blind, his own blind spot. Questions of visibility are the conjunctions between Lawrence the writer and Lawrence the painter. His painterliness is the cause of his work's richness in intensely tactile descriptions, which solidify into compactly memorable scenes and glow from within like coals. As Professor A. K. Thorlby has remarked, one remembers more self-sufficient scenes from Lawrence's writing than from the work of any other English author. Side-tracking for a moment to *Elective Affinities*, one recalls that Goethe stated that in his youth he had wavered between literature and painting; he was later to devise a Farbenlehre. The interest felt by both authors in the visual and the written is part of their sense of the mythical, for a myth is something that cannot be fixed once and for all, that flows over the barriers of the separate art-forms; the classic instances are the Wagnerian *Gesamtkunstwerk* and films. Overwhelming consciousness with its polysemia, it compels an artist to resort to various media to render some of its aspects, thus defining by negation its essence as the ineffably between. It is perhaps significant that in Lawrence's novel the one combination of the four fundamental personality-elements that is not permitted by the economy of the work is that of Birkin with Gudrun, of the writer's *porte parole* with the plastic artist who is his other self; their combination is taboo because each represents one of Lawrence's own two arts, each of which cast its own shadow in the real world (Birkin casts Ursula and Gudrun, Gerald). Their meeting would annul the polar tension Lawrence holds to be the basis of life (a belief that parallels Goethe's dialectical sense of diastole and systole and the necessary interdependence of Mephistopheles and Faust, Good and Evil).[10] The meeting of artists in Loerke and Gudrun is thus an incestuous disaster. (All chance of Birkin relating to Gudrun is dispelled by her being an unlabelled metaphor for Katherine Mansfield – another writer.)

Metaphysical, mythical novels require close readings and a dual focus. In *Women in Love*, the majority of scenes occur between two people, so everything becomes important, as the bifurcation of the world elevates the simply different (and realistic) into the elemental (and mythical): man and woman shade off and up into Man and Woman. The economy of the short story is transposed to the novel, which thus becomes very dense. Thus Goethe first envisaged *Elective Affinities* as a short tale, whilst the juxtaposition of short pregnant scenes in Lawrence's novel is part of its engagement with Katherine Mansfield (*Auseinandersetzung* might be the better term). The results are both critiques of, on the one hand, the short story's aesthetics of tight control and avoidance of waste, and on the other, of the novel's tendency to become a nameless wood of specificities, a 'baggy monster'. Short stories are generally honed to a moralistic point and 'tend to write about life's victims'[11]; the morals of the novel more often lie in the tale than in the teller, and its characters usually aspire to representativeness. These two works however are moralist novels, contradictions in terms. The moralist novel presents clear alternatives for action in the opposite characters and thus enacts a bitter awareness of the necessity for choice. Birkin wishes for a relationship with Gerald, and Goethe proposes an altered configuration of his four main personages, but the novels are bitter because the necessity for choice imposed by their moralism is countervailed by their aesthetic desires (desires encapsulated in Birkin and Eduard) for freedom from choice. The novelist is caught in a double-bind; he issues moral directives to reality, but the reality he depicts is a fiction, and his knowledge of this fact impregnates his Utopia with the dark hues of the Dystopia. He is forced, for instance, both to affirm and to deny the vocabulary of love and marriage – affirm its committed resolve, but deny the egotistic exclusiveness of that commitment. Lawrentian phrases like 'she had a full and mystic knowledge' or 'she was dark and fulfilled in silence' conflate religiosity with the banalities of women's magazines, rendering cliché indistinguishable from myth and so registering the equivocation between an overvaluation of relationships and a wish to ditch them because of their conventionality. It is the same dilemma that leads Goethe on the one hand to expound the sympathetic complementarity of souls and on the other to present it in grotesque terms: when Eduard and Ottilie suffer a headache, each suffers on a different side of the head. He can both 'place' the tastelessness of Mittler's legalistic notion of marriage and surrender to the poisoned farce of the birth of a child bearing the features of Ottilie and the Hauptmann (for it was of them that Eduard and Charlotte were thinking as they made love). Goethe portrays a marriage that is not a marriage, for it cannot have children (in this respect, his arrangement is again both Utopian and nightmarish). Lawrence's world (for all its rejection of Gudrun, who is unwilling to have children) is also a childless one, and this is part of its unremitting intensity and extraterritoriality *vis à vis* the English novel as a whole: an absence of children – no sources of light relief. All occurs within the closed phalanx of one generation, whose temporal isolation makes it brittle and apocalyptic. In both novels there is an element of jargon (Lawrence's pseudo-Romanticism; Goethe's eighteenth-century euphemisms whose stiffness derives rather from rigor mortis than from poise: for example 'das liebe Kind', 'das gute Mädchen', of Ottilie), and in both cases it serves an apocalyptic magic. Both authors deploy a language whose occasional exhaustion is an index of the deathliness of the rendered reality; the language seeks to call transcendent attention to the need to put an end to both this language and its adherent reality. Thus the apocalyptic elements in *Women in Love* signalled by Kermode reach down into the style's immanent self-criticism, and the hysteria at the close of *Elective Affinities* is a corollary of its earlier linguistic stiffness; the parallelisms are post-Romantic stylisations of eighteenth-century language as dead wood calling for the axe.

Goethe and Lawrence dance out the dialectic of enlightenment; 'just as the myths already practise enlightenment, so with every step enlightenment sinks deeper into mythology.[12] For 'men pay for the aggrandisement of their power with alienation from that over which they wield this power.'[13] 'Alienation' takes two forms: Marxist and Feuerbachian. Men reify things, and they project their own powers onto Nature. The mutual entanglement of the two varieties of 'alienation' is shown by the simultaneous rise of industrialism and of anthropomorphising Romanticism. Thus instrumental reason refuses to respect the otherness of nature (Gerald digs his spurs into the horse's flanks), and is alienated from it, whilst Ursula's Romantic alienation projects onto nature its own disavowed powers:

> She started violently. It was only the moon, risen through the thin trees. But it seemed so mysterious, with its white and deathly smile. And there was no avoiding it. Night or day, one could not escape the sinister face, triumphant and radiant like this moon, with a high smile.

The last sentence unmasks the projection: one does not see the moon 'night and day', and the face is no longer that of the moon but is simply 'like the moon'. It is an interior terror, and the passage is prose becoming poetry; could the terror be a childhood nightmare of Gudrun, spectrally prolonged? A later page in the same chapter, 'Moony', repeats the dialectic; Ursula describes a bird as 'a little Lloyd George of the air', but later realises 'after all, it is impudence to call them little Lloyd Georges. They are really unknown to us, they are the unknown forces.' Her retraction of her own remark uproots her points of contact with Gudrun. Similarly, in *Elective Affinities*, the rational view of the past that levels the graveyard into useful park-land as it were provokes the conquered myth into retribution, as the novel veers towards medievalism, records fantastic births and the avenging action of natural powers, and closes with a belief in the Resurrection. The dialectic of enlightenment is that of individuation and its impossibility. A review of *Elective Affinities* by Solger, which Goethe held to be the only cogent appraisal of his work, contains the following judgements: 'nowadays, each individual finds his only god in himself.': and 'the man who falsely understands and subdues his individuality or ... ignores the voice of conscience and follows sophistic reason – that man goes under. And this is the peak of modern art, the tragic novel.'[14] The first describes Birkin; the second refers to Gerald, using the tones of Goethe's Leavis. The novel traces the same path as *Women in Love* and the career of Lawrence himself: from enlightenment to myth, from the social novel (in Lawrence's case, via the folk novel with the rhythm of the seasons that is *The Rainbow*) to the anthropological and elemental. The compass of Enlightenment describes a vicious circle.

UTOPIAS: BUTLER AND WILLIAM MORRIS

The Utopia or philosophical fable arises on the border between fiction and philosophy. One could almost term it the Anglo-Saxon variety of modernist fiction, as it draws attention to its own origins by designating itself as an image of 'nowhere' (au-topos), as it displays an implicit awareness of the presuppositions and effects of fiction in general. But the form represented by the Utopia is misshapen and contradictory. The non-existent place is evoked in the language of present reality, and the real otherness of the Utopia cripples, or is crippled by, the language that seeks to encompass it. In Samuel Butler's *Erewhon*, the recurrent comparisons of Erewhonian features with European ones is embarrassing and contorted and blurs their specificity by indicating the inability of the European to see anything other than what he expects. In consolatory fashion they substitute Europe for Erewhon, unwittingly showing the degree to which Erewhon really is nowhere. Reading these comparisons, one suspects that the allure of the exotic has been exploited as a cosmetic to cover up the poverty of the imagination (Butler is not primarily a writer of fiction). Even as the comparisons render the otherness tangible and believable, they turn it into a montage of disintegrated bits of Europe, and this has its pathos; the narrator voyages to gather up the scattered bits of the exploded European house. Industrialised, Europe too is 'Nowhere', vanished completely. The Utopia is fiction making itself acceptable as a contribution to the archives of fact. It is clearly linked with the mirror, as is apparent from the title of Butler's book: 'Erewhon' suggests 'nowhere' when seen in a mirror (reversal transforms namelessness into a name). In Erewhon, time runs in reverse, from industrialisation to the twelfth century; crime is a disease, and to be ill is an indictable offence. Bellamy's famous Utopia *Looking Backward* also suggests the image of the mirror; in the mirror one perceives the area behind oneself, one is fixated upon that road, for the road forward is blocked. The reversals executed by the mirror seem both witty and mechanical as they free the author from contemporary civilisation and yet continually remind him of its inescapability; the systematic negation of civilisation reaffirms it by extending it into another place, like a shadow, and the mirror image mechanically corresponds to the rejected mechanical reality. It solders yet another link in the harsh chain of causality, which chafes all the more because there once were hopes of release.

Utopias appear as industry does, as images of its bright promise and dystopian threat. Hence Butler's satire is two-way, with both England and Erewhon as its objects. Since England was the first country to undergo industrialisation on a large scale, it was there that Utopias throve at the turn of the century. Butler, Wells and William Morris are simply the most renowned examples. They were accompanied by the emergence of images based on the exact symmetry of the mirror, such as Rossetti's painting 'How they met themselves', depicting the meeting of two pairs of identical lovers in a wood. One meets oneself as the product of alienated labour (not recognising in the object any trace of one's own participation in its manufacture). The otherness of the product interacts with one's subconscious awareness that it is one's own work to lead one to idolise it; in this sense, materialism is a religion. 'Basically', writes Benjamin, 'the feeling of empathy with the product ought to be the same as an empathy with exchange value'.[1] The mirror is the medium that transforms the person into exchange value; it is no surprise that its image should have dominated the works of the end of the nineteenth century and the beginning of the twentieth. As it transfers one personality for another, it represents in definitive form the interchangeability of people in the factory of existence.

The space in the mirror that seems to enlarge the world and grant it a new dimension is in fact 'nowhere', Utopia, and does not exist. It reflects the English fear of being bottled up in a tiny industrialised island. As this fear becomes general European property, as nations seek an outlet for the virulence of their own nationalism, they seek to escape from it in the same way as the English did: by imperialism and colonialism which, by extending the parent country beyond its own borders, achieve a paradoxical mirroring of the native land, both reproducing and denying it. Butler's narrator describes himself as the coloniser of an unknown country, as a quester for a sheep monopoly. He likens his own view over Erewhon to that of Moses gazing across the Promised Land he was forbidden to enter; entering it, he transgresses against the Biblical tradition to realise heaven on earth. But as he did so 'each moment I felt increasing upon me that dreadful doubt as to my own identity – as to the continuity of my past and present existence'. For like Alice he is in the process of stepping into the mirror.

The writer who lives in a society based on the division of labour may envy other artists their craft. I think it can be established that whereas the poets of the *fin de siècle* tended to admire and imitate musicians, the novelists were covetous of the painter's crown. This is partly because the painter could achieve the exactitude of rendition sought by the Naturalist. Lawrence, Wyndham Lewis, the Polish novelist and painter Witkacy, and, as we shall see, Morris and Butler, can serve as examples. Writers feel a yearning for the concrete image that will underwrite their words, which are coming to bear less and less relation to reality as reality undergoes the altering shocks of industrialisation and colonialism. The Utopia is the place where the fragmented body politic is put together, where painter and writer are one. Thus the painterly talents of Butler and Morris persuaded them both to privilege the eye. In their pastoral Utopias, writing becomes self-critical, for it is implicated in the intellectuality it criticises; this causes a dilemma in which one is forced to employ words as polemical weapons against the present, only then to find that the means have altered the end as the words one wishes to dismiss turn on their employer like unpaid soldiery. Hence the central figure in these Utopias is wrapped in ambivalent irony; this is fiction using realistic strategies, so one identifies with him, but the text's continual insistence on its own fictionality (it is a Utopia) simultaneously frustrates our imaginative efforts to follow in his footsteps. In the middle of Morris's *News From Nowhere* (the middle of a book is the place at which its author reaches furthest into the problems which beset him, and he spends the rest of the book fleeing from his own conclusions; to place an element in the middle of a text is to repress it, for beginnings and endings attract more attention) there appears the following complaint, uttered by an inhabitant of the ideal future: 'I have read not a few works of the past days, and certainly *they* are more alive than those which are written now; and good sound unlimited competition was the condition under which they were written'. If books are a sign of the diseased condition of his epoch, Morris nevertheless cannot forbear to express a certain pride in the products of his own era, a certain regret at the possible demise of the book; yet he has also prepared himself against desuetude in this future by adopting the parallel trade of painter. Morris cannot dispense with books entirely; when a girl throws open a window and cries of the trees and flowers 'look! these are our books in these days', the ecstatic note is partly the result of the author's gratitude at hearing the name of something he values uttered with respect, a respect that allows him to dream that he too could be accepted by the inhabitants of the future, that there is a way through the mirror and into the ideal.

Utopias are a variety of modernist art. This is why the question of the Utopian dogged Musil so relentlessly as he examined the links between Utopian projects and madness, between the form of the encyclopaedic novel and the autistic isolation of Ulrich, the man without qualities. By embracing the whole world, encyclopaedic knowledge erases the boundary between 'here' and 'there', as does the image of the Narcissus; to split the atom of space is to place the two sexes together, mingling them in the space of Musil's ideal hermaphrodite. The violence associated with physical love in Musil is the violence of this splitting, an earthquake in the world order. 'News From Nowhere' can also mean 'no news is available from any place', for all places have been homogenised, unified by the exclusion of otherness. There is nothing to draw attention, newspaper pages are blank; perhaps that is why there are no books in Morris's Utopia. To substitute the word 'nowhere' for 'Utopia', as he does, is to allow a note of anguish to betray the origin of the idyll. Utopias enact the threat and promise of the growing invisibility of the author in the face of his readers, the final loss if an oral culture in the era of mass production. Morris's narrator twice suffers dematerialisation. Once, to pass from the detested present to the future; once more at the close of the book, during a feast. On the first occasion he is unconscious of the transition; in the latter, firm reality turns into disquieting sand in his hands. The return entails the suffering of birth-pangs; it is thus an image of the painfulness of birth into the present world; he has been sucked out of the uterine repose of Utopia. The first dematerialisation, by way of contrast, is as instantaneous as a wish fulfilled. But even as he envisages a society based on community, Morris's narrator is sealed in the hermetic circle of a dream. He dreams of a collective dream. The Utopian writer chooses his invisibility in order to withdraw from the determined world in which his visible reflection would remind him that he is as mechanically dependent on others as his shadow is upon him. The narcissist becomes invisible to others by assimilating himself to the other, looking at himself in the other's place.

The apotheosis of the experience of invisibility is the situation of the film-watcher in a darkened cimema. It is no accident that cinemas appear in the period in which the question of invisibility, of the artist's visibility to himself alone (as a double), of his alienation from any possible audience, becomes of crucial urgency. The great Polish novelist and critic Karol Irzykowski writes: 'man has an innate desire *to observe in abstraction from reality*', adding that 'the more directly he has borne events, the happier he is to see them anew in a form from which he is detached'; both remarks come from his pathfinding book on the cinema, written early in the twenties, *X Muza*. Irzykowski indicates that the desire for invisibility originates in the experience of shock. The Utopian's total self-propulsion out of the immediate world is prompted by the shocks of urbanisation and mechanisation, which alienate him completely from his environment.

Utopias emerge in large numbers at the turn of a century because that represents the moment when time is completed and becomes again a white page for possibility to draw on. But the possibilities can only be imagined by using the forms of thought of the cancelled past, so the invocation of the future is compromised at the moment of its inception. Morris portrays it as a reincarnation of the Middle Ages, operating with a cyclical theory of history that casts a shadow forward across the permanence of his Utopia. The language of Utopia is compromised, like all descriptions of dreams, which are absurd because they stretch the dream on the Procrustean bed of a daylight chronology. The Utopian text hovers between an evangelical sermon and a modest description of an eccentric preference, between vision and dream. 'If others can see it, as I have seen it, then it may be called a vision rather than a dream': the poignancy of Morris's effort hangs in the balance of this equivocation. The Utopian text is affiliated to the dream-writing of Kafka, but it is also the purest naturalism: unremitting reconstruction of the face of society, and more justified than Naturalism inasmuch as that society is unknown to us. Denigration and praise can say no more than that it is the most realistic (the most English?) form of fantasy.

REPETITION: KIERKEGAARD AND PROUST

À la recherche du temps perdu and Kierkegaard's *Repetition* have a good deal in common; both are philosophical novels, and the category of repetition introduced in the latter parallels Proust's notion of involuntary memory both in its content and in the elusiveness of that content. Similarly,

Proust's use of repetition-as-imitation in his pastiches serves to deny the substantial unity of author and style, and this is reminiscent of Kierkegaard's habit of using pseudonyms. To state as one's aim the formulation of behavioural laws, as does Proust, is to act upon a belief in the possibility of repetition: actions form typological series (the Marcel-Albertine relationship perpetuates the mould of Swann's obsession with Odette), as do images and characteristics. And Kierkegaard seems to have other ideas congruent with those of Proust: 'the justified exception manifests everything more clearly than does the universal itself' declares Constantine in his letter to the reader at the close of *Repetition*, and this appears to parallel Proust's ability to unfold a totality (of scene or personality) from a single moment, his propensity for a synecdochic view of the individual, who gathers into himself several individuals, several generations. It is significant that Kierkegaard was an author deemed 'unreadable' until the nineteen-twenties, when the cult of his work began. But there are also clear divergences, and the similarity between the two authors is often only apparent; thus the previous quotation from Kierkegaard's novel establishes a dialectic of the universal and the particular that is alien to Proust himself, whose composite figures blur the difference between eccentricity and universality. Proust's engulfing mistiness is that of a clouded aquarium, and lacks the crabbed crispness of Kierkegaard's dialectical mind. So I will begin by enumerating passages in *Repetition* which accord with Proust, until I reach the points at which they part ways.

Early on in *Repetition* (I am using the Princeton text of 1941) one reads: 'in general, humane emotions in a person disarm the observer. Only where instead of this there is a hollowness, or where the coquette dissimulates, has one a desire to make observations.' (p. 8) Thus it is the malign and the snobbish who are transfixed and judged by Proust's incomparably mordant eye. Their actions are seen only once and are not considered worthy of repetition. They may themselves reappear, but when they do it is as different people, whose emergence from the cocoon of their old action disconfirms the narrator's knowledge and witnesses to the power of time – as when Madame Verdurin is seen to be capable of genuine benevolence towards the Saniette she has tormented so relentlessly in the past. The action whereby she gave pain in the past remains known, but she as it were sloughs it off; it is not surrounded with the incense and smoke of speculation that is offered up to the actions of those Marcel loves. The agnosticism with which the latter are considered cherishes them as tantalising ciphers of the nature of the beloved person; the various interpretations *repeat them* in the mind's eye. Thus in *Le côté de*

Guermantes, II, he presents a series of hypothetical reasons for his mother's unwillingness to look at his grandmother as she supported her in her illness. Here Proust does penance for the distance of his relationship to his mother, which prevented him from understanding her. The beauty of the action derives in part from his despairing knowledge that he will never understand even a person as close to him as his mother. He pores over the scene just as in *Blow Up* the photographer Thomas compulsively scrutinises the images he continually enlarges, until their 'reality' breaks up into a grainy confetti that reveals the abstraction, the unknowability, that floats between the particles of the event, and erodes it away. Penance for inattention and habitual blindness, benign refusal of the violence of understanding (which snaps the point of the darting lance of intelligence): Proust's procedure here is multiply determined.

Later in Kierkegaard's text a sentence begins: 'to explain to her the mistake by letting her know that she was only the visible semblance, whereas his thought, his soul, was seeking something else which he transferred figuratively to her' (p. 21): this parallels Proust's insistence that love is rendered impossible by one's search for an internalised archetype, perpetually projected, like a mass-produced slipper that will fit many a Cinderella. As in Proust, the poetic and the real are at odds. The figurative transference of which Kierkegaard writes is ever-present in Proust; all his girls are the momentary abodes of a Figure that plays hide-and-seek with him. Reality becomes a vast field of shifting metaphors upon which the metaphor wanders in search of an adequate referent. Marcel turns people into metaphors for their places of birth, for the past they have inherited, and for the absent ancestors whose places they have usurped; this infiltration of the excluded Other into the present would however be condemned by Kierkegaard as a symptom of 'the aesthetic'. Nevertheless, the project to associate people with localities has as its aim the equation of both Marcel and the Guermantes with Combray, which will place him on their level and so fulfil his social ambitions. The snob who has no past of his own seeks to submit time to his own element, which is space. There is no aestheticism that is purely aesthetic. But this spatialisation, like Proust's constant resort to metonymy, also seeks to counteract the time that has scattered the components of his childhood world. Proust allows the features of the past to shine through the present in the hope that this will make the present more comprehensible; but in fact, it is this very vision of several perspectives within one (the aesthetic vision) that prevents him from comprehending the present, and from acting within it. The self-evident force with which others act engenders in him a paranoia that is also a

mode of revenge upon the others by 'seeing through them' in a manner
that reduces them to pawns in the genetic game. But this seeing through
them is a failure to perceive them as they are. In Proust's world, the
seeing of an object precludes its comprehension. This is why he is driven
to inhabit the night, in which objects reveal their true aspect as dreams;
why he can possess the summer in all its fullness only by withdrawing to
his room and burying himself in a book; why the world can exist for him
only as language, as a book, so he lives only when he lives his writing.
The summer is grasped reflexively, becomes 'summer' (enabling one to
use the word 'summer') only under conditions in which it appears to be
over; when Marcel hears the drone of the flies punctuating the darkness,
interrupting his reading, he *remembers* that it is summer. For to sit inside
is to behave as if summer were already past, to identify with one's death.
And this mention of death may recall Rilke. As in Rilke, the object is
possessed only by the person who divests himself of it and *lets it be* (be
itself), undisturbed by the interference of his desire. As one turns one's
back upon a scene, one knows that, in its indifference to one, it is itself.
Meanwhile, one sees with the eyes in the back of one's head – *with the eyes
of the imagination*, which are brought to birth by renunciation – the
invisible scene. This scene is also the primal scene. For the wish to
perceive the hidden is bound up with Proust's voyeurism (one recalls
that the statement of Marcel's desire that a peasant girl materialise was
followed by the scene in which he stares voyeuristically at Mme Vinteuil's desecration of a photograph of her parents). It causes him to
conjure up the events that preceded his own existence: the love of Swann
for Odette, the previous generations of the Guermantes. For he knows
that his own death is imminent, that time presses, and that he can only
look backwards; as he does so, the repeated patterns of the generations
assure him that the signs of his life will not be erased utterly; but he dare
not consider the future, lest the pain of its imminent absence paralyse his
efforts, lest his presumptuous anticipation frustrate his chances of a
partial after-life. But in a sense, he has already absorbed the future; the
moment of involuntary memory expresses a materialism by virtue of
which the after-life appears in the shape of this life. The homosexual
knows he cannot have children; such is the strength of Proust's commitment to memory, to the weaving activity of contemplation, that one can
see in it the cause of his childlessness.

We have now reached the point of clearest divergence between
Kierkegaard and Proust. Kierkegaard writes: 'when one does not possess the categories of recollection or of repetition the whole of life is
resolved into a vain and empty noise.' (p. 34) So far, so Proustian. But

then Kierkegaard distinguishes between recollection, which he sees as characteristic of the pagan, and repetition, which he deems modern. (This distinction suggests the possibility that in modern conditions thought has been cast in the repetitive mould of industrial processes – but this is not what Kierkegaard has in mind). Proust, however, confounds this distinction, for the involuntary memory is both a recollection and a repetition. The whole of *À la recherche* is itself an involuntary memory, which does not so much order completed events as re-immerse itself in them so as to transpose them into the key of writing. And yet this remembrance is not the variety of involuntary memory that is commonly understood to be the novel's most characteristic feature. True, it is involuntary, unbesought, but it differs from what Proust himself terms *memoire involuntaire*, the moment of the past's mystical invasion of the present. The sole point of real confusion in the novel arises in the final section, where Proust juxtaposes the two (the experience in the Guermantes library, and his decision to write) as if they were different aspects of the same experience. In fact, the theory of the *memoire involuntaire* as a privileged moment is the least characteristic part of the book; its mystical joy is jarringly forced, and it is the fruit of Proust's violation of the subtle cadences of his own disillusion. Thus the madeleine section is marred by an unexpectedly crude rhetoric. Within it, grace is bestowed quasi-religiously, without reason, and in such a manner as to cast aside the more diffused, less ecstatic grace Proust has worked for and achieved by the spiritual exercise of *writing*. Over and against the aesthetics of absence that dominate the rest of the book, these passages assert a full presence. But the madeleine scene and the illuminations in the Guermantes library relate to the remainder of the work only problematically. For is repetition possible? Surely not if, as Proust says, the only paradise is the one we have lost. The widespread anthologising of these incidents is an index of how the official optimism of culture betrays the books it accounts the prime objects of its veneration. (Such anthologising has only one valid aspect: it implicitly recognises that these passages are embedded in the novel like foreign bodies. It also, significantly enough, concentrates on the one means of access to the past the work offers to those who are not themselves writers; the isolation of these passages constitutes a populist denial of the necessity of writing).

The madeleine episode rings false because it contravenes Proust's own aesthetics. These state that the imagination is necessary in order to make fleetingly present the absent world withheld from Proust by his asthma. The long sentences are invested with an immensely authoritative pathos deriving from the manner in which all available stylistic powers are deployed to capture a reality that is itself an absence, a fiction. 'Reality' is a *fata Morgana*, and the Baroque flourishes and whimsies of the prose are tell-tale symptoms of the impossibility of shedding style to reach 'life'; there is no life except through the creation of a style. Proust's intuition of the final ineffectuality of his wilfully engulfing style persuades him to insert a self-parodic sub-text, the comic and yet also grotesque self-undermining Roger Shattuck has seen to be present in passages like the description of Marcel kissing Albertine for the first time at Balbec. Proust extends the sentence so as to postpone its ending, when it will again become necessary to confront the problem of how to begin. The long takes are heroically futile attempts to elide the gaps in experience that seduce the eye into an abyss of regret. The long sentences of the asthmatic Proust are part of the fiction that there exists a world in which he can breathe freely, a world in which the force that attracts him to Reynaldo Hahn will be the similarity in their mastery of breath-control, not the terrible difference between the long phrases of the real singer and Proust's 'petite phrase'. The tactile, oneiric quality of the visions he beholds in his dark room is that of the film he develops, an art that embraces all life and lifts off its death-mask.

Despite the flaw in *À la recherche* I have already mentioned, Proust is more honest in the face of his own experience than is the Kierkegaard of *Repetition*. Kierkegaard-Constantine allows the young man of his story to align himself magically with Job, in the hope that the similarity of their afflictions will induce a common end. The young man sits – a compound avatar of Eliot and Kafka – awaiting 'the thunderstorm that is to make me a husband'. He adds: 'if the thunderstorm does not come, I shall resort to cunning – I shall make out that I am dead'. This is what Kierkegaard himself does in actuality: the thunderstorm does not come (he does not marry Regina), and so he has to play dead (he adopts a pseudonym). Nevertheless, he also applies a compensatory fictional salve to the wound of his private experience, the wound of the betrayal, the marriage of the young man's beloved. Although he closes with a final hymn of triumph by the young man, the eventuality he foresaw and proclaimed averted has in fact come to pass; the real outcome is the feigned death. There are two symptoms of this death. Firstly, the way in which the young man's hymn subordinates the category of the religious to the category of the aesthetic; Kierkegaard here renounces his own rigorous distinction between them. And secondly, the fictional suicide which leads him to sacrifice his own name and replace it with 'Constantine Constantius' (which states his continued fidelity to Regina even as the repetition mocks it). And at this point in the text he leaves the young man (the young man actually 'dies') and reverts to Constantius, who derides all hopes for a transforming thunderstorm. Having collapsed himself into 'Constantine', Kierkegaard then cooks the book by altering 'Constantine's' character in the letter to the ideal reader that follows; for *here* his narrator-projection suddenly accepts the validity of the young man's belief in transformation. In fact, Kierkegaard here melts his two figures into one, solders together the split components of his own voice, and allows the nominal 'Constantius' to enunciate in a style that is suspiciously close to his own non-pseudonymous one. The word 'repetition' is itself repeated compulsively throughout the text, and its stickiness is the basis for its irrational fetishisation; the bad faith with which he uses this term is obvious in the simultaneous rejection of Hegelian pieties and the desire to defeat them on their own ground of systematic philosophy by proposing that repetition constitute the true content of 'mediation'. One part of Kierkegaard realises that his own self-hatred cannot provide any reasonable basis for prescriptive moralising; it was this aspect of his personality that attracted Kafka to him, for Kafka's own enigmatic parodies of religious discourse also refuse to found a religion. This side of Kierkegaard ascribes opinions to pseudonymous personalities and implicitly admits the impossibility of removing the aesthetic substratum from didactic writing. This half of his mind executes fine and objectively disinterested attacks on the perversion of Christianity he dubs 'Christendom'. The critique is negative, but that is the source of its coherence and strength. On the other hand, the clear-sighted Kierkegaard is shadowed by a double whose despair makes objectivity unattainable, and it is this double whose endorsement of the fragmentation and fear (sickness unto death) of one stage of Christendom itself leads him to ignore the specific historical differences between Early Christian and nineteenth-century conditions. But these two strands – the critical strand of the genius, the edifying will of the apostle – are inextricably interwoven in his work.

There is one passage in *Repetition* which draws a clear line of demarcation between the projects of the two writers. 'He who would only hope is a coward, he who would only recollect is a voluptuary, but he who wills repetition is a man'. (p. 5) In this context Proust can resemble the voluptuary – especially so, since he seems to have unwilled repetition by inscribing a sharp caesura in his life: by commencing *À la recherche*. He sees ahead of him a nightmarish infinite regress of relationships reiterating the same configuration – obedient to the pattern established by Gilberte and Albertine – and he wishes to arrest it. (Could this be the result of unconscious guilt feelings, as if he were responsible for the death of Albertine and wished to halt the murderous syndrome?) But here Kierkegaard's 'either/or-ism' overlooks the dialectical truth. True, Proust is a voluptuary who unwills repetition and wishes only to recollect, but he also wills repetition by re-enacting his own life, by arranging people – himself included – into typological series. Even writing offers no sanctuary, for Marcel-the-writer's tendency to de-realise real people into the characters of a dream (to melt them into other people) repeats his past inability to respond to their specific being in the moment. But this inability is not Marcel's alone; his work gains its greatness from the truth of its testimony to the erosion of nineteenth-century individualism in the early twentieth century. The waxwork faces of a freakish past are caught as the flame dissolves them and they weep their substance into formlessness, shed their individuality. Repetition is written into the associative movement of the style, as the typological cards are shuffled again and again by the hands of time; each new game is played with the finite material of the old. In the past, Marcel's addiction to speculation had been the source of his torment, an index of the impenetrability of the other, but in the realm of writing speculation comes into its own. Proust uses speculation to justify the stitching together of various people he believes to exemplify the same charac-terological law; he classifies hybrid species. Doasan, La Rochefoucauld, Sagan and Robert de Montesquiou are mixed to make the colour 'Charlus'; 'Elstir' is a compound of Monet, Moreau, Blanche, Turner and several other figures; 'Albertine' is Alfred Agostinelli, Marie de Chevilly and Marie Finlay. Thus Marcel's inability to comprehend others derives less from the over-determination of actions than from the fact that the various depicted deeds are amalgams of the gestures of several people, and their superimposition is conducive of a blur. This moment of blurring marks the point at which the individual becomes a crowd: a triad, as in Freud, a dyad, as in the stories of Poe, or a swarming mass, as in the making of a film, which has a multiple author. Nor is Marcel himself a single consciousness, for the narrator is a subtly shifting mixture of Marcel in the past, an older Marcel, 'Proust', and an objective narrator-moralist whose readiness to plunge his friends into a fictional melting-pot (does the Jew scarred by the Dreyfus affair revenge himself upon French society by defacing the outlines of its most lustrous inhabitants, all those who once attracted him?) has put him beyond the pale, in the space of death. For the written word is the only voice with which the dead speak to us.

Proust records the débâcle of the individual at the beginning of this century; the individual was to vanish into the crowd, as it did in the mass

movements and revolutions initiated by the First World War. The crowd
attracts the individual because he sees in it an image of his own split
nature. On the one hand, Proust analyses the individual into the features
bequeathed him by others (at certain moments the flesh of Charlus
quivers with the expressions of earlier female Guermantes; and his
homosexuality then migrates in its turn into the frame of Robert de
Saint-Loup). But this de-mythologising breakdown of the individual is
accompanied by a compensatory myth-making formation of new individuals out of the components into which human beings have been
dissected. Proust's realism casts a shadow of mythical stylisation; thus
the intense poignancy of his grandmother's voice over the telephone,
perceived for the first time when isolated from her other features (the
dissection of the individual mentioned above), is attended by the
flippant defence mechanism that refers to the switchboard girls as
Naiads. One could say that in Proust in general, the myth is an heuristic
device that allows him to distance painful experience so as to analyse it;
but the pain is itself the distance from others that transforms them into
mythical beings. The two procedures are dialectical aspects of the same
phenomenon. For Proust is a crowd, possessed of a multiple personality;
psychologist, historian, novelist, autobiographer, sociologist, etymol-
ogist and metaphysician consort within him. Together, they frustrate
each other's designs and so delay the beginning of work on *À la recherche*.
But Proust is also a lonely and incredibly idiosyncratic figure whose love
for Albertine is simply a distilled personification of his love for the little
band of 'jeunes filles en fleurs'; this affection can be displaced to other
members of the same group, for at its roots there lies a desire for an
individual who will convey to the isolate the warmth of the crowd. His
composite figures are also wish-fulfilments of such people. His interest in
family heritage, genetics and even etymology is a strategy for multiply-
ing the personality of the other, the meanings of a single word. He thus
dispels regrets at the way the choice of one person (or word) precludes
enjoyment of others, grants the other the numerical superiority to the self
that permits that self to submit to masochistic engulfment (there is a
deep link between masochism and snobbery), and overcomes fears of his
own marginality by deducing from the number of persons akin to any
other the fact that there must also be people like himself. When Proust
renounces the world in order to write he admits that in everyday life
people are not experienced as crowds; only in the realm of aesthetic
contemplation, of recollection of their various gestures, is their multiplicity revealed. Marcel's inability to know others had resulted from his
misapplication of speculation to real events, which thus became mystify-

ing; only once he begins to write does his propensity to speculate find its vocation, its voice. Proust's decision to fuse different personages into new unities is a result of his self-analysis and self-dispersal, which evaporate him from the scene of wordly pain by distributing his characteristics – legacies after the death of the individual – among the characters of his novel. Thus he bestows some of his own attributes upon Bloch and accords Mme Vinteuil his own vice of inviting his friends to spit upon a photograph of his parents. He detaches – disavows – his own parts and attaches them to others. Thus characteristics become masks. This is why the role played in events by the elusive narrator so often passes unrecorded; his part in the conversations cannot be transcribed, for he is speaking through others (writing pastiches), and is really elsewhere. This dispersal of the self is a homosexual indirection, ventriloquistic camouflage. It compensates for the sterility of the homosexual by disseminating him in space. And it tallies with Proust's evocation of the homosexual's fear of exposure. He analyses at length the belief of one type of sodomite that he alone suffers from his vice, a conviction that leads him to repress it for many years until chance reveals to him that others too share his leanings. May not this man in the meantime have combated his isolation by projecting his own characteristics onto others, even as he realised that his constructions were fictions? Could this be the source of Proust's own fictional technique?

But for all one's awareness of the divergences between Proust and Kierkegaard, there remains one essential convergence. They are united in their consciousness of the rarity and even near-impossibility of repetition. And when each allows repetition to occur, the inner logic of their work declares it to be false. Thus we have the compromised tone of the young man's pseudo-poetic ecstasy at the close of *Repetition*, or the subtly discordant notes of the madeleine episode in Proust. Proust's involuntary memory, the intact sliver of a shattered past, is but an accident momentarily accessible to taste or smell or hearing (the less-frequently used, less habit-deadened senses), but it cannot provide the basis for the practice of a lifetime (habit would dull the receptivity of the sense organs in question), and it cannot be engineered or prepared for. Its moment has nothing to do with writing; it is not writing that re-gathers mystical time. And in this respect the title of Proust's final volume is misleading. The incidents in the Guermantes library do not belong to the essence of his task, but have been dragged in by the magnetic force of association of ideas.

One can now return to Kierkegaard. Just as some commentators have read *The Concept of Irony* as a parody of philosophical discourse, so it may be possible to interpret *Repetition* as a parody. But of what? The fine and witty account of Constantine's visit to his old lodgings in Berlin, which seeks to determine whether or not repetition is possible, is a two-edged parody. It subverts the dignity of the philosopher who tests concepts existentially ('But, alas, here no repetition was possible. My host, materialist that he was, *hatte sich verändert.*' (p. 39)). But this parody is also self-parody, a mockery of the very notion Kierkegaard himself is anxious to expound, that of repetition. His satire is directed at a certain mode of philosophical discourse (Hegelian, systematic, dialectical and unworldly), but it threatens to engulf all philosophy, including that of Kierkegaard himself, who shares the dialectical vocabulary of his opponents. In this context, the pseudonym is used to place brackets around the work and define a space within which self-doubt can have free play without impinging upon the integrity of the hidden self. Fiction allows him both to develop and to criticise his own concepts; it generates sentences such as the following: 'then it was that time and again I conceived the idea of repetition and grew enthusiastic about it – thereby becoming a victim of my zeal for principles.' (p. 77) Kierkegaard employs fiction to measure philosophy against everyday life. The difference between his dialectic and the dialectics of the Hegelians is that his is a dialectic of vulgarity – in a sense, truly Early Christian, affiliated to what Nietzsche would have termed a slave morality – whereas the Hegelian dialectic is an abstract, non-vulgar, non-existential one. (Hegel may have believed the truth to be concrete, but his own analyses are abstract). Thus one recalls that Kierkegaard was considered vulgar by his professors; that existentialism marks the entry into the arena of philosophy of the *petite bourgeoisie*, with its fear and sense of imminent threat, an entry prepared for by the diffusion of education. And one recalls Pauline Kael's remark that the innovator is the man – or woman – who has 'the wit or crassness or desperation' to do what others had the 'good taste' not to do.

This vulgarity causes Kierkegaard to be interested in popular art. He empathises with the actors of the Königstäter theatre; 'they have the courage to do what the ordinary man dares to do only when he is alone by himself.' (p. 55) – when writing, for instance. His passion for the theatre parallels Proust's fascination by the stage – life as a play in the arena of hypocrisy, which in turn corresponds to Proust's willingness to consider Françoise and the other servants as significant as himself; hence also his love for Albertine, which is not the conventional young man's initiation by a chambermaid. Theatre and writing are the natural homes of the displaced; theatre is a cipher for the alternative reality he wishes to inhabit, writing is a sign of his inability to find others with whom to exchange speech. Because of the outlet it offers the multiple personality, the theatre is fundamentally vulgar; the reader of a novel is a bourgeois who exercises the habits of domination and self-domination as he identifies with the masterful solitude of the hero, but the spectator of a play is split into the crowd to which he belongs. The reader employs language, the instrument of command, whilst the onlooker faces images and is told the language belongs to the others upon the stage. 'Surely there is no young man with any imagination who has not at one time been captivated by the enchantment of the theatre, and desired himself to be carried away into the midst of that fictitious reality in order to see or hear himself as an *alter ego*, to disperse himself among the innumerable possibilities which diverge from himself.' (p. 42) He loses and finds himself in the crowd.

This is what Kierkegaard's own associative writing does; it runs off in various directions, towards travelogue, literary criticism, philosophy, theology, psychology, fiction and autobiography, and is as unclassifiable as Proust's great 'novel'. He praises the ability of farce to throw one simultaneously into opposing moods, and his prose has the same effect. As Nabokov has remarked, nothing is more exhilarating than philistinism, and Kierkegaard's fast transitions mimic the effervescence he praises in farce. His is the outrageousness of dialectical shock; when he writes that the theatre 'was not contaminated by the sweat of an audience moved by sensibility to art' (p. 61) there is a nice dialectic in the vocabulary, for 'sweat' would normally be associated with the farce-watching rabble, whilst the refined sensibility would be assumed to have shed the cumbrousness of flesh and to 'perspire' at worst. A phrase like 'the authority of genius' (which indicates the mutual implication of apostle and genius in his work) Romantically asserts the power of the (vulgar) genius to confront self-complacent establishments. To associate him with Romanticism may seem perverse, for in *The Concept of Irony* he subjected the German Romantics to violent criticism, and the normally persuasive Gabriel Josipovici has seen his works as having an entirely anti-Romantic thrust. Nevertheless, it was the very Romantics criticised in *The Concept of Irony* – Schlegel and Tieck – who developed the associative, rhapsodic-digressive forms he himself employs. The digressions reflect the interactions between the components of the self – the interior drama whose exteriorisation is frustrated. Instead, there is only 'inwardness', which cannot be adjudged to be simply positive; for associative logic (as in Proust) is the logic of memory, which stands at the close of time, in the space of death. Different characters struggle within

Kierkegaard, and hope to be parted by an Ideal Dramatist (God) who will lend them independent life. Thus he invents the idealised scenario of the religious leap, which will enable him both to recognise the presence within himself of various impulsions and to achieve unity by granting one of them ultimate hegemony. But in reality, he cannot ultimately arrange his religious, his aesthetic and his ethical selves into a hierarchy of transcendence – just as one cannot ultimately distinguish Proust from Marcel and the Narrator. The multiple personality that lurks within these individual authors parallels the emergence of media with multiple authorship: of film and the *Gesamtkunstwerk*. Like films, these works exemplify the problematic status of the author, and thus of all authority. The pseudonymous texts of Kierkegaard, the writings of Marcel Proust, subvert the fiction of identity, the identity of fiction.

A NOTE ON METONYMY IN PROUST

In a fascinating essay on metonymy and metaphor in *À la recherche* (*Figures III*), Genette has argued that all Proust's metaphors ultimately resolve themselves into metonymies, that the steeple near a cornfield will be likened to a haystack, whilst the one near the sea will have titles like the scales of a fish. This argument seems to me to be both indubitably right, and subtly misleading. Genette is right: there is no means whereby the object in Proust can break through the magic circle of its origin, and the metaphor is tethered on a short leash; however high Marcel may climb on the ladder of society, he will never be able to shed the past or remake himself utterly. Similarly, when a person's unwitting gestures of intonations proclaim the presence of a hidden self, they reveal the suppressed origin; Berma as Phèdre is still Berma above all. Nevertheless, in one respect Genette's analysis is misleading and even wrong-headed. His uncritical acceptance of the current distinction between metaphor and metonymy ignores synecdoche, in which the part becomes the key to the whole. The metaphor cannot simply be translated into a metonymy, the attempted poetic transcendence cannot always be disenchanted by its reduction to a narrative context that renders it prosaic. For metaphor and metonymy are less characteristic of Proust than is synecdoche. As Paul de Man notes in his excellent essay on Proust[1] 'synecdoche is one of the borderline figures that create an ambivalent zone between metaphor and metonymy and that, by its spatial nature, creates the illusion of a synthesis by totalisation.' This ambivalence is central to Proust. The transference between steeple and cornfield is both subjective delusion, a Baroque whimsy, and a sign of a deep underlying, mystical – poetic, metaphorical? – unity between objects perceived as differing in time and space. The movement between haystack and steeple is a double movement in both space and time; the passage of the individual object beyond its native position, and its return or reduction to that position. The part becomes the whole – the steeple becomes the cornfield. The effect is like the work of Cézanne, in which different objects become similar inasmuch as they possess the same geometric shape: a house becomes a rock, and vice versa. The ambivalence of the object of perception is the very heart of Proust's novel. The metaphors cannot be reduced to metonymies – for the entire work is an examination of the consequences of a suspension (by means of synecdoche, part for whole, madeleine for a complete period in a life) of the distinction between them.

When Genette ascribes the dominant role to metonymy, he commits the narrativist heresy and values prose over poetry; he believes that sign and referent must always be disjunctive, that there can be no moment of correspondence or rest; like Derrida, he ignores the existance of ideographic writing, founded upon a resemblance between signifier and signified. The disjunction generates the forward movement of the writing, but it is characteristic of Proust's work – as Paul de Man notes – to proceed both backwards, to a moment of revelation or troubling ambiguity, and forwards, in flight or search. This duality is surely evident in the manner in which Proust revised his novel; when the First World War delayed its publication, he modified it extensively and doubled its length, moving forward in time by going back to a text that already existed. Similarly, he composed the first and last volumes almost concurrently, and having done so, proceeded backwards in time to write forwards towards the last book. Movement forward requires the continual backward glance of memory. Memory is drawn backwards to the sense of happiness in the reading/writing that is successful interpretation – of the books Marcel reads, of the events of his life. Success is apparent whenever he lights upon the one feature that is the key to the totality of a life or series of occurrences. It comes unbeckoned, like a dream, and is called 'involuntary memory'. The happiness exuded by the madeleine is the result of the emergence of a world out of Marcel's teacup, enabling him to stop writing and take a breather. Otherwise the writing would become merely automatic and symptomatic. But the moment of involuntary memory is non-writerly (which is why in the writing it seems false), the achievement of the senses of taste, touch or smell, as the body Marcel has repressed by his decision to live for writing alone briefly awakens. Involuntary memory and the doctrine spun around it by Proust may be what George Craig had in mind, when, in a brilliant lecture delivered at the University of Sussex under the title ' "La Petite phrase" and the long sentence', he talked of there being lights scattered throughout the darkness of the Proustian text, lights lit by Proust himself, which were nevertheless not the only ones available. So involuntary memory may not be the only way into Proust; in fact, Gilles Deleuze's book suggests that it may be the quickest way out of Proust. Returning to George Craig's metaphor, may not the true lights be will-o'-the-wisps – roaming all over the marshy text, never stable? By abolishing the distinction between living a life and recounting it, Proust has dissolved fact into fiction. The final outcome is not 'le temps retrouvé' but the vertigo with which it is both absent and present in the Albertine volumes.

DOUBLES: CONRAD, IRZYKOWSKI, POE, HAWTHORNE

In the introduction to his interesting psychoanalytic study *The Double in Literature*, Robert Rogers quotes Albert J. Guerard's assertion that 'no term is more loosely used by casual critics of modern literature. As almost any character can become a Christ-figure or a Devil-archetype, so almost any can become a double.'[1] Having cited this warning, Rogers bears it in mind for two chapters only to fall then into the overweening generalisation criticised by Guerard; Rogers loses control of his subject as he passes from overt doubles to concealed/latent ones, since the latter are obviously more pliable to his psychoanalytic urge to read off the hidden signature of the text and melt it down into an archetype. His a-historicity fails to perceive the relationship between the image of the double and the genesis of modernism, which revolved around the question of the status of external reality and questioned the degree to which it really was 'external', out there; Impressionism, for instance, was both a response to the increasing fleetingness and transitoriness of events *and* an extension into the domain of perception of a creationist urge to transform the given shape of things. Whereas 'concealed' doubles appear in traditionally 'realist' works, 'manifest' ones are characteristic of stories in which the writer is conscious that to write a story at all is to decompose the self, and that changes occurring in external reality are altering the very nature of perception, exteriorising that which seemed condemned to remain locked within the self as an aspiration or dream. Lines between realism and fantasy, selfhood and otherness, begin to dissolve. The outcome includes a concrete intuition that the look is no longer the preserve of the other, that the self is other too. Rogers quotes Tymms's *The Double in Literary Psychology*: 'doubles are among the facile, and less reputable devices in fiction'[2]. He adds that the use of manifest doubles severely inhibits the degree of identification between reader and character and so leads to aesthetic failure: 'a crucial drawback lies in the reader's awareness that some kind of decomposition is being represented. The lack of aesthetic distance resulting from this transparency allows incipient guilt and anxiety feelings in the reader to inhibit deep identification with the characters.'[3] In applying the categories of a particular kind of realist fiction to the proto-modernist works that deal with the double, Rogers perversely ignores their transitional status and fails to realise that they abandon identification in order to produce embryonic theories of the origin of fiction, of the evolution of an organ capable of perceiving the invisible. In accordance with the American individualist tradition, Rogers interprets the abandonment of identification purely negatively, as a sign of the demise of the individual – not as a simultaneous image of the birth of society within the individual. He overlooks the double's ironic critique of individuality, the dialectical reversal whereby isolation employs the imagination to generate company out of itself even as it remains real solitude. The solution that resolves the problems of the individualist yearning for companionship is a parody of the desired synthesis of crowd and hermit: one creates society as God created Eve out of Adam – by splitting the self.

A key example of the way in which the transition from realism to modernism generates uncertainty in writers is Conrad's short story 'The Secret Sharer'. Conrad cannot decide whether his doubling should be discreetly latent (realistic) or manifest (proto-modernist); driven towards the modernist problematic by the independent logic of his subject-matter, he shies away from direct confrontation with it. His work is laboured and indecisive, hovering between realism and fantasy, unable either to unite them or to separate them. (Unlike Poe, who – to anticipate – unites them triumphantly in 'William Wilson'; this success is achieved by presenting the narrative in the first person; only when placed outside society can a man be insane and yet seem normal, for there is no standard of comparison to help us determine his status). Conrad's narrator is not impelled into obsessive individuality by an extremity of isolation: the crew does not clearly reject him, and his identification with the criminal is only partial. If the story has a point, it relates to the regret felt by the acceding ruler at the necessity of revoking his ties with his old compan- ions, the regret of Hal as he becomes Henry V. But Conrad's story is too ready to give hostages to the moralism that sees in it merely a *rite de passage*; he interprets the decomposition of the personality as merely a temporary phase – teething troubles of the captain's first command – detached from the deeper level at which there exist fundamental rifts in the structure of character. Conrad hides the trail that leads from his captain-hero to the self-conscious narrators of modernist fiction. The captain's insistent references to 'my double' thus come to seem unmoti- vated, for the sole apparent similarity between him and the rebel is that both are young and both are Conway boys. When he remarks 'it was, in the night, as though I had been faced by my own reflection in the depths of a sombre and immense mirror', he is playing with the idea of identity so as to create a fictional companion; his desire to fictionalise is both a response to his solitude and an exercise of power. One recalls that Canetti has seen in the hidden explosiveness of the secret the kernel of power in general; here the double is the captain's secret. But his fictional play is implausible because he cannot yet handle the elements of power with assurance; hence the figure concealed in the cabin is not only the secret but also an image of the captain's wish that he could be somewhere other than on deck, where he has to prove himself. On a psychoanalytic level, the murder carried out by Leggatt is the necessary prelude to the captain's assumption of power, a parricidal usurpation of authority.

Conrad's use of the double is a reaction to the crisis of realism in the late nineteenth century, when the disintegration of once hermetic com- munities cast in doubt the validity of the rhetoric of gestures and appearances that allows one to 'place' a character on a mental map. Stories about doubles raised the acute problem of the extent to which one 'sees' the characters in a work of fiction. Two alternative solutions emerged: the Jamesian point of view (which problematised the interpre- tation of gestures by demonstrating that for the foreigner their meanings are far from self-evident) and the Naturalists' registration of external signs (which dispensed with character and presented the individual under scrutiny as a bundle of symptoms). The double combines these alternatives, forcing them into a dissonant unity. At one and the same time he both sees and is seen.

For Conrad, as for the Symbolists, language is also silence: the silence of the objects with which one is confronted, of the people reduced to the level of objects by the processes of industrial capitalism, of one's past self which spoke another tongue. The foreign language is the speech of one's own childhood and is inaccessible to memory. The plenitude of language in Conrad is the fullness of the distended sun before it sinks behind the hills of silence. In 'The Secret Sharer', Leggatt represents the repressed anger that underlies the hallucinatory irritability of all Conrad's dialogue; one is annoyed by a double that requires one to speak to it, for his identity with oneself should establish unanimity ('oneness of souls'). The captain styles Leggatt his double in the hope of escaping the necessity of talking to him. Conrad himself ceases to address the Poles, for he is afraid of his own voice (he buries it underneath another language, where it smoulders like the fire below the volcano in *Victory*, Titanic and suppressed): the disavowed voice of the murderer Leggatt, of the attempted self-murderer Józef Konrad Korzeniowski. It is significant that the portion of his name discarded by Conrad should contain the Polish word for 'root' (korzeń). The Pole's repressed double is another Pole, a rebel in the Polish tradition, not a merchant seaman applying himself to his duty. The eerie calm of *The Shadow Line* is experienced by a man who has muffled the Siren song of self-destruction with two plugs of wax.

If works involving doubles tend to be short, this is not because the introduction of the double evokes a facile and necessarily short-lived *frisson*, but rather because it freezes the dynamism of character interaction into an emblem. It is no accident that doubles should have been prevalent in a period in which more and more novels came to be illustrated, for the double is the point at which the writerly meets with the visual. The questioning of subject – object relationships questions language itself, from which it takes a short sample for experimental observation. In 'The Metamorphoses of Mójski', Karol Irzykowski's story about a misanthrope who fashions a dummy of himself and then addresses monologues to it, one can find the sentence: ' "he" provided "me" with material.'[4] The inverted commas relativise language. Stories about doubles have to be brief because of the immense amount of tension focused within them, and because their asceticism implies a critical distance from the practice of literature in general (it may be no accident that Irzykowski is better known in Poland as a critic than as a writer of stories and novels, or that E. T. A. Hoffmann wished above all to be a musician; each man has a double identity). In stories about doubles, the fact that personal pronouns have the primary status of shifters is allowed to dialecticise individual sentences. Irzykowski writes (Mójski to the mannequin): 'You're a free man, do as you please. I'll run in horror behind the chariot of your Satanic triumphs, wringing my hands and crying out: Alas!'[5] The dialectic is not dispersed throughout the story as the moving principle of a narrative but is fixed as shock. Individual sentences acquire the mirror-structure typical of the paradoxical antitheses of Baroque literature, which gravitates towards anti-literature: 'the Baroque is that style which deliberately exhausts (or tries to exhaust) its own possibilities and borders on its own caricature.'[6] The metamorphoses of Mójski are potentially endless; his name (derived from 'mój', the first person possessive) is namelessness, so he is infinitely labile and extensible. His multiplicity can be correlated with Irzykowski's interest in the cinema; his *X Muza* is one of the key books on cinema of the first two decades of this century. For the cinematic author is also a multiple personality: 'Griffith' subsumes into a single icon: D. W. Griffith himself, Bitzer, Lillian Gish, Mae Marsh, and a horde of backers and actors.

Stories about doubles demand a double reading and thus lie on the boundary that divides 'prose' (the linear, read once only) from 'poetry' (the Beautiful upon which one is fixated). The distinction is of nineteenth-century provenance, though it has been perpetuated in Jakobson's description of the metaphoric and the metonymic codes: it is strange that Post-Structuralism should have retained the distinction, for it has no meaning in the context of the modernist literature it propagates. *S/Z*, which encourages endless re-reading of an extremely prosaic piece of Balzac, demonstrates a rare consciousness of the nullity of the distinction. For the literature of modernism is the nameless work of 'l'innomable'. Stories involving doubles engage with poetry and prose in a manner that anticipates modernism (they are the small scale models that are later enlarged by Proust, Kafka and Musil): 'le developpement de la poétique littéraire depuis la fin du 19-ième siècle . . . efface désormais la distinction faite par la rhetorique traditionelle entre "prose" et "poésie"', writes Julia Kristeva.[7]

A fine example of this is Poe's 'William Wilson', though one should add that the story tends less to 'erase' the distinction between poetry and prose than to to exploit their dialectical conflict and interdependence. The very title employs effects of poetic suggestion and prosaic anticipation of the themes of the story it introduces: the letter 'W' is a homonym for 'double you' and itself appears twice in Wilson's name. As in poetry, even the most minute features of the text gather significance when read attentively. Will-I-am Will-son: the will's son is the conscience that criticises the criminal will. During the necessary second reading, text and sub-text change places, and that which seemed merely incidental, narrative redundancy or waste, assumes a clear poetic function. Innocent remarks take on a grisly irony: 'Wilson and myself were the most inseparable of companions'[8] becomes frighteningly knowing, and the phrase that speaks of his 'consummate self-conceit' glows with a metaphysical wit as it rehearses the theme of narcissism. To occupy two places at one and the same time is to be both visible and invisible: invisible like Hermes, the patron of thieves, or the criminal whose favoured time is the night; visible like an ordinary person. Wilson's tormenting conscience 'had so contrived it, in the execution of his varied interference with my will, that I saw not, at any moment, the features of his face'[9]; similarly, the reader does not see the face of the writer, and this is the basis for the story's subterranean identification of writing with criminality or transgression. Prose transgresses the boundaries of poetry; Wilson oversteps the bounds of his own body. He is both the will and the will's son: he is invisible because otherwise justice and criminality would wear the same aspect, and because we cannot imagine any place from which the story could have been told, nor any teller. For at the end it is disclosed that he (who? Will, Will's son, or both of them?) is already dead. 'Everything in Poe is dead: the houses, the rooms, the furniture, to say nothing of nature and the human beings.'[10] The story ends with Wilson stabbing himself in front of the mirror; reading his tale becomes in retrospect a seance, a communion with the living dead. After its long silence, conscience eventually speaks: the narrator remarks 'I could have fancied that I myself was speaking while he said . . .'. [11] The story sets in the mould of a labyrinth with this moment as its centre: earlier on in the story there had been talk of 'mazes' and of a 'wilderness of narrow passages', for the text is a labyrinth whose heart is the moment of overt duality when the self confronts a mirror. Here word and image deadlock at the limit at which the code of writing is demonstrably inadequate, having been party to a mystification: it is evident here that the entire text should have been composed in the present tense of our reading, not the preterite that sets the seal on a comfortably completed past. The last page is an eerie opening of the grave of the past. Had there been a dimension of images from the very beginning, the text could not have come into being; the modernist text eschews the illustrations (and the attendant popularity) that would be its downfall. As it annihilates itself, the text reveals the underside of absence below its presence. Thus its subsequent real absence becomes the double of its inauthentic presence. This absent text is the silence of the Sirens – as Kafka noted, more deadly than their song – which lured the Symbolists onto the rocks of sterility.

Not until the close of Poe's story is the narrator accorded his true, inalienable and endlessly alienated name: I. He has felt persecuted by 'Wilson''s mocking mimicry, which has deprived him of his own identity. The narrator states that odious circumstances had rendered his name so closely akin to that of 'Wilson' that the name and deeds of the one were generally ascribed to the other, and vice versa. Neither of them is 'the real Wilson', for 'Wilson' is a fiction. Both Poe and the narrator create fictions; the true double of the narrator is the unamed Poe. The narrator states that for the purposes of the story he has assumed the name 'William Wilson', and adds that it does not diverge greatly from his true name. One may ask whether it diverges at all. Or whether he possesses any name. Because 'Wilson' is a fiction, neither the narrator nor his shadow can be held responsible for his deeds. As if in fulfilment of Flaubert's ideal, the story is about nothing – written by no-one. Thus one cannot blame the (non-existent) narrator for the incoherence of the recounted events, nor for the murkiness that results from the superimposition of allegory upon realism. In order to shatter the limitations of his private existence, the narrator creates a double, one who will not have his own hated, unmentioned, plebeian name. Similar reasons, and a similar snobbishness, lead Proust to forge his own double, 'Marcel'. One creates the Other by bifurcating the self.

At the beginning of this essay I sketched a distinction between post-modernist stories in which the use of the image of the double is overt, and traditionally realistic ones in which the identity of the characters is subterranean and occult. Although the distinction functions well enough as a working hypothesis, I would like to conclude with a text which indicates the point at which it becomes inadequate, Hawthorne's strange novel *The Blithedale Romance*, which floats between the two camps. One can start by noting that its final chapter, 'Miles Coverdale's Confession', includes the following remark: "As Hollingsworth once told me, I lack a purpose. How strange! He was ruined, morally, by an overplus of the very same ingredient, the want of which, I occasionally suspect, has rendered my own life all emptiness.' [12] Like the inexplicable friendship which once prevailed between the self-absorbed Hollingsworth and the speculative , Jamesian Coverdale, the sentence suggests a hidden identity of the two men, and the possible interchange of opposites is reinforced by the duality of both their characters: Hollingsworth is both egotistic and philanthropical, Coverdale other-directed and self-enclosed (a very Jamesian combination). But although an identity is suggested it remains merely a suggestion, shimmering between possibility and improbability. However, the idea of the different self is thematic in the work: Moodie was once called Fauntleroy, Zenobia's true name is unknown, and she spectrally outlives her own death in her half-sister, who also loved Hollingsworth. Characteristically, Moodie and Zenobia are the only other figures apart from Cover-

dale himself who recount stories (Zenobia's is a veiled threat, whilst
Moodie's is an unveiling). This suggests that Coverdale too is shadowed
by a different self: within the story, Hollingsworth, and outside it,
Hawthorne himself. (The triangle is closed between them by the mutual
echoing of the letters of 'Hawthorne' and 'Hollingsworth'). But it also
intimates a quasi-identity between all these figures – a suspicion perhaps
justified by the manner in which the 'Fauntleroy' chapter is narrated,
not in the first person of authoritative revelation, but in the third person.
Thus the omniscient author speaking of Fauntleroy is identified with
Coverdale and with Moodie speaking of his old, disavowed self. The
mixture of events revealed by Moodie and events later uncovered by
Coverdale himself cements the identity, which is also the source of the
circular equanimity and indifference of the narratorial tone. There
comes into being a regress of narrators. Thanks to this regress it is no
surprise when Coverdale first imagines a drowned figure in the
Blithedale pond and then Zenobia actually drowns herself there; nor
does it surprise us to see Zenobia and Priscilla appear at the boarding
house window opposite Coverdale's hotel directly after he has left them,
as if they have been materialised there by his obsession. *The Blithedale
Romance* enacts the process whereby the writer discovers that his story
exists independently of him and has its own logic. One expression of this
is the recalcitrance of Coverdale's characters; another, his vengeful
violence towards them. These characters are, of course, primarily
Zenobia, Priscilla and Hollingsworth. At one point he remarks:

> Was mine a mere vulgar curiosity? Zenobia should have known me
> better than to suppose it. She should have been able to appreciate that
> quality of the intellect and the heart, which impelled me (often against
> my own will, and to the detriment of my own comfort) *to live in other lives*
> [my italics], and to endeavour – by generous sympathies, by delicate
> intuitions, by taking note of things too slight for record, and by
> bringing my human spirit into manifold accordance with the compan-
> ions whom God assigned me – to learn the secret which was hidden
> even from themselves.[13]

The secret is hidden from them in the form of their other, unacknowledged name. Zenobia however resents his authorial insistence, his will
to power over his puppets: 'It is dangerous sir, believe me, to tamper thus
with earnest human passions, out of your own mere idleness, and for
your sport.'[14] She discerns in Coverdale 'a most irreverent propensity
to thrust Providence aside, and substitute one's self in its awful place.'[15]

But if she resents Coverdale's interference it is because she herself is an author, contriving a plot for the disappearance of Priscilla. Her story of the Veiled Lady foretells the danger to Priscilla, just as Coverdale's vision of the skeleton in the mud foreshadows the fate of Zenobia herself. Since, in this convocation of authors, Coverdale is the meta-author, it is he who has his will, frustrates her plot, kills her off, and even suppresses her real name. She makes no mention of a wish to commit suicide, and it is as if the death is simply an imaginative extension of Coverdale's brooding on the drowning pool. The 'dale' suffix common to both author and book, however, suggests the presence of a maker other than Coverdale, of a maker who frames a clumsy jest at Coverdale's expense. For Coverdale provides a 'cover' for his own disaffected double, Nathaniel Hawthorne.

JÓZEF KONRAD

The statement that Conrad's works display features common to Symbolism and Decadence seems – and is – absurd, but it is also true. It can be both because of the split nature of the Conradian personality. Attention has been directed away from this duality by the moralistic bias of English criticism – a bias ultimately shared by Conrad himself – which leaves intact and 'organic' the self perceived as split by the Symbolists. The main trait he shares with the Symbolists goes unperceived by the English reader because it is so omnipresent: this is the fact of his having written in a foreign language. I have tried to draw attention to this in my title, a hybrid of his English and his Polish names. One of the reasons why many artists in the modernist period felt themselves to be possessed of (by) a dual personality lies in the frequency with which they undertook translations. The language of surrounding society was becoming so foriegn to them that texts in a different tongue – texts that made no secret of their foreignness – became more congenial to them. The translator is perpetually tormented by the possibility of putting things a different way (the modernist concern with unrealised potential), and in some artists this fostered a tendency to place invisible inverted commas around completed statements (Mann), and drove others to quotation (Eliot and Pound). In Conrad there is a triple process of translation at work: from Polish into French, from Polish into English, and from French into English. This is why studies of the relationship between his English syntax and the syntax of Polish are so unrewarding, for there is too much French syntax and semantics intermingled. Just why Conrad should have written in English when his French was more fluent remains a point for endless debate, but I think one can present a few plausible hypotheses. Firstly, French was too close to Polish; France has been the haven of many Polish writers (one thinks in particular of the Great Emigration of 1831), and up to the beginning of the last war most cultured Poles learned French as their first foreign language. Moreover, Polish is studded with words borrowed from French (e.g. 'abazur' or 'zaluzja'), even sharing nasalised vowels with the French. Thus to write in French would have entailed only a partial departure from the sphere of Polish culture – and Conrad desired a more radical break. French must also have been associated in his mind with the traumas that precipitated his attempted suicide in his youth in Marseilles: putting French behind him was a symbolic means of disposing of the knot of experiences that had brought him close to self-extinction. It also, symbolically, re-enacted the self-extinguishing gesture. Finally, of course, English was the language of the sea; and the man who flees his own culture and himself must stay in constant movement, like the Flying Dutchman. To settle and write in England was to step off the continent in which Poland and France are linked and into a new reality.

The fact that Conrad employs a foreign (doubly foreign) language can spark in the reader a continual, often subterranean awareness of the presence of the author, a self-consciousness such as is characteristic of modernist texts. This is perhaps most evident in *Lord Jim*, where the narrator's pretence that we are hearing colloquial English only underlines its disquietingly subtle difference from everyday idiom. Conrad peoples the novel with foreigners speaking an obviously un-English English to disguise his own difference: he too wishes to be 'one of us', though he can admit this desire to consciousness only in the camouflaged form of a fiction. For to surrender his linguistic independence, his independence of language, would wound his pride. *Lord Jim* is his first really significant novel because the loosening of the pressure to achieve linguistic correctness (attained through the use of a narrator) frees his imagination to explore the murky underside of heroic obsession; the narrator is Jim as his own narcissistic admirer. The form of narration that places even the third person narrator at one remove is a smoke screen. In Conrad, the theme of the absence of language (inscribed both in the fact that he uses English and in his colonial settings) attracts the themes of darkness and privation, key Symbolist concerns: darkness that is both the grubbiness of objects coated with industrial grime and the obscurity of the exotic realms into which anthropology was only just beginning to penetrate. But this absence is also a presence, a form of richness. It is rich in the secrecy of self-presence, in which the self knows itself to be itself and is known by no other person. This is the secrecy and darkness of self-alienation sought out by 'Mistah Kurtz'.

In *Heart of Darkness*, Marlow hears the savages calling through the mist in which the ship is enfolded, and it is 'as though the mist itself had screamed'. Thus language is deprived of expressiveness, detached from the person; and the silent person, like Kurtz, is reified into a Symbol by the look of the Other (of Marlow, the speaking side of Kurtz). In connection with the image of the mist, it is interesting to note that Leavis pillories Conrad's vagueness: 'the vague and unrealisable, he asserts with strained impressiveness, is the profoundly and tremendously significant.'[1] The vocabulary of vagueness has its source in the writer's suspicion that the alien tongue he employs is not fully under his control (just as the other half of his personality shades off into darkness), that its most intimate corners withhold their secrets from him. The writer drawn to a foreign tongue is one for whom writing involves continual failure, as it does for Beckett, who has long proclaimed the artist's prerogative of failing more comprehensively than any other man. The portentous vagueness of much of Conrad's writing is a sign that all attempts to bring into the light the heart of darkness are doomed to failure; Kurtz's silence is the silence of the other selves within Conrad that do not speak English, that do not speak at all. In Conrad, the foreign words that struggle merely to exist stand as mutilated trophies of the triumph of the will. The heroic fact of their existence quelled any doubts about their right to exist, as they do for a man who considers a dubious enterprise simply from the point of view of the techniques one must master in order to carry it out. Writing in a foreign language was for Conrad (as it probably is for Beckett) a narcotic administered to a suicidal self-consciousness. Yet writing in an alien tongue is also – dialectically – itself a form of suicide, of living death, of alienation of the forms of self-expression; everything is relegated in advance to the level of the secondary or foreign (to write in a foreign language is to state that language itself is ultimately foreign to the deepest, wordless core of selfhood); pessimistically, one forecloses the possibility of communication in one's primary tongue. This masochistic relation to language may have a correlative in Conrad's image of encounter with the other sex, during which man proves incapable of interpreting the tight-lipped, predatory tension of the foreign girl.[2]

For Conrad, all encounter is enigmatic. The other is both a man like oneself and something demonically different, the very existence of which poses a threat. In *The Duel*, the reason for Ferraud's incessant issuing of challenges to D'Hubert is suppressed because Ferraud is practically a foreigner (he is a Southerner), and the faculty of speech is by implication attributed to D'Hubert alone, for the narrative verbalisation is from his point of view. Here anthropology and sociology meet; a member of one's own nation can appear as alien as a South Seas islander. Ferraud fears to become an object of mockery by using language, for he could only use it clumsily, and he vents in action his rage over his own inarticulacy. The duel between the two men recurs with absurd regularity on the successive rungs of their promotion because the possession of a secret (the cause of the duel itself) is the source of their power. By their enigma and legendary persistency they are magnetically drawn towards the higher reaches of power, eventually disappearing into the mists whence power stems, where they will no longer be questioned about the reason for their feud; their silent challenge to authority's right to know becomes the basis of their own eventual authority. Thus Conrad himself sees in Kurtz's taciturnity the source of his authoritative mystery.

Conrad composed in ornate mosaic manner, word by agonising word, and the process of composition left him drained once it was completed. The agonising results in a highly adjectival style. Each adjective and adverb allows the author to rest in the middle of the sentence he is writing, momentarily to suspend the narrative (it is a microscopic image of those larger landslides of time in Conrad, when an entire narrative face suddenly crumbles away); for to write in a foreign language requires great effort and is the source of the sense of strain in his work. 'Incomprehensible', 'mysterious' and all the other portentous adjectives use their spendthrift emptiness to grant him a breather from the process of careful construction of signification. Adjectives show how the simplicity of actions is lost in a fog of qualifications; enterprises of great pith and moment lose 'the name of action' (the title of one of Greene's most Conradian novels). The pearly strings of adjectives also represent a fetishistic lingering over objects, the difficulty the narrator has in taking his eyes off them; for Conrad, the real hero-villain of *Nostromo* was Silver. This fetishism of bejewelled splendour is a primary feature of Symbolism; it is the reason why the *fin de siècle* spawned so many adjectival styles. Ultimately, however, Conrad rejects his tendency to kinetic fetishism and opposes to the brightness of the silver the darkness in which language and communication come into being. In the boat that sails across the blackened bay in *Nostromo*, the objects that would normally distract people from each other have disappeared, so contact becomes possible. The lighthouse is the key symbol in *Nostromo* because it embodies the dialectic of dark and light, of darkness and silver, of communication and miserly lingering over objects, that lies at the heart of the novel. The flashing alternation and mutual punctuation of light and dark is that of the beating heart of darkness.

In the blackness, events occur suddenly; the blinded, scarfed reader does not perceive the potholes in the narrative, the time-slips and disjunctions in Conrad's novel, down which he tumbles. Paradoxically, the discontinuous text, the text recounted with nonchalant violence and a cinematic sense of the shock of the cut, this text is the one that is read unbrokenly by a reader anxious to clear up the mysteries. This is the basis of modernism's complicity with the detective story, the reason why Kafka could term all literature a series of variations on the theme of the detective story. In *Nostromo*, political events break like a tidal wave; Conrad has concentrated on the individual rather than the mass, so the Monterist revolt in Sulaco really does seem (to use one of Conrad's favourite adjectives) incomprehensible. It breaks over the reader just as it does over the characters. The silence of the bay has given one the feeling that one can perceive everything of relevance, but in fact this tranquillity has been the artificial product of the province's mountain-bound isolation, and its fate has been determined on the other side. By concentrating on individuals and then demonstrating how this concentration overlooks the really significant events occurring elsewhere, Conrad de-mystifies the individualism of the classic realist novel, undermines the novel from within. The mountain is an image of the impossibility of passing from the realm of the individual to that of the mass; the novelist can define mass events only by negation. The revolt on the other side of the mountain demonstrates the fact that History has a logic of its own that is separate from, and ultimately overrides, the logic of the individual. The demise of the individual is however forshadowed in the attribution of several names to many of the characters: Nostromo is also the Capataz; Charles Gould is Don Carlos and El Rey de Sulaco. By implication, the individual is breaking up; or rather, there are masses beyond who refer to him by a language that is not English. Sulaco's stupored blindness to the coming catastrophe is that of foreigners for whom the alien environment does not really exist; but the emigrés themselves are the real living dead. Most corpse-like of all is Nostromo himself; it is a consummate irony with regard to the implicit individualism of the novel form that he should be the hero of this anti-novel. Action in a foreign land always tends either to be ghostly or symbolic, rooted in illusion. The Goulds are English; Giorgio and Nostromo are Italian; Decoud is French; and Antonia has shed local conventions. The revolt is the moment at which their tomb is opened and they disintegrate in the fresh air.

Earlier in this essay I remarked that Conrad's is an adjectival syle. Now is the time to show the relationship between such a style and the dreams of empire. Adjectives form a constellation around the object, defining it by negation; one has the feeling that a noun in need of an adjective is one that has lost its properties and passed into the realm of 'lessness' (Beckett); that the adjective is its ghostly after-life, and haunts its grave. The object forfeits its properties, of course, in the process of ruthless exploitation. The frequency of adjectival styles round the turn of the century is a reflection of the omnipresence of a colonialist mentality, of the widespread nature of the dream of exploitation. Conrad's sombre, Baroque imagination surrounds objects with darkness so as to isolate them; he then submits them to a process that extracts from them their properties. The following sentence from *Lord Jim* is just one of many of which a single object is surrounded by darkness:

> Only one corner of the vast room, the corner in which stood his writing-desk, was stongly lighted by a shaded reading lamp, and the rest of the spacious apartment melted into shapeless gloom like a cavern.

The sentences he appends to it are equally revealing and characteristic.

> Narrow shelves filled with dark boxes of uniform shape and colour ran round the walls, not from floor to ceiling, but in a sombre belt about four feet broad. Catacombs of beetles. Wooden tablets were hung at irregular intervals. The light reached one of them, and the word 'Coleoptera' written in gold letters glittered mysteriously upon a vast dimness. The glass cases containing the collection of butterflies were ranged in three rows upon slender-legged little tables. One of these cases had been removed from its place and stood on the desk, which was bestrewn with oblong strips of paper blackened with minute handwriting.[3]

Here, as Conrad's writing moves away from the colloquial, it gains an exalted assurance; he is no longer cramped by the difficulties with dialogue that dominate the first half of *Lord Jim* and correspond to the individual inability to master his fate. The mastered fate is associated in the second half of the book with the eye ranging over objects, with the evaporation of the embarrassing compulsion to speak. But then, at the end of the novel, when speech is reactivated as Jim addresses the brigand Brown, he becomes aware of his foreignness, of his inability to explain himself to the tribe that finally kills him. In the passage quoted above, virtually every sentence contains a reference to darkness – there is even 'blackened paper', as if the paper were a carbon, or as if writing were the source of a variety of defilement. The darkness that here exerts such a strong pull on Conrad's imagination is widely present in the paintings of the late nineteenth century and is caused by a shame similar to Jim's: a wish to veil the reality that testifies to one's crimes, to lower industrial smoke and euphemistic mist as curtains before the scene of exploitation, and narcissistically to mourn one's lost innocence. (One can only leap off a boat containing *foreign* pilgrims, who have been de-humanised by the imagination – just as Conrad allows the German captain to appear as a baby elephant or Cornelius as a beetle). In the passage I have quoted, language is treated as an acquired material possession; the words have the materiality of objects, each one weighed like a coin. The sheer voluptuous density of Conrad's descriptions is more European than English and this reflects the fact that European languages are more highly structured grammatically than is English, and so require more thought on the user's behalf. The European is accustomed to weighing every word – at least half-consciously – to ensure that it agrees with other words; Conrad writes English with the intense deliberations of a European. In the passage quoted, the amoral eye mentions colours but does not name them, for it is drawn instinctively to the area of sharpest contrast, where darkness meets gold (whenever Conrad *does* mention colours, they are often contrasting ones, e.g. red and green on the face of a cliff). He throws everything into darkness and then lights a single torch which provides a source of heroically isolated order; similarly, he hurls all men but 'the great' into the gulf; he is capable of a quite withering disdain, such as he feels for the revolutionaries of *Under Western Eyes*. In creating this contrast he is both criticising and preserving heroic Polish individualism, showing that is is valid to act as if there were no one else only if there actually is no one else, if one has renounced society to become – in Aristotle's phrase – 'a beast or a god'.

A theatrical, stage-lighting dialectic of light and dark, of extreme contrasts, fascinates Conrad. Thus the opening of *Victory* meditates on the fact that carbon contains both coal and diamond, the imagined diamond shines all the more brightly against the background of the imaginary coal. *Victory* progresses from the pinprick of Heyst's cigar against the darkness to the magnification of that flame, as human reality rivals the volcanic eruption in the burning pyre of Heyst's house at the novel's close. *Victory* is more slangy and casual than *Nostromo*, and this difference brings both losses and gains; the mordant precision and angular, Cézanne-like clarity of the earlier work is lost, and much lurid writing is perpetrated, but by placing his own customary *vanitas* theme in the mouth of Heyst, he is able to achieve a comic, though tired, detachment from his own pessimism. By placing in Heyst's mouth phrases like 'the game of life', he admits their sentimental exhaustion (something his disciple Greene was never to realise). The book is a study of the dangers of relationships: Schomberg preys upon his wife and talks of Heyst having similarly drained Morrison of his bodily fluids; Ricardo uses helping Jones as a licence for a boyish, provocative callousness towards everyone else, and his unnatural activity is the counterpart of Jones's bored civility. Heyst has tried to avoid the snares of such vampirical relationships, but paradoxically enough this is because the spectre of his pessimistic father has dictated the tone of his life (is there an image here of Conrad's own feeling about his own father?). Heyst may in fact be trapped in the most dangerous of all relationships, that with a phantom. The volcano is a symbol of the suddenness of action (a theme found in *Nostromo*), but it is also introduced because places near volcanoes are usually deserted; Heyst wanders the streets of a private Pompeii. As elsewhere in Conrad, the foreign environment represents the inexplicability of the world, but a dual focus is operative; it is only to the foreigner that this world is incomprehensible. This is the thin trickle of optimism running through the darkness of Conrad's works. The book comes down both for and against solitude. In his eremitic retreat, Heyst is the only character who is not duplicitous. Rodrigo hides the girl's existence from Jones; Jones conceals his health under a mask of tactical invalidism; Schomberg seems blustery but is timid within, and his wife seems a broken woman but is in fact possessed of great courage and defiance. Only Heyst is at one with himself, and apologises to Lena for having hidden something from Jones. Solitude breeds honesty. The question whether or not relationships based on truth are possible is raised by Heyst's love for Lena but then dropped, as Conrad amputates the story before one can reach any conclusion. He may well have feared that a positive answer would undermine his own belief in the virtues of solitude; the title suggests this. But the ending is not arbitrary: it is a sign of the discontinuity of all life, all narrative. Conrad is interested in people whose lives contain deep rifts, as does his own. A life withdraws from its previous form and assumes a new one just as his works all withdraw from their titles: others thought *Nostomo* a misleading title, and one may doubt the felicity of *Victory*. This is because the experience they seek to gather slips through the net of language. Of his works one could fittingly say what Gabriel Josipovici says of modern fiction in general: they are *negatives* of reality, reality both registered and denied, black undeveloped images of a perishing world. There is no time to develop them, for the convulsion intervenes. In the hints of transmigration that dot his works (the changes of name indicate the birth of a new personality), Conrad is at one both with the Polish tradition (the mysticism of a Słowacki, for instance) and with the turn of the century, with its indebtedness to hinduism. In Conrad, man is always reborn on earth, in the form of a dog, for dogs are faithful, but 'dog' is a term of abuse. He is the first of the modern race of extraterritorial writers and yet also the last of the old, for which language was indifferent. He is caught between transmigrations. For no framework can hold him – no language.

THE LATE HENRY JAMES: SUBSTITUTION, PROJECTION AND THE GUILTY EYE

I. Relativity

The master is the person who keeps everyone in their places. Where there is no master, people lose their places. This is what happens in Henry James's famous story *The Turn of the Screw*, which I would like to consider here less with regard to the probity or possible villainy of the governess, than as a web of substitution and exchange, in which, as in relativity theory, people are mobile in time and space and glance backwards and forwards at their own selves and see them as other. These other selves are disavowed incarnations of the evil in their beholder – like the image of the self that might have been perceived by Spencer Brydon at the close of *The Jolly Corner*; it is such an image as hovers round the edge of Strether's vision in *The Ambassadors*, as he confesses: 'I'm always considering something else; something else, I mean, than the thing of the moment. The obsession of the other thing is the terror.' The terror of this other is that it is the alienated figure of the self. It is, perhaps, primarily felt by the late James, who fears he has lost himself as an artist.

Let us return to *The Turn of the Screw* and the theme of the loss of the master, of the master key and master image. The house in which the governess takes charge of the two children is one without a master. The master is perpetually absent, and one of the conditions of her continued employment is that she should never write to him, regardless of what difficulties may arise. The theological implication of the self-sufficiency of this world is that it has been given over to the demonic, which – and this is the source of the story's equivocation and ultimate failure – may or may not be the human irrational. The place of the master has been usurped by the servant: Mrs Grose reports that Quint used to wear the master's waistcoats; and it is just after the governess has wished to see the master that she glimpses Quint above her (in the position of the master) at the tower window. The Quint-master relationship resembles that between the real and the symbolic body of the king in medieval political theory: the one subject to corruption, the other lodged in ideal glory. Behind James's use of the motif of the double body lies the theme of the double itself. The loss of the master is what Derrida would term the loss of the Ultimate Signified, the accent of dominance.

When the governess first sees Quint a complicity between their looks is implied; he 'seemed to fix me, from his position, with just the question, just the scrutiny through the fading light, that his own presence provoked'. The exchange of looks is like an exchange of places. On the second occasion when she observes Quint, as he stares at her through a downstairs window, she rushes out after him:

> It was confusedly present to me that I ought to place myself where he had stood. I did so; I applied my face to the pane and looked, as he had looked, into the room. As if, at this moment, to show me exactly what his range had been, Mrs. Grose, as I had done for himself just before, came in from the hall. With this I had the full image of a repetition of what had already occurred. She saw me as I had seen my own visitant.

And on the third occasion on which she sees Miss Jessel – she is accompanied by Mrs Grose and Flora – she remarks that the apparition 'rose erect on the spot my friend and I had lately quitted'. At the end of section XV she witnesses the image of a woman seated writing as if to her lover, and naturally enough, at the end of section XVI, she herself sits down to write to the master she would like to have as a lover.

These quotations indicate the extent to which the pattern of looks built up by *The Turn of the Screw* is based on substitution and projection. The degree to which the governess is unconsciously jealous of Miss Jessel, who possesses the master-substitute Quint, is evident in her unwillingness to name the rival; she does not name her when she first sees her, and later she sees only the back of her apparition, head bowed, at the foot of the stairs. As she considers the other from behind, the back is an image of her own alienated self. (Compare the paintings of Munch or the films of Antonioni). In her own eyes, the image of the governess herself is self-styled: 'Then, with all the marks of a deliberation that must have seemed magnificent had there been anyone to admire it, I laid down my book.' Here of course the regret is mere sophistry, for an ardent admirer is indeed present, she herself, prolonging her own gesture for self-delectation. When the governess sits and writes from the position of Miss Jessel – 'my vile predecessor' – she is shunted into it by the train of the story's substitutions. What she sees opposite herself, in the place of the other, is herself in the future, and she fears that self as if it were another person, since its presence testifies to her non-identity with herself (her incompletion, her forbidden desire for a lover to fill the gap that is the place of the self-as-other). This is why she demonises the other.

Here one becomes conscious of the relationship between the mechanisms of projection and the dualist attitude to reality. It is because the governess sees the children as absolutely and angelically good that she is simultaneously able to view them as totally depraved; the opposites switch places. She compensates for her unhealthy conscious unwillingness to believe any evil of the children by arraigning them in the dock of her unconscious. In some respects, her love-hate relationship to them is typical of an American sense of inferiority to exquisite European manners and European decadence, those key themes of James's work. When she remarks 'it wasn't for ugly feeding that Miles had been expelled from school', the vulgarism strikes a very American note of mockery. In fact, her covert violence towards the children appears in the wording of much of the narrative. Flora 'is not a child: she's an old, old woman' reflects the theme of the movement in time in the story, but it also mirrors a common American prejudice about Europe, whose children are wizened from the cradle on. At another point she writes of her own relationship to Flora: 'why not break out at her on the spot and have it all over? – give it to her straight in her lovely little lighted face?' Here the 'lovely' is ugly and aggressive. Here 'the threat to the children makes them interesting' is more the phrase of the Jamesian villain than of the tender governess. Thus she is seen to stage, and revel in, the psycho-drama of her own envy.

Throughout *The Turn of the Screw* the governess remains nameless. It is this unnamed status that makes it possible for her to migrate into the place of the other. She is possessed by others because she lacks a place of her own; she stands for the principle of narrative circulation. Several incidents demonstrate the frailty of her identity. In rushing out after Quint she herself slips into the place of his terrifying apparition in the eyes of Mrs Grose, and in the following passage she herself disappears as a speaking subject.

It added to the interposing cry, as if to stay the blow, that Mrs. Grose at the same instant uttered over my violence the shriek of a creature scared, or rather wounded, which, in turn, in a few seconds, was completed by a gasp of my own. I seized my colleague's arm. 'She's there, she's there!'

Here the speaker of the last words is not named. The words happen, as it were, independently of the governess, and survive her, like her own narrative. And she projects her own uncertainty about identity onto others. As Flora abuses her, she remarks that the little girl 'buried in her skirts the dreadful little face'; no pronoun is attached to the face, which thus comes to seem like a mask, the most substitutable type of visage.

As I have said, one of the primary themes of *The Turn of the Screw* is the way the establishment of an absolute good (in the master, in the children) generates the evil that overthrows it. The idolatry of the children causes a suspicion that they are too good to be true, that their goodness is 'really' evil Luciferically masked. The governess's will to renunciation is shadowed by an equal will to total possession; she will renounce the master, but compensates for this by claiming absolute control of the children. The deliberate repression of the past on the level of language, the prevailing refusal to speak of it, to mention Jessel and Quint, leads to the symptomatic return of the repressed in the form of images, which bypass the blocked channel of language. But language itself provides the basis for the ambiguities in which the story is steeped; since every text requires a context (usually implicit in the form of genre), it becomes ambivalent when the accompanying text is removed. Thus the letter declaring the fact of Miles's expulsion gives no explanation of the reason, and so acts as a catalyst, a Rorschach blot into which the governess can read what she wishes. The indeterminacy of personal pronouns augments the ambiguity; both the frightening Quint and the master are 'he', and the namelessness of the governess means that in a very real sense it is she who is 'Quint', the unwanted *fifth* person in the Quint-Miles-Jessel-Flora group. But as the meanings of the text disappear into the gaps with which it is littered, vanish into the silence of the portentous, unidentifiable image, the text itself suffers a breakdown in its own identity and coherence, for it fails to thematise the relationship between language and image (a constant theme in James) by bringing the motif of the double onto the surface of the narrative.

Thus for all its rich fascination, *The Turn of the Screw* is less ambiguous than confused. The loss of the identity of the text is grounded in James's own loss of identity as its narrator. *The Turn of the Screw* has often been praised as a marvel of sustained equivocation. Edmund Wilson remarks that 'almost everything from beginning to end can be read equally in either of two senses'; Dorothea Krook, otherwise critical of Wilson, concurs with him on this point. However, there is a substantial group of critics who see the tale as devoid of any ambiguity (Heilman and Reed, for instance). It seems to me more accurate to describe the story as one that contains various signals, pointing different ways. It is incoherent, for it imitates Hawthorne's formula of multiple possibilities whilst remaining insufficiently detached and saturnine to allow of the fluctuating and ordered play of these possibilities. The incoherence largely results from the retelling of a simple tale by a sophisticated author who flatters himself on his ability to refine the original *frisson* without dispelling it. Two of the opposed signals mentioned above are the statements regarding the goodness of the governess in the prologue and various hints of the real possibility of her guilt; likewise on the one hand the similarity between her vision of the dead Quint and his actual appearance implies that she is trustworthy, and yet the lack of evidence that the children ever see the spectres casts doubt upon her testimony. In his preface, James talked of his wish to evoke the power of Evil in the intercourse between the servants and the two children, but the tale itself is full of evidence suggesting that the spectres are merely projections. One has to conclude that James was not fully aware what he was doing. On the one hand, a belief in sin, a preacher's wish to scarify a certain kind of reader; on the other, an awareness of the hysterical psychological mechanisms of hallucination, combined with an ambition to create a complex literary artefact to please, and baffle, the connoisseur. The two elements do not so much fuse into 'ambiguity' as undermine each other. The outcome is a tissue of mixed motives, a story that is neither pre-Freudian nor post-Freudian, which oscillates inconsistently between innocence and knowledge. It is symptomatic of a larger failure in James's work, to which I will revert at the end of this essay. The haze of Romance that smears opposed literary modes into a sort of unity in the work of Hawthorne is fatally dissipated by the epistemological scrupulosity of James.

II. The Guilty Eye

One of the key themes of *The Beast in the Jungle* and of *The Figure in the Carpet*, as of many of James's works, is the inability to see, or to say, the crucial thing. Seeing and saying this thing are identified in the very title of *The Figure in the Carpet*. The hidden embroidered figure, the deep-sunk secret that unifies an author's work, remains a tantalising web of vagueness. Its simultaneous presence and absence, existence and non-existence, poses the problem of the nature of James's narratorial aware-ness. When the first person narrator of *The Figure in the Carpet* recounts the death of Corvick, the sole possessor of the secret, in a manner so curt as almost to be callous, we do not judge his character but as it were glide over the point, for the death feels as if it has been engineered onto the story by James himself (like the letter slipping under the – this time figureless – carpet in *Tess*) to defer indefinitely the revelation of the likelihood that there is no figure, or at least, none perceptible to the author (though it may after all be evident to the critic trained in depth psychology). The narrator of this particular story represents an ambigu-ous hybrid of James the sovereign executioner and the James who is almost comically fine-spun and frustrated; he it is who mystifies us, but he is also mystified himself. Here the ambiguity of the person who is excluded and so excludes others in his turn is blurred by the quasi-identity between James and the narrator. In *The Beast in the Jungle* it is to some extent possible to distinguish between them.

The first fourteen pages of this story[1] are pure mystification, as James indulges in feline teasing of the reader. He bars the reader from knowledge of the shared secret of the two characters. This incident at the beginning, when an old acquaintance re-emerges from the past, is itself probably a mystifying transposition of the experience of meeting another American in Europe. But after these first fourteen pages the writing begins to describe Marcher's predicament, and it suddenly becomes very direct. The access of self-awareness in 'an auditor would have wondered what they were talking about' lifts our spirits, for in it the author concedes that he has alienated us earlier on. It is as if the story, like the narrator (and like Marcher?) has wished to protect us from itself, has sought up to this point to bore the reader and exasperate him so as to shake him off and not to have to bear any responsibility for the effect upon him of initiation into its secret. The strategy is Kafkaesque; one wonders whether James himself may not have left America in order to protect all those he felt best equipped to hurt, or whether his sentences wrap up their intentions because intentionality is felt to be grounded in violence. (*The Jolly Corner* certainly suggests that James feared that his American self may have become an image of evil.) But although *The Beast in the Jungle* has been convoluted like a maze as if to protect us from the thing that inhabits its centre, one may feel that the rhythm of the sentences is spinsterly and that the only beast that will spring is a cut-out, pop-up paper tiger. All the same, a decisive event does occur in the course of Marcher's story, however little it may actually seem to do so. But it is not – as Marcher and many critics seem to believe – the moment at which he fails to realise the possibility of love for Mary as she props herself up against the mantelpiece; the beast springs at a far earlier point, in slow motion, when they agree 'to watch together' for the crucial moment of change. This watching is constant in James. The importance of observation in his work is formalised in his theory of 'the point of view'. Thus saying is identified with seeing and the boundary between James and his narrators becomes a fluid one. The eye that watches is commonly guilty of projection. Just as Ralph Touchett watches Isabel in *The Portrait of a Lady* to see what will become of her, so Mary and Marcher observe the alienated self of Marcher himself. This watching is a dangerous voyeurism that half wills disaster on the figure under observation. The projection of a possible future for a person becomes in a sense a plot against that person, an attempt to use mechanisms of suggestion to force the future into a particular form; in James, as later in Pynchon, to plot a story is to plot against the independent life of the characters who inhabit it. Thus the watchers project a fate onto Nanda in *The Awkward Age*. Kierkegaard would have condemned this attitude to life as 'aesthetic', a tendency to judge lives not according to their morality but according to the degree of their interestingness. In *The Portrait of a Lady* the guilt that is common to both Ralph and James himself (it is he who chooses the title 'portrait', which betrays a merely aesthetic interest) is displaced onto Isabel's aesthete husband, who really does treat her as an *objet d'art*. However, the guilt of watching is not simply distructive. There is another side to the mentality which treats another person as 'interesting', a side overlooked by Kierkegaard: the wonder over the very fact of the existence of the other, an enchantment that charms into contemplation and precludes action. Thus in Book Five of *The Ambassadors* Strether reacts to the first sight of the daughter of Madame de Vionnet by feeling: 'What was in the girl was indeed too soft, too unknown for direct dealing; so that one could only gaze at it as at a picture, quite staying one's hand.' The wording here is intriguing, for it expresses both a repressed violence (the girl becomes 'it'; the implications of 'staying one's hand'; the sinister undertones of the avoidance of 'direct dealing', of which there is very little in this novel) – a violence towards the beautiful that is repressed in the conscious action of the governess in *The Turn of the Screw* and yet determines the actual effect of those actions – and a sense of wonder. Hence it can be stated that Chad likes Madame de Vionnet's daughter too much 'to be willing to do anything with her but be immensely kind

and nice – really tender of her'. The withdrawal contrasts with engagement of *The American*; one may conclude that the pain of Christopher
Newman's unwarranted rebuff by Europe led James to approach it in his
later fiction with anthropological wariness and repressed rage (the
strings of 'wonderfuls' in the late fiction protest too much). But Chad's
enigmatic tenderness surely also has something to do with James's
repression of the theme of homosexuality, which is part of his unwillingness *explicitly* to formulate the theme of the double. The fear of too close
an encounter with women (both homosexual fear of unmasking and
reluctance to engage with women) recalls James's very early romance *De
Grey*. The first female love of every De Grey has died upon receiving that
love. In this case, however, it is De Grey himself who dies, as the girl
survives. He dies in part because had he lived James would have been
compelled to prolong his work into a tale of repeated picaresque
vampirism, but also because to marry is to die as a writer – a motif from
Kafka. Most important however is James's survival through his perennial identification with the feminine, through his mental transvestitism.

In *The Beast in the Jungle*, Mary adopts the standpoint of the
narrator, withholding from her character Marcher the knowledge of
what will happen. She conducts her experiment in narration from on
high. Her watching, like all watching in James, induces in the person she
observes a paralysis between a desire for self-destruction in order to
divert the kindly observer and conclude the agony of being scrutinised,
and a determination to freeze, partly so as not to crack up, partly so as
to cheat the predictive narratorial observer. When under observation
one feels both that one has to do something to assert one's independence
of the evil eye, and that one should play dead until its searchlight moves
on. But as a counter-narrator within the narrative (the initiator of a
mise-en-abîme) Mary is also an objectification of Marcher's habit of
watching himself. His self-observation to make sure he does not become
too egotistical itself reinforces the egotism it opposes, just as the creation
of a counter-narrator reinforces the narrator himself, by duplication and
opposition. In his notebooks James refers to her as the 'second consciousness' of the story. Her inability to tell the secret (compare *The Figure in
the Carpet*) is due to the narrator's existence upon a different ontological plane from that upon which his characters move; the difference
between these planes recalls a poem by the great Polish Symbolist
Bolesław Leśmian, *Sen wiejski* (*A Village Dream*), in which the poet
dreams of milkmaids who, as they return home, talk of how they are
dreamed by the poet himself and of how, because they are his dreams,
they cannot meet him in reality. But Leśmian's poem is far more explicit

than James is prepared to be; he remains at the stage of Hawthorne's *The Blithedale Romance*, and what is advanced in Hawthorne becomes a sign of artistic regression in James himself, forty years later. One never becomes fully aware of the extent to which *The Beast in the Jungle* is really a study of the survival of the fittest of two narrators. Just as the planes upon which Mary and Marcher exist are disjunctive, so are the planes upon which there exist Dencombe and the doctor who enthuses over his work in *The Middle Years*. Dencombe does not reveal to the doctor his true feelings about his own work, for the doctor is, as it were, his own character (as is apparent from the fact that *The Middle Years* is the title both of James's story and of Dencombe's work). The circumlocutory style of James himself enjoys the possession of a mystery, the ownership of which – as Canetti observes – bestows power on its possessor. Like Dencombe and like Mary, James occupies a dual position, both above and below himself; the placement of the narrator in the story implies the existence of a meta-narrator, recounting the story of Henry James.

The interdependence of Mary and Marcher is almost vampirical, and this too is an aspect of the theme of the double. Mary is a *femme fatale*, but she is also the unattainable princess, a rich investment because she is so difficult of access. Their interdependence is that of a narrator and his characters, which is apparent in James's frequent use of *style indirect libre* – the stylistic equivalent of 'point of view' – which is an inherently ironic device; the narrator who deploys it is saying that he can assume a person's viewpoint and yet still leave a part of himself unoccupied by that person, whose mental frame is too puny to contain him. Thus it is thanks to this stylistic device that Marcher appears so small a character. But as often in James, the final irony is on the narrator, for his style is now indelibly contaminated with the idiom of its victims.

The last few pages of *The Beast in the Jungle* are very explicit about the waste of Marcher's life, his inability to be – as Eliot would have put it – man enough to accept damnation. But one should be wary of this explicitness. It is all very well to say that Marcher ought to have loved, to have forsaken his egotism, and so on, but the story offers no point at which he could have done so. His feeling that he ought to have loved Mary is a masochistic self-dramatisation after the event and continues the pattern of self-wounding submission to her; from the grave her image preys upon him, now truly vampirical. His vision of the leaping beast – the very notion of 'The Beast' – is an attempt (by him, and by James) to smuggle into the narrative a concreteness that will make the 'it', the figure in the carpet, the vague apocalyptic thing that ought to have happened, more convincing. It is melodramatic and rather dandified and forced, like Eliot's hard-bitten comments about damnation. (The link between James and Eliot is a very obvious one: each is particularly conscious of the vehemence of the eye, each seeks to become an 'invisible poet' by leaving the country of his origin, and each has been designated a 'case' in his late work by F. R. Leavis). Even at the end, Marcher is still dramatising himself to himself (he has to, for he is the agent of the narrator's self-dramatisation) – his continued duality as doer and spectator of his own actions is shown in his regret that he is not 'markedly bereaved', a nice ambiguity (often associated with 'marked' in James) that stresses both his lack of grief and his desire to be seen (and indicates that they are linked); it is also evident in his feeling that he is walking arm in arm with his younger self. The story is divided against itself, as *style indirect libre* always is; it is a narcissistic style, admiring the other in oneself, and a paranoid one, for the line of demarcation between the narrator and the engulfed other, between the authorial tone and the tone of the quotation, is not at all clear. The title licks its lips both moralistically and melodramatically at the final come-uppance. Like the title of *The Middle Years*, it is compromised by a double usage, both by the narrator and the figures he judges within the story. Thus James's story is deeply compromised. It presents the vampirical people as they are, but it also resorts to mystifications akin to those used by Mary, as well as to self-mystifications (*style indirect libre* does not so much reveal egotism as disclose the narrator's inability fully to detach himself from his egotistical protagonist) reminiscent of those employed by Marcher.

If, despite their distinction, James's later stories fail, it may be because he is unwilling to draw the necessary conclusions from his own complicity with the narrator and unable to develop a form that will connect autobiography with fiction, as they are connected in Proust's great novel. The fact that his engagement with the *fin de siècle* theme of the double is an implicit one preserves him from many period automatisms, but it also prevents him from unfolding all the implications of his themes. He cannot admit the presence of autobiography within his fiction, and so remains as mystified as he is mystifying.

Like James himself, James's characters do not know where they stand. This is perhaps most apparent in Strether, who always identifies only partly with the place he occupies. 'He was burdened, poor Strether – it had better be confessed at the outset – with the oddity of a double consciousness'. In *The Ambassadors*, James attributes the speculative attitude to relationships, usually considered typical of himself, to women. Is this mere sleight of hand? Strether is continually nonplussed by the abysses of significance visible to the eyes of women. Similarly, the

fictive primal scene of *The Turn of the Screw* is constructed by the
governess, and Marcher's future is predicted by Mary. Here James may
be demonstrating an awareness of the relationship between hysteria and
the making of fictions. But he camouflages the near-identity between his
female plotters and himself. Critics may talk of his psychological trans-
vestism, but this is something both less interesting and less radical than
the actual bisexuality proposed by Proust, who raises the whole question
of the genetic basis of the narrative of history and of the possible end of
time in the moment of the disappearance of gender. Proust's questioning
of the conventional distinction between the sexes equips him to interro-
gate his own narrative; he arrests the sexual history embodied in the
sequence of 'who begats'. Even so, James comes very close to self-
interrogation of a kind in the marvellous desolate luminosity of the latter
part of the eleventh book of *The Ambassadors*. Lambert Strether's chance
meeting with Chad and Madame de Vionnet at the Cheval Blanc, and
the terrible momentary possibility of their cutting him, restore his
awareness of the physical nature of intimacy and of the exclusive
violence that carves out a clearing for that intimacy, both of which had
been repressed by his rather etiolated imaginative identification with
them. Retrospectively Sarah almost seems to have been right to see
Madame de Vionnet as hideous. Strether has been identified with the
imagination, and in unmasking the limitations of his character's imagination, James indicates the possible evasiveness of his own circumlocu-
tions. For it is Strether's lack of the violent exclusivity required for real
intimacy that puts him in such simultaneous plaintive relation with so
many women.

> With whom could *he* talk of such things? – unless indeed always,
> almost at any stage, with Maria? He foresaw that Miss Gostrey would
> come again into requisition on the morrow; though it wasn't to be
> denied that he was already a little afraid of her 'What on earth – that's
> what I want to know now – had you then supposed?' He recognised at
> last that he had really been trying all along to suppose nothing. Verily,
> verily, his labour had been lost. He found himself supposing innumer-
> able and wonderful things.

As the author confesses his own defeat by the limits of his own
imagination, for a moment he steps outside those limits into truth.

5 Fictions of Identity: Modernism in Germany

THOMAS MANN: THE MYTH OF *DOKTOR FAUSTUS*

It is possible to be over-ironic about Thomas Mann's aspirations to the status of *'praeceptor Germaniae'*. Michael Hamburger has been justifiably scathing about Mann's tendency to bury his real comic artistry under a prestige-seeking ponderosity [1], and Musil applied the devastating tag of *'der Grossschriftsteller'*, a sort of cultured philistine. It can indeed be argued that the majority of Mann's artistic life was expended in virtuoso, acrobatic strutting along the fence that divided the great modernists from a popular public. He thirsted for both varieties of success, popular and select, but the means he evolved to achieve it, though dazzling, were dubious and shifty. The magician – Cipolla in *Mario and the Magician*, the writer's *alter ego* (for although Cipolla officially represents Mussolini, one recalls Mann's own 'brother Hitler') – is always an ironist, for he knows that the feats his audience takes for magic are really tricks. Nevertheless I think a change came over Mann at the end of his life, a change caused by his realisation of the degree to which his work was compromised by its ambiguous genealogy – a suspicion that in one respect Hitler, if not his brother, may have been a not too distant cousin. The shock led him to turn himself inside out as an artist. The result was *Doktor Faustus*, his much-misunderstood masterpiece.

Doktor Faustus is often described as an allegory that parallels the demonic turn taken by the art of the composer Adrian Leverkühn with Germany's adoption of National Socialism and regression to a barbaric, cultic reality. It is easy to see whence this view stems; Mann himself contributed to it in the form of statements like 'what he inflicts on Rudi is a premeditated murder required of him by the Devil'[2], whilst his anti-war broadcasts and deliberate parallel with Goethe's great drama would lead one to expect an ambitiously programmatic statement. But a

141

'statement' is just what the work is not. Mann's reference to the 'clear-ambiguous' relationship between Zeitblom's despairing account and the pressures of war[3] should have made readers wary of identifying it as an allegory with point-by-point equivalences in actual historical reality. Ronald Gray teeters on the edge of a subtler understanding, only to retreat; he remarks that 'the confusion of *Doktor Faustus* derives from the fact that Zeitblom operates always with a dual conception of Leverkühn.'[4] It is almost embarrassing to have to point out the simple fact that this confusion is Zeitblom's and not Mann's and to draw the necessary critical conclusions: namely, that Mann's astonishing, resonant work is neither an allegory nor the failure it is commonly held to be (*pace* T. J. Reed) but rather a close analysis of the conditions under which people resort to myth. It analyses the extreme situations of deprivation and isolation to which people respond by myth-making, and whatever Mann's conscious intentions may have been, the allegories in his work stem from his two narrators (*two*, for Leverkühn narrates the encounter with the presumed Devil) and are so shaped as brilliantly to express their impulsions. It is Leverkühn who mentions the Devil and calls his last work 'Doktor Fausti Weheklag', whilst it is Zeitblom who picks up the cue and terms the music hag-ridden. Leverkühn's full statement of the consequences of his 'pact' is uttered before his gathered acquaintance and is chilling because its conscious recapitulation of a myth sounds insane; indeed, a doctor present remarks that Adrian *is* mad. Adrian's words cannot be taken literally. Mann's description of him in *Die Entstehung des Doktor Faustus* as 'deliberately and darkly playful'[5] suggests that Adrian has donned a mask he is now unable to separate from his face. The central theme of *Doktor Faustus* is the breakdown of personality, which recurs on all levels of the book. Leverkühn sees himself as Faustus, adopts a pseudo-Lutheran dialect and frames his account of his meeting with the Devil in terms borrowed from Dostoevsky. That he does this, and that Mann painstakingly composes his character of fragments of Hugo Wolf, Schoenberg, Nietzsche and various other artists, is less a consequence of Mann's own defective powers of imagination than a means of suggesting the elusiveness of Adrian's personality, which evaporates in the gaps between the echoes. The use of people and places as leitmotifs sends ripples criss-crossing through the entire narrative, reflections of the theme of breakdown. This serves a dual purpose: on one level it expresses the way Zeitblom's obsessions mould and probably distort the material (it is he alone who is alarmed by the similarity between Buchel and Pfeiffering and he who persuades one to consider Adrian as purely and simply demonic by voicing the unease he feels when his friend is too 'human'); on another level it shows how ideas that seem harmless in one context can circle back into history in a virulent form, just as Kretschmar's ideas (and Mann's own?) bear in retrospect an unsettling similarity to those of the Kridwiss group. Thus Modern Germany melts into its medieval forebear, as Kaisersaschern emerges as the kind of place where one expects to see haggard old witches walking the streets, as the habit of book-burning returns, and as intellectuals advocate a cultic civilisation. The nightmare extends from time into space; the Devil moves without transition from one part of Adrian's room to another and seems at moments to be Schleppfuss redivivus, Kretschmar, or even Adrian's own double.

Dualism is a constant feature of Mann's works. Here it is movingly related to the themes of insanity and mutual unknowing, rather than – as usual – being employed to generate a series of endlessly dissipated and reiterated polarities. Here the dualism says that even childhood friends are strangers. Where knowledge is insufficient, myth enters; Leverkühn is no doctor, so he mythologises his disease, of which he exhibits no comprehension; Zeitblom's lack of continual intimacy with his friend makes him use myth to create the illusion of knowledge, both for himself and for others. By dissociating himself from the narrator, Mann underlines that the creation of myth is part of the Teutonic malady. Zeitblom is the child of a myth-making era and cannot escape its fundamental assumptions. Like the later Wittgenstein, Mann traces the bounds of sense by letting his characters overstep them, and lest this seem complacent, he implicates himself in the objects of his critique by attributing many of his own ideas to a generation which becomes lost through seeing itself as lost. That Mann's work was read as a myth or allegory by the civilisation he suspected of being diseased is hardly surprising; the readers projected their own ailment onto the work. Mann breaks the vicious circle by showing how a *present-day* man, even one as apparently sober and unbiased as Zeitblom, is driven to myth as an attempt to explain the inexplicable. Myth is self-hypnotising pseudo-explanation.

Mann remarks that he employed Zeitblom in order to bring about 'a certain lightening of the dark material'[6], but the narrator's deeper function is to relativise Mann's own words and so to preserve him from the presumption of attempting to explain whatever complicities may have obtained between German high culture and National Socialism. By placing the accusation in another's mouth he avoids the fatuity of art about the danger of art: for to question culture truly is to question the questioner who assumes that he can stand outside culture. Adorno has written of the 'enigmatic irony, which cannot be reduced to any conceptual mockery' in Mann's style[7], and in the earlier novels this tendency often infuriates, for the narrator is perpetually on the verge of becoming a discrete personality but never actually does so, which produces a tantalising sense of the wilfully withheld. The emergence of the narrator as a separate character brings the sub-text of doubt out into the open to make it actually functional in the text. Incorporating non-Mannian ideas into the text becomes the ultimate extension of his realism and represents the dialectical point or border case at which the writer relinquishes control over his characters. Here Mann really does recall Dostoevsky, as was his intention. The narrator's ignorance, which drives him to myth in an attempt to produce a pseudo-explanation, is undermined by the way the ideas held by the characters are more powerful than those of the narrator. Mann gained this effect by inserting many of Adorno's ideas virtually verbatim into his text. Kretschmar's 'Da – wird – die Sprache – nicht mehr von der Floskel – gereinigt, sondern die Floskel – vom Schein – ihrer subjektiven Beherrschtheit'[8] (There – the language – is no longer – cleansed – of flourishes, but the flourish is cleansed – of the illusion – of its subjective – control) is Adorno on Beethoven's late quartets.

Mann's decision to give his narrator his head (or enough rope to hang himself with) makes reading him much more like living with any other person; at times we empathise strongly with him, whilst at others he leaves us lukewarm or even cold. His nature is not fixed and he is no easier to classify than Leverkühn. His moving accounts of the histories of Ines and Clarissa Rodde are rapt and passionate. Similarly impressive is the domino-like collapse of the interdependent characters, in which the final symbol of the community is the apocalyptic image of the Munich tram discharging infernal sparks. But there are also moments when one is suspicious of him, which is why Mann holds the process of narration at arm's length. Zeitblom's frequent references at the end of the paragraphs to his 'Erschütterung' seem in the end to protest too much, and it seems disingenuous of him to feel thus about Adrian's actions whenever his friend behaves 'humanly'; his parallels between Buchel and Pfeiffering, Kaschperl and Suso, and the maids with mud-caked feet, seem in the end like tasteless doodles. Perhaps the area in which he is most suspect is that in which he analyses Adrian's reasons for sending Rudi Schwerdtfeger to present his suit to Marie Godeau. It is at this point that he confesses his absence from these meetings, and so instantly undermines his own claims to authority. And the possibility that the German defeat he is experiencing as he writes predisposes him to a pessimistic, 'demonic' interpretation should also put one on one's guard. Moreover, Leverkühn's enigmatic reserve makes all categorical explanation dubious.

Whilst reading these passages, I felt that the account was left open and that it was part of Mann's mastery to present the narrator's relationship to his material as ambiguous whilst allowing one to separate the one from the other and attempt to decide for oneself. Thus I felt convinced that Zeitblom's reading was wrong – partly for the aforementioned reasons, and partly because Leverkühn is drained and dejected when he receives no reply. His action in sending Rudi seems to be a despairing wager to determine whether or not the dice of reality are loaded against him, and it has a child-like magicality. It is as if Leverkühn has said to himself that if, despite everything, a flirt like Rudi proves capable of self-sacrifice and his own belief in Marie Godeau's love for him proves correct (something his isolation makes it hard for him to determine), then reality will be seen to be beneficent and he will be justified in coming out of isolation. It is Adrian who notices that Marie's voice resembles his mother's, and his suspicion that spiritual incest underlies his fascination by her may make him desire to keep his distance. A romantic, implicitly incestuous love, is the only affection that offers a *Durchbruch* (breakthrough – a key word in the novel) from isolation, but the fixation on the past it establishes relates the self back to an internalised archetype and so consolidates isolation. So devilish is this procedure that one is tempted to see behind it an actual devil who indulges one's desire to escape oneself by immuring one in a tower of obsession. One may be tempted to demonise the whole proceeding, as does Zeitblom, but he has no warrant for believing that Adrian deliberately removed from his presence the only two people who could have mitigated his isolation. Rather, Leverkühn's behaviour here recalls Kafka instructing Max Brod to incinerate his works – he seeks a way of acting without acting, for he is unsure of the legitimacy of any of his impulses. It is this self-uncertainty which has led him to music, which speaks but without committing itself to any meaning.

Only by having his narrator consistantly refer to music that does not exist could Mann establish his structure of ambiguities. The 'speaking unspokenness' attributed to music by Zeitblom is such that when he speaks on the same page of how a certain feature is *unverkennbar* (unmistakeable) we suspend assent, for Mann leaves us to choose for ourselves whether to believe or to doubt. The fact that Adrian's music exists for us only in this form stresses the unity between Zeitblom and himself, to whom Mann referred as the two halves of one self (which is why neither of them can be visualised) and whose connectedness is underlined by the *du* with which Adrian addresses both Zeitblom and himself. Had Mann chosen an existing composer (Schoenberg for

instance, who clamoured for Mann to credit him in *Doktor Faustus* with
the invention of twelve-tone composition) this hostile complicity between narrator and subject would have been impossible. Moreover, he
would have violated the general principle of the book, which in its
concern to diagnose the Zeitgeist eschews the search for scapegoats. And
since all writing about music belongs to mythology in the sense that it is
desperately difficult to validate (except on the level of technical
analysis), Mann can use music both as an image of the kind of experience
that can seem so ineffable as to generate myths as verbal approximations
to it (an experience that would render the Germans, 'the musical nation',
the nation most prone to myth-making) and as a means of preserving us
from an easy scepticism about the nature of Zeitblom's motives. His
position is that of the stained glass that both transmits and alters the
light. Through him Mann sums up his own life-long obsession with the
description of music, since it is in such description that the suggestion of
inverted commas worn by his style is most appropriate. He confronts his
own critical language with that of actual musicians (the composite figure
Schoenberg – Adorno – Leverkühn – Kretschmar), allowing the two
languages to complement and criticise each other. Mann develops two
opposed forms of virtuosity: he assimilates modern ideas about music
and he creates an impressionistic medium to refract its heard complexity. The opposition precludes fetishism, for music is experienced both by
professional musicians and by non-musicians.

When at the end of the novel Adrian talks of his pact with the Devil, it
is his other-wordliness which is unnerving, not the mention of a possible
demonic inspiration, and the chill is intensified by the fact that his
understanding of himself is so mythological and so portentous as radically to diverge from the kind of understanding embodied in the biographi-
cal novel. Mann refers to Adrian as 'repeating a myth or a cliché with
dark, deliberate playfulness'[9]. To suspect that the hero has lost himself to
a cliché rather than a myth is to face the frightening possibility that his
very heroic self-stylisation is on the same level as a manipulated response
to an advertisement, in this case, to an advertisement for 'Kulchur'. In
Mann's work, the novel is eroded from two sides by the myth that
preceded it and the cliché into which it is degenerating, so it can only
yield a negative image of what would constitute an understanding of
Adrian; psychology has been leeched of all meaning. Mann once ex-
plained his predilection for parody by terming parody the expression of
love for a form that is no longer viable. The explanation is plangent and
beautiful, but in *Doktor Faustus* Mann comes to terms with the self-
indulgence with which it is also tinged. For in Adrian and in Zeitblom,

the parodistic fixation on the past becomes a means of amputating oneself from the present. Together, they throw his life away by casting it in the mould of the Faust legend. In Mann's novel, as in Adrian's final work, parody explodes itself from within. Adrian's quotation of Faust's phrase 'for I die as a good and bad Christian'[10] is so ambiguous as finally to burst the mythical framework that has supported it. Ambiguity becomes a means, like music, of talking silently, and represents the paradoxical moment at which the exhausted language of a devastated culture lies fallow before it can be used again. Here the partial, and hence inauthentic, ambiguity of Mann's earlier works becomes total, and it does so through a dissolution of his rigid categories – art versus life and so on – which corresponds to the eerie fusing of characters and ideas. Moreover, the genuinely modernist, dialectical (rather than dualistic) aesthetic at which Mann finally arrives makes it quite possible to see Leverkühn as Zeitblom. This is the most mysterious side of the novel, a radical sub-text that has passed unnoticed in Mann criticism. The identity of the two is possible for the following reasons: (a) both the novel and Leverkühn's music have the density of twelve-tone composition; (b) Zeitblom occasionally remarks that he is recounting scenes from which he was absent (e.g. the scenes between Adrian and Marie Godeau), as if dropping a hint for those who have ears to hear; (c) the co-presence of two ways of writing about music suggests the presence of a dual personality; (d) it seems strange that Zeitblom, the serene humanist, should express unease whenever his friend is too 'human' (here Zeitblom sounds like Nietzsche – 'Human all too Human' – and hence like Leverkühn); (e) Leverkühn enjoys composing parodies, as when he apes Lutheran accents in the scene with the Devil; (f) Zeitblom is the only person Adrian ever addresses by the intimate 'du' (thou); and (g) Adrian's fear of the nakedness of the voice may have led him to clothe himself in the mantle of an alien voice. The novel may be the terrifying spectral after-life of his sanity, its narrator a madman. This would account for the myth-making elements in 'Zeitblom' 's early evocations of Halle as a demonic medieval town whose lengthened shadow extends into the twentieth century. Yet this reading remains only a tantalising possibility, which is why I have relegated it to the end of this essay, rather than pronouncing it 'the true reading of *Doktor Faustus*'. The reader is drawn to participate in the book's making, so he can never be sure. The despair of Mann's book lies in the fact that its definition of sanity and truth is a negative one; its hope is that by embodying inadequate, myth-ridden means of understanding and demonstrating their inadequacy, he can indicate the existence of a point beyond them.

He is not so presumptuous as to assume that he can occupy such a point. Novels allow authors both to speak and to remain silent behind the volubility of their characters, the silent image of the page. To exploit this to the full, as Mann does, is to reveal the impotence of art's power, the power of its impotence. For art alone is aware that the language it uses is fictive. By means of self-negation it transcends its own fictions.

SOME ASPECTS OF *THE MAN WITHOUT QUALITIES*

Non-Identity

In a chapter of *The Man without Qualities* about the 'Friends from Youth', Walter terms Ulrich 'a man without qualities'. Musil approves of the phrase, for it is the title of his own novel, but he criticises Walter's self-interested use of it as an anti-Ulrich slogan. Strangely, Walter's conception of the crisis of the modern era (the locution begs for inverted commas) is akin to Ulrich's, as Clarisse notes when she remarks that despite the similarity 'he [Ulrich] does not take it as badly as you [Walter]'. Thus Walter is less a character than a personification of a mood – a particular declension of the fundamental impasse Musil sees in himself and in the age. These moods are disavowed allegorical embodiments of parts of Musil. His original intention of naming Ulrich 'Anders' (Other) shows that even the 'hero' is not immune to the distancing effects he himself administers to the self-deluded females he re-names to reveal their real nature: 'Bonadea' (named after a goddess whose chaste palace degenerated into a brothel) and 'Diotima' (Plato's schoolmistress of love). The characters are flat cards with which Musil plays patience, and Ulrich is the joker in the pack. Ulrich mediates between Musil and the other characters (between the separate modes of autobiography and novel); he is both Musil's *porte parole* and a character who is himself broken down into other characters, variously inflected.

Whilst Ulrich's experiences are simultaneously undergone by the other characters, who do not recognise their experiential quality, they do not seem to be fixed in any distinctive or specific manner. Thus there develops a solipsism without ipse, a world of depersonalised personality-elements which do not congeal around the unity of the person about which stories continue nevertheless to be told. This world can however be represented by anchoring these elements in characters whose hollow consciousness prevents them from reflecting on the elements, from recognising that they too lack qualities.[1]

The hero of the novel is 'one' – what Heidegger terms '*das Man*', the non-entity who incarnates the consensus – *Das Man*, the bureaucratic committee whose members are the extended phantom limbs of Ulrich's body of thought. Diotima's desire for an event that will unearth a new unity – a desire shared by the entire committee – is the hope that the alienated parts of Ulrich, a man of parts, will rediscover their community. Ulrich's wishing for his true self and the Collateral Campaign's quest for the true Austria both postulate the same apocalyptic will-o'-the-wisp. As usual, Musil presents two different forms of the same experience, each of which is reduced to a metaphor for the other. Thus all reality becomes metaphorical, a referent for an absent other – and the absent otherness required by this reality is the ideal of 'the other state' (*der andere Zustand*). But that which is comic when stated of a committee steeped in a common madness is tragic when it applies to the individual alone; Austria is a mad, mad world, but Ulrich's negative capability is close to the insanity of Moosbrugger; both hear voices. So although the other characters refract Ulrich, they own the frozen qualities he does not possess. If he were just like them, he would be merely a character in a novel; as it is, he is the Archimedean point from which Musil dislodges his own novel and the world held captive in its mirror.

Simile

Musil deploys similes at frequent strategic points in his pages because a simile is neither an 'image' (in the modern sense discussed by P. N. Furbank) nor an idea. Musil's ideas and his images thus come to question each other by means of an elegant symmetry mingled with mystery and arbitrariness. A train of thought that recurrently slides into the metaphorical is a perpetually weaving flirtation with hermeticism, symptom of a desperate frivolity deriving from the fact that there is no audience. Musil's similes do not claim the vatic significance of the metaphor, nor are they recuperable to pure reason, as metonymies would be. As in Godard's essay-fictions, there is a consistent rupturing of tone. The rigour common to both men requires that every sentence doubly validate and disqualify itself, be both language and meta-language. The similes are the result of doodling to take one's mind off boredom or despair – they constitute the element of automatic writing ('the irrational') which makes us value the reasoned assurance it threatens. The similes express psychological truths whilst side-stepping the language of the emotions, considered contaminated by Ulrich. The language attempts to over-leap its own shadow and render states with a greater exactitude than is available to conventional notation, but again and again the disclaimer built into the form of the simile prevents one from being quite sure what (if anything) has been described. The often slender basis for the analogy may be a hint that Musil is playing games with the reader, testing the degree of his rationality by offering him take-it-or-leave-it cues to perceive similarities where none are actually present. The similes may be hallucinations, like the voices Moosbrugger hears. Thus the precision is also a radical unknowing, aimed at infiltrating the Utopian into discourse by showing that the surrealism of the negative is the foundation of the photograph. Because of their doodle aspect, Musil's similes can seem like compulsive, unmotivated ornaments. They and the surrounding prose exchange a blank stare. This blankness can provoke a panic of associations in a critic who attempts to recuperate into the text (turn into a pregnant metaphor) the simile that projects from it at a jagged angle. Thus Dietrich Hochstätter, in an otherwise interesting book on Musil's *Sprache des Möglichen* (Language of the Possible), lavishes an entire page of hypotheses on the comparison between Graf Leinsdorf's eyes and a pair of stones in two soft furrows.[2] Hochstätter's excessively fine-spun reading shears the simile of the margin of difference from its object that is as important to Musil (as a source of provocation) as is its correspondence. The similes do not so much illuminate their environment as perversely flee it into a masochistic blind alley. They alternate with sober prose according to the rhythm of a neither/nor-ism founded on the pleasures of pain. They resemble red herrings. Musil uses resonant pseudo-Expressionist images (the piano behind Walter as a bed whose sheets an insomniac has rumpled) and then deflates their claims to represent a shrilly transcendent reality by prefacing them with 'like'; the image is prevented from stepping out of its frame and engulfing reality, as it does in Kafka. Instead of a fusion, the simile presents both a difference and an identity: the fundamental duality of the novel, in which all the real characters are simultaneously de-realised by their similarities. The similes are *Vexierbilde*, disconcert us because their intermittence suggests that they will be absolute images, drenched with evocative resonances; in fact, they are far more casual than that and seem rather to be negative indices of the fissures in rationality than revelations that have seeped through them from the beyond. Ulrich and Agathe consider the possibility of speaking in metaphors alone,[3] but the outcome is a combinatory arrangement of various metaphors, none of which is privileged: Musil terms the metaphors themselves 'Gleichnisse', i.e. similitudes or parables. By establishing an opposition between their own 'metaphorical' language and the language others employ, Ulrich and Agathe arrest the dialectic of interwoven private and public idioms, clichés and speculations, which had been the motor of the first half of the novel. Agathe is a magnet to draw Ulrich from the society of others who are only partial metaphors for him. She is to be his only adequate metaphor, i.e. transferred self. Her very existence is Utopian; Musil's own sister died when he himself was aged only eleven months, and Ulrich's 'lost sister' is the extended shadow of the dead sibling. With her emergence, the book modulates from transformed autobiography into pure fiction. The ideal metaphor is a fiction. By draining himself of his own qualities, Musil/Ulrich gives birth to her; the lost qualities are Adam's lost rib. The search for an original unity of the sexes leads to the origin of fiction in Musil's own experience: the 'what if' with which the child examined the possibility of his sister having survived (a romance motif) reinforces his struggle to understand the strange *ménage à trois* of his family, in which the presence of his mother's lover was tolerated by his father. Musil's obsession with sexuality is part of a secret project to imagine the primal scene and discover which of the two men is really his father.

Fiction in transition

Musil's inability to finish his novel would suggest the failure of his tactic of letting himself be swallowed by cliché in order to release ironic acid into its belly, the tactic of the spy (one recalls that he intended Ulrich to be a spy during the war). Cliché has a very strong stomach, and at times one can sense the virulence of his combat with banality – carried on, for instance, in the way he sometimes surrounds the more empty and high-falutin' words with inverted commas: 'culture' or 'spirit' often suffer this indignity. The occasional resort to inverted commas is worrying, for it suggests that Musil has two conflicting conceptions of the reader; idealistically, he imagines a reader who will grasp even an implicit irony, yet he fears that the reader will require that everything be spelled out. 'The book is neither easy nor difficult', he remarked, 'for that depends on the reader'. The inverted commas are distressing for another reason; they present the point at which the work's two styles meet and cancel each other out, as the irony lavished on Kakanien and its appanage of second-hand emotions collides with his own readiness to use a similar rhetoric in the private, a-social context of his hero's mystical experiences. It is as if at these moments he has strayed too early into the positivity locked up with a time device at the back of his mind, not to be opened until the ending. (This anticipation of the ending may be what prevents the actual ending's arrival). He then has to extricate himself from the temptation to identify with the language of Kakanien; he snatches the words back from those he feels misuse them, such as Diotima, and reserves them for his own personal use. Yet for a second he has been perilously close to Diotima's own viewpoint – as he is, for example, at the end of the novel's second paragraph, where the reference to 'the important' strikes an attitude prescient of hers. The danger and fascination of a private language is evoked and examined primarily in the figures of Clarisse, who develops her own cryptic sign-language, and Moosbrugger, who devises the word *die Eichkatze* by combining the High German and the dialect forms of the word for 'squirrel'. Musil is ambivalent towards this aspect of *Möglichkeitsdenken* (thinking in possibilities) as it appears in characters for whom *der andere Zustand* sends its light through cracks in the wall of sanity. Yet one can oneself exercise *Möglichkeitsdenken*: the ambivalences in the novel make it possible that the lack of an ending is itself an Utopian feature (just as Benjamin sees the endlessness of Kafka's texts as a sign that grace has been bestowed on them). The multiple possibilities come into their own and subvert the fixed purposiveness of linear narrative. This development is one of which Musil was not himself fully aware – it was apologetically that he stated that the novel remained unfinished because none of the characters wanted it to end. One can see this faulty awareness as the tragedy of his project – as an inability to realise that even as he thought he was losing sight of his goal, he was actually very near to it. He only needed to discard traditional notions of the book and arrange alternative versions of the same event, like Robbe-Grillet or, later, John Fowles. But may not Musil's blindness be a necessary corollary of his intensity and not tragic at all? Is it not the strength of his commitment to the artefact of the book, the book of his life, that permits the tidal wave of his work's resonance to drown the tiny ripples generated by a mere Robbe-Grillet?

Masculin/Féminin

The man without qualities is attracted by women who are his intellectual inferiors, and he designates them with private names which mockingly stress his superior cultivation (Leona, Bonadea, Diotima) and yet also hold these women at a tender distance: the name's cosmetic fog is an alienation device that compensates the narrator's sentimentality regarding the female (as in Pynchon), holds a particular woman at a distance to be admired, whilst also preserving Musil/Ulrich from being drawn in. The names are spells against feminine magic. Early in the novel Ulrich is drawn to Leona, a late incarnation of an outdated ideal of beauty, but this beauty – being dead – can be perceived only in reified form. The astonishment with which Musil registers many of his characters' moves, and which Michael Hamburger has commented on, is a reaction not to their autonomy but to the fact that they are dead people paradoxically able to breathe in the amber of their superseded traditions. The undead do not merely walk the streets, their corpses litter the language too. The signs of their spectral persistence are clichés, which have the same pull for Musil as Leona does for Ulrich, the magnetism of the living dead. The following sentences occur very early in *The Man without Qualities* and are symptomatic of Musil's attitude to cliché in general. 'A new age had just dawned then (for a new age dawns every second), and a new age demands a new style.' (p. 20) 'That–an affair that did not seriously touch on him – was the well-known disconnectedness of insights and their unfocussed extension, which is so characteristic of the present.' (p. 20) 'This is the well-known matter of the contradictoriness, imperfection and inconsequentiality of life.' (p. 27) The first sentence is typical of the manner in which Musil's sentences both advance and retreat at one and the same time, doing the intellectual splits and then rebounding onto the spot with an exhilarating click of the heels. The latter two are interesting in that they illustrate Musil's flirtation with cliché, his propensity to turn his own ideas into sententious banalities; this tendency is the stylistic equivalent of his ability to semi-alienate himself into Ulrich, to uncouple his past self, make of it a different personality, and attack it with an ironic fable. In the sentences quoted, the adjective 'well-known' (*bekannt*) defuses the idea in advance – but one wants to ask: '*bekannt*' to whom? Musil ironises the concept because what was once '*bekannt*' to himself alone, an original thought, has become a generally devalued cliché in the course of the first quarter of the century's vulgarisation of the intellect; the idea has become '*bekannt*' to others and so lost its force. (It can also be said to be 'well-known' to the collective consciousness of '*das Man*', the novel's group-subject.) Musil takes into account the effect time has had on his own ideas by creating an Ulrich, other than himself, to hold them; like Adorno, he is concerned with the effects of 'the ageing of modernism'. Ulrich's quasi-identity with Musil (e.g. the vowels are the same in both names) means that the novel is being composed according to the combinatory laws of a *Möglichkeitsdenken* it also disowns. This contradiction is one reason why it could not be completed. Once the adjective *bekannt* has appeared, the sentence extends like a phantom limb; the novel itself is the ghost of the novel. There is a weariness in the adjective, tiredness of having to explain to people who in any case do not understand (Ulrich's weariness of life). Yet the 'bekannt' also contains a statement of aristocratic disdain by Robert Musil, scion of a family ennobled by the Emperor, for any idea so unaware of its pedigree as to consider itself 'new'. Self-parody dictates many of the wittily empty sentences that end the chapters – but it is with bitterness that Musil executes upon his own ideas the sentence of intellectual vulgarisation, which enables him to remain true to the impulses behind them only by jettisoning them. Many generalisations of an apparent neutrality really mock the common sense they imitate. Musil ironically notes that the banalities of the fathers become new thoughts. The dialectical irony of modernity is that opposition to cliché culminates in acquiescence in it, for Ulrich's commitment to fluidity foresees so many possible styles that none can be actually adopted: Ulrich leaves the decoration of his house to his contractor. The entire novel documents the cliché's power to absorb opposition to it; it is a perverse hymn to the Empire's capacity to neutralise whatever threatens it with rejuvenation. In describing Leona Musil bluntly remarks that she is a prostitute, only to add that 'she had her romantic side too'. The proverbial two-sidedness of the personality turns the characterisation into a pseudo-characterisation, as the narrator punctures his own tone, much as he does at the end of the novel's second paragraph, where logic is invaded by pseudo-logic. Sceptical about the clichés of 'a new age', Musil finds himself in the paradoxical position of having to consort with the old clichés in order to anticipate the next modernity; he takes commonplaces and modernises them. This neo-classicism governs a sentence like: 'He had come back from the moon and immediately rearranged everything as if on the moon still.' Musil employs cliché to be a jump behind himself, to camouflage his radicalism from both himself and others. A similar sentence to the above concludes Chapter Seven: 'Two weeks later Bonadea had been his mistress for fourteen days.' The apparent movement forward in time moves back to the day which initiated it and so cancels itself out. The step forward is also a step back. It is an absurdly circuitous and wittily Zen-like way of saying that Bonadea became Ulrich's mistress that very same day, but it is also typical of the type of euphemism Bonadea might herself use to screen herself from the bare fact of her infidelity. The futility of the time taken to read the sentence is the futility of time in general, which runs on a treadmill of eternally recurrent banalities.

Where cliché rules there shall be timelessness also. The sentence presents a deadlock, as the same institutes itself in two places. This tendency is related to the novel's obsession with bureaucracy, which homogenises different places, and narcissism, whereby the self splits to establish the same in the place of the other (it erects a mirror or a wall of water between itself and the world, in which the threat of otherness abides).

The Narcissist who is the ghostly hero of the modernist period bifurcates himself so as to overcome castration anxiety; the Other, who is usually a woman, whose lack of a phallus indicates the possibility that he too may be deprived of it, here becomes a man, who is anatomically inviolate. The privilege Musil accords the cliché that allows itself to be sodomised is the same as the privilege he grants women, a doubly ironic gift. He adores them, for they are other and represent the promise of a Utopia outside the bewitched circle of self-hatred; and he revenges himself on them for withholding their otherness by allegorising them, and thus Leona, Bonadea and Diotima are reduced to the level of the known past that engulfs their potential otherness. This is in line with Musil's overall leaning towards the allegorical. Either one has no qualities, or one is so possessed by a single one as to become a caricature. Given this will to allegory, Musil was almost bound to allegorise the name of an author like Mann and to dislike him, as he did; the word 'Mann' personifies a masculinity that questions both his own masochistic identification with the female and his more considered intellectual championship of the Bisexual. (The female is stabbed by the jabbings of the male organ. Thus it is interesting that Ulrich should wish to stab Arnheim on being touched lightly on the shoulder by him, or that Moosbrugger should knife girls to death. In both cases, stabbing is a panicky assertion of masculinity by characters who fear that their helplessness, their loss of the initiative, is placing them in the position of the female. Musil believes that if this helplessness is accepted it can become Utopian and non-pathological, as in the second half of the novel.)

The Bisexual or the Hermaphrodite (who encompasses all knowledge by embracing both sexes and so becomes the author of an encyclopaedic novel) are commonly seen as alternatives to the sterility of Kakanien. But of course both these images are the epitome of fruitlessness. The mixture of man and woman in Clarisse merely unhinges her reason. When Diotima appears at a fancy dress ball as a Napoleonic colonel, it is the prelude to her weeping breakdown. In the eyes of Moosbrugger, a chambermaid becomes a disguised man the moment before he kills her. The slide into a unisexual style accompanies loss of orientation. The theme of incest between Ulrich and Agathe generates an obsessive re-writing of chapters; incest suspends narrative, the linear continuity of the race. The permutations of the stylistic switch-back arise from the fact that Musil's work has no audience (the discouragement that follows from this is one reason why the work could not be finished). Incest arises when the endogamous and the exogamous are so mutually contaminated as to eliminate each other, so that even a sister can seem to belong to an alien race, to the family with which one has ceased to identify. The alternative versions are extorted by the necessity to write both endogamously, as if for the family, and exogamously, as if for foreigners or one's extra-familial lover. Endogamy and exogamy become one in the paradoxicality of the German language in Musil's time; a language shared by two rival empires, one emergent and one in decline. The screws of paradox are tightened on Austrian German by the fact that when compared with Prussian it is a non-militaristic tongue, but when placed alongside the other languages of Kakanien, it embodies structures of domination. Ambiguous sexuality halts the time of the novel; the superimposition of styles is the superimposition of one sex upon the other. The image of Ulrich's castle as compounded of styles that blur each other like a multiple exposure applies to Musil's novel too; temporal succession has been spatialised, and the variants congregate on a single obscured spot. Ulrich is devoid of qualities, for he is part of a series that superimposes Ulrich upon Walter, Arnheim upon Ulrich and so on, and comprises a potentially infinite chain of mediations. One 'character's' meditations can invade the mind of another, for both are pseudo-subjects. Musil stockpiles variants as a compulsive delaying tactic because he is too close to Ulrich to be able to circumscribe him in a fictional fate. He can neither fictionalise him nor mythologise him. Thus the whole novel hangs in abeyance between the exploded realistic novel that precedes it, which it quotes, and the mythology towards which it tends; it enacts an inability to pass from the negated referential to the Utopia which cannot be represented figuratively. Musil's very guarded *style indirect libre* renders the collective consciousness, but it has an aftertaste of bitterness, for it hints at what the collective consciousness represses. The unisexual style dissolves in the intermediate space that separates Ulrich's scientism from Diotima's emotionalism. The binary structures are the two sides of the abyss in which identity vanishes.

The Posthumous Life (Nachlass zu Lebzeiten)

The Man without Qualities is over even before it begins. Ulrich has rejected several careers already (soldier, engineer, mathematician), and the

Fictions of Identity 157

remainder of the novel is his pre-death reflected in reverse. The characters are personifications of possibilities he has rejected; their tiny satellites circle his dead planet. The novel is written from an Archimedean point outside life and styles. Its perspectivism absorbs and rejects impressionism, expressionism and neo-classicism (Diotima and Arnheim) – Ulrich's holiday from his life is an excursion into death. It is of no importance that the novel has no actual end; in its beginning is its end. It reverses the film of reincarnation that has finally broken its own karmic cycle by entering the mystical space beyond opposites. For there is no fundamental difference between any of the characters. In the Thirties Musil published a work entitled *Nachlass zu Lebzeiten*: posthumous works in one's own lifetime. This paradox designates the essential experience of *The Man without Qualities*. As F. G. Peters observes, 'such action as does occur is often retrospectively reported'.[4] The fact that the novel's life is stifled in the cradle was even more pronounced in an earlier version of the first chapter, in which the man killed in the car accident was Ulrich himself. 'To have to await one's death in order to start living: that's a real ontological star turn', writes Musil. It is the trick performed by the spectral tumblers of *The Man without Qualities*. At one point Musil describes the effect Ulrich's 'essayism' is intended to exert: 'the apparently solid would then become a porous pretext for many other meanings, the occurrence would become a symbol of something that had perhaps not occurred, but was sensed through it'.[5] Musil's book is a mirror of this 'something', this after-life of the object, clouded by the closeness of its breath.

Quotation/Speculation

The Man without Qualities is riddled with transformed quotations. Many of Clarisse's statements derive from Nietzsche's *The Birth of Tragedy*; Arnheim is Hegel/Walter Rathenau; Agathe's mysticism feeds on an anthology of ecstatic texts complied by Buber; and Klages and Jung lie behind many of the Utopian excurses. The use of quotation can recall Walter Benjamin's intention of writing a book that would be solely an arrangement of quotations. It is significant that the major projects of both authors – the *Passagenarbeit* and Musil's 'novel' – remained fragments. For the quotation either discredits the voice of the individual who employs it, or it represents a tonality rejected by that voice. The former is the case with Benjamin; the latter applies to Musil. In Benjamin's essays, the individual voice emerges only indirectly, via the speculative juxtaposition of quotations; in Musil, the author's voice generates speculations that are condemned to eccentricity and marginality by the ingrained unthinkingness of the world represented by the quotation. For Benjamin, the quotation is explosive and auratic; it blasts its way out of the original text, the life trapped in the past is released into the present, which it invades from below like a diver. But for Musil, language becomes quotable only once the passage of time has demonstrated its shortcomings – he construes sentences in a dead language. He cannot complete his work, for he knows that his own speech will soon be as irrevocably past as the idiom he dissects; he turns his eyes to the past all the same because he is both a scientist carrying out a post-mortem and an artist who hopes that the future will turn its eyes to him. In the Sixties, the German satirical magazine 'Pardon' sent a random selection of pages from *The Man without Qualities* to Rowohlt, Musil's publishers, as if they were the work of a young and unrecognised author. Musil's fears for his own work appear prescient when one reads the outcome: the publisher rejected the work. Musil himself may have suffered a crisis of will in the Thirties, when the possibile political consequences of mysticism became evident. He could not have foreseen that a dialectical engagement with ideas found in Nietzsche, Jung or Heidegger might tempt readers to place him in the bad company of a set of authors congenial to the National Socialists. The lesson of the Collateral Campaign is that the future one plans for does not exist.

FRANZ KAFKA: THE IMPOSSIBILITY OF WRITING

Writing is the cipher of an absence, a buoy floating above a hidden reality; below it lies the hidden author. By virtue of his dislocated position at the crossroads of German, Czech and Jewish cultures, Kafka was the first writer to realise that in an age of technical mass-production writing ceases to represent an extension of speech; so much print is being produced that people are beginning to read silently. The late-nineteenth-century concept of the isolated artist was not just a mystification, for the unpredictability of change was snipping through the conventions that spun frail webs from author to reader; where the writer is by definition unknown, all his words hover between fact and fiction and fiction is fused with autobiography (as in, say, Mann and Proust). All that remains is 'writing', homogeneous as print. Kafka draws conclusions from this by allowing the form of fiction to terrorise its content. Thus one has the third sentence of the *Schlag ans Hoftor* (*The Knock at the Manor Gate*): 'Ich weiss nicht, schlug sie aus Mutwillen ans Tor oder aus Zerstreutheit oder drohte sie nur mit der Faust und schlug gar nicht'. (I don't know whether she knocked at the door out of mischievousness or out of absentmindedness or merely threatened it with her fist without knocking at all).[1]

The possibility that she never knocked follows the statement that she did because this statement was fictional; doubt seeps from the existence of fiction in the form of *oder ... oder* (or ... or) until it assumes complete ascendency. Fiction becomes immanent self-criticism. What here constitutes a single sentence slowly isolates itself as the most important element in his work, which moves from Expressionism's cryptic fragmentation to an examination of the source of those displacements and their relationship to the system that makes possible his own writing. An equally apt example is 'Wunsch, Indianer zu werden':

> Wenn man doch ein Indianer waere, gleich bereit, und auf dem rennenden Pferde, schief in der Luft, immer wieder kurz erzitterte ueber dem zitternden Boden, bis man die Sporen liess, denn es gab keine Sporen, bis man die Zuegel wegwarf, denn es gab keine Zuegel, und kaum das Land vor sich als glatt gemaehte Heide sah, schon ohne Pferdehals und Pferdekopf.
> [If one were only a Red Indian, ever alert, upon a galloping horse, perched high in the air, continually, rapidly shuddering over the shuddering earth, until one dropped the spurs, for there were no spurs, until one cast away the reins, for there were no reins, and hardly saw the land before one as smoothly trimmed heath, already without the horse's head or neck.][2]

The wished-for horse dematerialises because the subjunctive act of wishing makes the fulfilment of the wish impossible, the wish exists to be a wish and not to be an instantly forgotten bridge to a concrete reality; it is itself a materialisation of fiction. When the wish is complete one no longer needs a real horse, only the words that embody it and, by simply representing it, admit the impossibility of simply wishing things into existence. Kafka is perpetually aware that whatever is made can be unmade (the lack of 'aura' around an industrial object allows one to reshape it and do as one will with it, as the Surrealists discovered), just as a man can be unmade into a dog or vermin or divested of the substance of his name. He runs the evolutionary film in reverse and unmakes his own existence in the hope of starting again. And every moment unmakes a

fiction, modifies a viewpoint. His addiction to disorientating interpolation unmakes the sentence even as it is being written; the individual
sentence harried by counter-sentences is like K. unable to obtain privacy
with Frieda. In the same way as the maids march into his room as he tries
to make love to her, so the interpolation kicks down the door into the
secluded room of the single sentence; just as the interpolation is itself
curtailed, so Joseph K. shuts the door on the whipping. Since writing is
the sign of an absence, it imports and attracts absences like the court or
the castle which become the invisible moving principles of the writing.
The castle's bureaucrats are perpetually surrounded by mounds of
almost forgotten protocols; like Kafka, the institution has dematerialised
itself into paper bearing contents it would perhaps rather forget. The
fictionality of fiction relates it to delusion. Kafka's mode of composition
is probably more purely fictive than any other; historical props and real
people are markedly absent from his writing. His customary purity
emerges in this truth to fiction; those who inject real experience into their
work may be offending against the laws of probability or using the story
as an arena for compensation or revenge, though in any case they are
masquerading as fiction writers when much of their material is factual.
He looked in the mirror and did not see himself. As a reward for his
faithfulness to it, fiction recomposed for him the autobiography he tore
up, wrapped in lead and hurled into the sea; for it clearly emerges from
his work that he suffered from a traumatic relationship with his father
and worked as a clerk. The autobiographical image of Kafka deducible
from his works is more complete than that of any other author; it was
made whole by the sea into which its fragments had been hurled, and
came up rich and strange, cast onto the beach of consciousness like
amber after the most violent of storms, the storm of self-obliteration. He
is sympathetically critical of the mind in which fiction and reality have
become entangled: sympathetic, for he too was human once and under-
went this dilemma; critical, for he has shown how to disentangle the two
by suppressing fiction until it bursts forth volcanically as a dream that
could never be taken for reality. Such minds belong to the mouse that
need only change its direction to save itself[3] or to Joseph K. justifying his
inability/unwillingness to help the *Waechter* (guards)[4]; in the latter case,
the simultaneous source of sympathy and criticism is the fact that the
conclusions seen as *offenbar* (obvious) may be spurious because of the
time taken to reach them (just long enough to forget the original
stimulus) and because Joseph K. is trapped in an onlooker's position.
The double focus is characteristic.

   In order to ascertain the limits where fiction ends and reality begins,

Kafka invents hybrid forms that are both practical linguistic philosophy and fiction. He extrapolates from casual, banal phrases in order to determine what forms of consciousness can live in the moribund, apparently innocent corners of language. *In der Strafkolonie* (*In the Penal Colony*) is built around the phrase 'er erfaehrt es ja an seinem Leib' (he feels it on his body, a German saying) incidentally uttered by the officer during his disquisition on the machine's workings; language has become so deadened in his mouth (his culture only reacts to writing as death – a little like *Tel Quel* – writing as a bloody spectator sport) that he can no longer connect it to reality. Here proverbs and sayings have become the dead heart of culture. Kafka quotes it not to show how fertiliser poured on the roots of language can revitalise it, but rather to demonstrate how the leaden weight of such phrases pulls back to earth even texts that seem fantastic means of escape from them, like Kafka's. He is grimly aware of how little his writing matters or 'redeems' the terrible reality it embraces. *Die Verwandlung* (*The Metamorphosis*) is obviously based on 'diese Leute sind wie Ungeziefer' (these people are like vermin), where the *wie* (like) has been removed, unmasked as a means whereby anyone uttering such a phrase conceals his own brutality from himself. *Das Schloss* (*The Castle*) plays on the title's other meaning of 'lock' and *Josephine die Saengerin* (Josephine the Singer) derives from 'ich pfeife auf euren Schutz' (I whistle at – i.e. spit on – your protection). Kafka attends to the undertones of language in order to prove that one cannot speak with assurance about anything; he hangs the millstones of banality around the neck of a text because it is better for him to fling himself thus attired into a pond than lead anyone astray. The deader the phrase, the more likely it is to be of great age and to have concealed by its exfoliations the tiny seed from which it emerged. The speaker who uses such a prefabricated phrase without considering what order of reality it posits and anchors in the depths of consciousness is not speaking but being spoken through. Kafka's inability to clear his texts entirely of such dead wood made him despair of the cities of words eroded into dust that whirled up in his face in the form of metaphor. One is being spoken through; thus the dead captain's words govern the conduct of the officer in the penal colony, and for the same reason all Kafka's subsidiary characters melt into their functions and appear in pairs, walking proverbs, assembly-line products. Clothes are mass-produced and *Kleider machen Leute* (Clothes make the man); Klamm's clothing is the one feature everyone recognises as unequivocally his. One could even claim that K.'s inability to become his function – land surveyor – is a token of his humanity. When work is dehumanising, to be alienated from it is to preserve one's identity; hence his name is only K. and he refuses to manifest himself through action. The name's remainder is buried treasure.

Kafka's characters, on the model of the mythological figures to whom he often refers, frequently have only one name. This increases the claustrophobia by turning the world into a huge family in which everyone is known by first names only, though the family is also an army where only surnames are employed. Thus there is no privacy. Yet nothing links the names with each other, so society is also a series of unrelated monads. In Expressionism, the use of single names is ambiguous; the world reduces one to a function, but it is also the stuffy family whose walls one must shout down in order to gain room to breathe. Expressionism is mostly sentimental because it avoids the juxtaposition of these contraries. By holding them together, Kafka creates a work more insidiously violent than all other Expressionism; the ambiguous work leaves shrapnel within us by demonstrating that the only valid image of reality as a whole would be incomprehensible to any one of its constituent parts.

The desire to realise what one is saying – which results in a critique of speech by removing it from interpersonal relationships and tying it to a page – leads memory to search out all time. Here all time is one place, like the sprawling multi-styled Victorian house which is the castle, with its labyrinthine cunning corridors. Kafka's philological memory is more honest than, say, Heidegger's, since Heidegger arbitrarily stops at the Greeks whereas Kafka carries on back even when he has given up; in this he is like the Chinese emperor's messenger. His castle is the nineteenth century through a mist; he takes all types of writing under his wing – myth, parable, fairy tale, poetry, allegory and the novel – for he is aware that their poverty unites them (his eclecticism lacks the previous century's pride, and the genres' acceptance by such a pariah as himself seals their destruction – all are wanting as explanations, yet memory requires that they all be summoned.) Synthesis is due to the ghostly abstraction of the separate synthesised terms. He summons these impoverished forms just as he migrates into the ignored forms of animals and insects, once the messengers of the gods. Memory photographs the novel as it dissolves into the archetypal dust whence it arose. But memory is too short to reach the origin. It comes up against the skeleton of an unknown creature, Odradek. And in Chapter Five of *Das Schloss* an official has fearful difficulty in finding the original document relating to K.'s appointment as surveyor. The snowscape outside is an emblem of forgetting, as in *The Waste Land*[5]; the letter K. is like a sign in a snowdrift whose initial letter alone is visible. The warm winter rooms are slumbr-

ous. That K. has come from a distant land and yet never uses the
customs of his homeland to indict the castle's strange procedures shows
the inadequacy of memory and also leaves open the possibility that he is
simply amnesiac; it is also possible that the violence of the present, whose
every moment has to be removed through rationalisation, is so intense as
to provide no leisure for remembrance. The comparison between the two
orders of time has been suppressed – one can only state the fact using the
impersonal form – and as a result K. behaves in the new environment as
he would have done in the old. Given Kafka's oriental obsessions, it is
possible that K. has been reincarnated into a land that will punish him
for the sin of striving. K. seems to have forgotten the journey and expects
to be at home in an alien society. The paradox of perpetual change is that
it prevents one from seeing any one change as radical. K. is active
because no weight of memories pins him down – he has excised the past
to prevent memory's self-petrification. The way memory is related to the
impossibility of movement is adumbrated succinctly in *Das naechste Dorf*:

Mein Grossvater pflegte zu sagen: 'Das Leben ist erstaunlich kurz.
Jetzt in der Erinnerung draengt es sich mir so zusammen, dass ich
zum Beispiel kaum begreife, wie ein juenger Mensch sich entschlies-
sen kann, ins naechste Dorf zu reiten, ohne zu fuerchten, dass – von
unglueklichen Zufaellen ganz abgesehen – schon die Zeit des
gewoehnlichen gluecklich ablaufenden Lebens fuer einen solchen Ritt
bei weitem nicht hinreicht'[6] [My grandfather used to say: 'Life is
incredibly short. As I remember it it becomes so compressed that I can
barely understand, for instance, how a young man can decide to ride
to the next village without fearing that – setting aside all unlucky
accidents – even the duration of a life passed in contentment would be
far from sufficient for such a ride'.]

The fact that the grandfather always reiterated the same phrase
reinforces his remark about the difficulty of completing an action; it is
always turned aside by some inescapable bureaucracy. There is a
paradox here in that the grandfather's sense of time is also perpetually
changing, so that he now lends time the physical tiredness and short-
windedness of old age. The view is dependent on change and yet denies
it. Similarly, the narrator begins as if the remark were illustrative of an
argument only to disappear behind it; one can only present facts, not
interpret them, though the quotation destroys the basis of one's own
discourse by submitting it to a tradition that renders it superfluous, so

one cannot continue once the quotation is complete. The work enters one's mind as innocently as a Trojan horse; the interpolation within the quotation opens up an infinite regress that swallows up any further remark. Something happens to the narrator behind his own back whilst he quotes; to quote is to be vulnerable, and perhaps Benjamin's art of quotation was one of the generators of his bad luck. Like all Kafka's pieces, it is profoundly concerned with memory, in that one feels that to hold all the elements in the mind simultaneously would solve its riddle. By telescoping all the events of one's life into a timeless point, one achieves an immanent transcendence, for all the events cancel each other out. Benjamin has compared Kafka to Scheherezade. This is a beautiful and illuminating metaphor; it allows one to see his concessionary phrases as memory of the situation in which one is telling the story prolonging it so as to ward off execution, and also accentuates the oriental elements in his work. Nevertheless, it seems to apply more to the novels than to the earlier works.

In *Der Geier* (*The Vulture*), *Die Verwandlung* (*The Metamorphosis*) and other early pieces, Kafka is fashioning exquisite images of his own irrevocable desolation, but this is possible only because he does not yet feel fully out of touch with people. A similar paradox is operant in the entire *avant-garde* of the period and caused reactionary approaches once that period was over; only a sense of a secure order gives one the courage to protest and make daring experiments. It was once mockingly said that 'all you need to be a Surrealist is to come from a "good" family.' One can condemn oneself by proxy only if there is a chance of escape in life; condemning oneself appears as removing a dead weight to let new life emerge, as it does, however qualified, at the end of *Die Verwandlung* – although the ending is ironised, it is the end of the writer as well as Gregor, for he steps back into the bounds of realism. Thus the apparently suicidal *Das Urteil* (*The Judgement*) is subtitled 'Eine Geschichte fuer Fraeulein Felice B.' (A story for Miss Felice B.). But as tuberculosis encircled him, closing off the access to others, he had to sustain himself through art alone, beyond the conflict between writing and marriage, since the latter was no longer possible. Kafka probably requested Brod to burn the unpublished later works because he saw them less as art than as a life-support system, useless to anyone else after his death. Thus the novels are extensive where the earlier works are intensive (the telescoped infinite regress of the interpolation in *Das naechste Dorf* has been moved out of the middle of the text, placed at its end and the telescope extended). The earlier epitaph-like concision and poetic suggestiveness disappear. There is an interesting fragment which marks the transition:

Joseph K. dreams of his name being inscribed on a grave and experiences a strange satisfaction at the thought. Kafka excised this from *Der Prozess* (*The Trial*) because it belongs to the earlier climate of willing self-destruction. In the novels the cataleptic protests at being buried alive and the outrage below the epitaphs bursts forth. At the end of his description of the castle he appends the following sentence:

> Es war, wie wenn ein truebseliger Hausbewohner, der gerechterweise im entlegensten Zimmer sich haette eingesperrt halten sollen, das Dach durchbrochen und sich erhoben haette, um sich der Welt zu zeigen. [It was as if some melancholy tenant, who ought by rights to have kept himself shut up in the furthest-flung room, had broken through the roof and raised himself up to show himself to the world.][7]

It is Kafka breaking out of his self-erected mausoleum, the unconscious becoming conscious as the individual seeks to deduce the branding iron from the scar.[8] Obsessive though much of this writing is, his decision to live by it alone prevents it ever degenerating into mere word-spinning. There is instead a deeply moving sense of writing barely surviving. That one suspect's Frieda's speeches of being prolonged by her in order to keep K. present creates rending pathos, as of lovers who can never become completely one. Both K. and Joseph K. plead actively on their own behalf, and this insistence is new. The exact nature of the obstacle they encounter is cloudy, but rather than reckon this a fault (the work is supposed to be 'not fully achieved', though this remark is valid only in so far as it points to the work's incompleteness; conceptually, it is fully formed) I would insist on its merits. By never specifying his metaphor, by leaving it unlabelled, Kafka evades the reductivism attendant on allegory and liberates the work from an insistently sentimental dependence on awareness of his own fate. The letter K. is not an exception; it appears only to prove his objectivity since he can allude to himself and maintain the coherence of art.

Kafka wrote because of the intense excitement he experienced in racing across the tightrope of an inspiration during a few hours. Thus *Das Urteil* (*The Judgement*) was composed in a single night and left him in a state of joyous self-extinction. This excitement appears in his characteristic prose rhythms, in the movement from shorter to longer clauses as the ramifications of the first sentence diversify and as the premises that underlie the apparently objective statement come to light. As in logic, the proposition is followed by the sub-propositions it organises. This is a passage from light to darkness during which one's eyes begin to see the dark as akin to the light, becoming accustomed to it. Thus *Die Verwandlung* (*The Metamorphosis*) ramifies from its first sentence with the calmly insane literalism of a child as it monomaniacally applies the new idea by which it is taken. The excitement is due also to the repression of words in others' presence which causes them to erupt in privacy. Hence writing becomes an enigma, a statement that is no statement because it occurs outside the conversation it continues by other means. Enigma seems to be a method for ensuring that one is not forgotten, despite the ease with which one has been passed over; it is the sting in the tail of silent acquiescence. Tradition that fears time will erase it turns into enigma. It does so to protect itself but becomes thereby the executor of its own destruction as it emptily mirrors the irrationality the opposition ascribes to it, as it provokes attack like a cobra's question mark. Kafka's work has been similarly attacked and suffocated with interpretations in the process Adorno terms 'the fatal parody of that forgetting Kafka wished upon himself with bitter earnestness'.[9] In Kafka, tradition is an enigma, for it persists whilst no longer understood; what does *Vor dem Gesetz* (*Before the Law*) mean?

Literary history demonstrates a movement from explicit moral purpose and stylisation towards realism. If an account has a moralistic aim, as do Biblical stories or fairy tales, the fact that the events never happened exactly as the story's cues would lead one to imagine becomes irrelevant; the sole important element is the patterned architectural interdependence of crime and punishment. Reject this moralism and one is driven to create narrative as an exact photography (in James Agee, and later in the *nouveau roman*, novel becomes screenplay) where one increasingly cultivates description to specify exactly what happened. Sartre is right to complain of Flaubert's tyranny, as Leavis does of Joyce's – the novelist suffocates the reader's imagination under rich weaves of description so as to permit neither participation nor doubt (for he is aware how doubt is burrowing under tradition, is resigned to being his only reader). The isolation of industrial society (its duality poignantly underlined by Freud when he marvelled at the telephone which would link him with his son and added that he would not have needed it had the motor car not carried that son away) transforms the novelist into his only certain reader. In Kafka's sentences it might even be possible to register the point at which he broke off and read the sentence (even if he didn't actually do so, he read it in his mind's eye by remembering it). As an example I will use the earlier extract from *Der Schlag ans Hoftor* (*The Knock at the Manor Gate*) quoted on p. 159. The last phrase 'und schlug gar nicht' (and did not knock at all) is produced by re-reading the sentence and re-writing it within its own confines. Another way of saying this is to state that the full stop often appears before the end of the sentence, whose actual end ought to be the trailing dots of amazement. Change is so rapid that things vanish even as they are being evoked. The religious equivalent of this is the possibility that the Messiah has already arrived, thus undermining all the Jewish books that anticipate his advent. A Jew living in a predominantly Christian culture could hardly overlook this disquieting irony, resolved by most Jews in the alternatives of Zionism or secular assimilation; Kafka leaves the Gordian knot uncut. Titles like *Das Urteil* (*The Judgement*) or *Die Verwandlung* recount stages in the death of an exemplary victim and inevitably sound like captions to The Stations of the Cross. '*Das* Urteil', for there is only one judgement, only one life, since Christ lives again in the Christians who imitate Him.

Kafka's style is a two-edged amalgam of bureaucratic protocol and its parody, just as his characters are both alienated from society and self-alienated: they speak the same spare language as the society that frustrates them (spare perhaps because of a deep anger that withholds speech; perhaps because the other is one's projection and both are unanimous, i.e. of one soul). Such duality is common in first person narration, but its agnostic sting is usually removed and its bad faith revealed by the ease with which it is assimilated to the self-portrait. Kafka provocatively preserves the sting by injecting the uncertainty about others' motives of first person narration into third person narrative. By thus fusing omniscient narration with first person narration, so that the latter can no longer be seen as a ditch of uncertainty running along the royal road of the novel's vocation, he preserves his work from the virtuoso mimesis to which first person narration is irresponsibly prone. His omniscient narrator knows nothing, for the character in the story is the self he tries to unknow by writing the story (this is the most serious form of what later became cheapened in the device of *mise-en-abîme*). Hence the full stop after the letter K. to suppress his presence. Kafka wrote a series of aphorisms about himself called *Er* (*He*), and according to Max Brod much of *Das Schloss* was composed in the first person and then transposed into the third. Such self-representation appears in the many reflexive forms, as in *Die Verwandlung*, where *sich vorstellen* (imagining oneself) is what Gregor Samsa's imagination has achieved by turning him into vermin, though this inaugurates a process and he is at first unable to grasp the consequences of his new state; he is his own modernist art-work, acquiring meanings in the course of time. The degree to which reflexive awareness is possible introduces the problem of his characters' responsibility. If Gregor Samsa has turned *himself* into an insect, may this not be for a masochistic *frisson* rather than to exact justified self-punishment? Thus the Marxist argument that by doing so he comes to consciousness of/stands as mute emblem of/the degradation imposed upon him by the nature of his labour becomes ambiguous. The warders in *Der Prozess* (*The Trial*) remark: 'Er gibt zu, er kenne das Gesetz nicht, und behauptet gleichzeitig, schuldlos zu sin'. (He admits to ignorance of the Law and at the same time protests his innocence).[10] Our ignorance of their reasons for saying this prevents us trying either the trial or Joseph K.; we choke on our laughter and watch attendants wheel away our own corpses who died laughing. Where the Law has become enigmatic, it is possible to feel accused by it without knowing why, or to disown actual guilt by mystifying it with relativism: Kafka is dealing with the split in consciousness which makes it possible to speak both of an objective and of a subjective morality. The Law must exist, for the word 'law' persists, though the concept's vagueness turns every deed into a potential trespass. Perhaps the lost order of scribes and Torah has suddenly begun to operate anew. One could distinguish between K. as inarticulate everyday feeling and the court's intellect, capable of sophisticated rational argument, though the distinction breaks down, for the court's arguments may just be rationalisations and thus obey emotion rather than any impartial reason. Joseph K. could be seen as an unconscious novelist of himself, hallucinating objective correlatives of his own guilt. (Perhaps all of Kafka's characters tell each other stories that never coincide to maintain a separate identity and if they came together the overlap would reveal that they were basically the same person, that *all* the characters were the same person: Franz Kafka). Joseph K.'s conviction of guilt is the outcome of a long development – the restriction of relationships in his life so far has been the result of self-doubt, self-criticism, and it is natural that he finally surround himself with fictional characters who will take him away and so protect other people from him. Kafka's inspirational, fragmentary writing institutionalises self-doubt; one is chosen by what one writes, thus escaping hubris, though like Jacob one struggles with God by ramifying the original statement (the divine rupturing of silence) so that it destroys itself. By destroying writing he hopes magically to destroy the isolation from which it stems. The name Joseph K. or K. is the ruined name that can serve as a new beginning. Yet the name has also ended with its beginning, and this leaves him functioning with some vital unspecifiable part missing. He only partly perceives the world because he only partly acknowledges it. Thus there emerges the intensely adolescent (I do not mean this in a pejorative sense, I simply intend it to evoke a process that is incomplete) ambivalence of inability to enter the world, because to do so would condone its evil, or to remain a child. One lives on two levels: to escape the dilemma one reverts to childhood, the 'love at first sight' K. experiences with Frieda. But K.'s unconscious total dependence on women is deadlocked by a conscious recognition of a patriarchal world of writing (the women all speak), of power and secrecy, for one does not know what lies in the piece of paper the official holds and which protects him from attack, for he can always use the paper as an alibi and refer one to another department. Kafka postulates a society alienated from itself, suffering from a collective neurosis; language is alienated from itself by becoming writing.

More than any of the other works, *Das Schloss* is dominated by lengthy monologues between the characters. At the turn of the century the dramatic monologue represented a common artistic solution to the problem of the expression of alienated subjective experience. Alienation is cogently expressed by the way others' voices speak through the self (the device thus stems from the same source as the allusion). If statements lack objective truth, language can only be preserved by referring them back to the speaker to demonstrate their truth for him, so language can display subjectivity even though unable to build bridges to it. Kafka, by placing these monologues in a suspension unable to crystallise into narrative, insists on the partiality of such truth. People radiate in static desolation at fixed intervals like street lamps; putting them in a row shows that none of them is *the* light. By trying to place the monologue in a narrative, to prevent the self's relation to its projections being simply the static one of a planet with its entourage of satellites, Kafka insists on revealing by its absence what the monologue leaves out: the possibility of story, of interaction. He thus indicates the absence of society that is the vacuum into which the individual expands. The reader seeks to escape the concrete claustrophobia of the monologue by entering into metaphysics, but on doing so feels guilt as well as relief, and hurries back under the street lamps, out of the disembodying dark.

The major concern of *Das Schloss* is self-forgetting, which can be the result of either solicitude or guilty repression. Phrases like 'die Worte kamen ihr wie gegen ihren Willen hervor' (the words came out of her as if against her will)[11], 'er vergass sich in der Eile des Erzaehlens' (he forgot himself in the rush of the narration)[12], and Olga's statement that speech 'reisst uns fort, wir wissen nicht wohin' (tears us away and we don't know where to)[13] evince the theme clearly. Kafka explores the ambiguity of this by using two separate forms of presenting speech: monologue and reported speech. He can alternate between them because each – by virtue of the duality of any encounter – presupposes the other as a transformation, a transposition of self into the key of the other and vice versa. Monologue displaces the author, but reported speech creates an image of him as a tyrant forcing utterances onto a Procrustean bed. Yet he also seems trapped as he does so; reported speech reveals the author's (or the other's) impatience with his characters, his testy and grating tolerance of them. Monologue gives the authorial self full rein even as it seems to be giving others *carte blanche*, and the disguise makes its lament movingly impersonal. The unparagraphed speeches are sustained by a strong will to jam the fragmenting interpolations of Kafka's unconscious as he seeks here to transcend or ravage systematically his earlier method of writing. Kafka is near to his characters yet uncomprehending; their isolated utterances are steamrollered into the oppressive texture of a single paragraph. The form of the book dictates the novel's content; since the written page is the result of the impossibility of direct communication, its subject must be non-communication. Speech – the realm of human interchange – becomes invested with the monolithic quality of monologue; reported speech is monologue for two voices. Where there is no reader there can be be no dialogue, so there is no paragraphing and isolated remarks are crushed into a homogeneous mass.

One logical consequence of the theme of self-forgetting is the erosion of the novel's basis in narration. The narrator's presence in Kafka's early work laid it open to charges of arbitrariness – disconfirmation could be seen as purely wilful and authorial, with the safety of the author's perspective travestying the experience of his degraded characters. Even so brilliant and sustained a work as *Die Verwandlung* (*The Metamorphosis*) seems finally to be simply a monstrous *jeu d'esprit*, and the ending did not satisfy Kafka himself. But excising the narrator and permitting others to speak places uncertainty in the nature of existence and precludes the psychoanalytic reductivism that would see Kafka's visions as merely idiosyncratic; the advent of such a style accompanies a greater generosity towards the characters. *Der Prozess* (*The Trial*) and *Das Schloss* (*The Castle*) move consistently away from narration and towards the juxtaposition of statements (the flaws and inconsistencies in the early stages of *Das Schloss* are the result of the transition; for example when K. talks of his imminent battle with the castle, the predominance of narration at this stage makes us expect some explanation of what he means, and its absence is dissatisfying). On the basis of the chapter 'Im Dom' (In the Cathedral) in *Der Prozess* one may postulate a relation between the two novels similar to that Leavis has discerned between *The Rainbow* and

Women in Love[14]: the former work opened up dimensions it could not manage, so the author tacked on a summary and regressive ending in order to move on quickly to the problems raised by the new discoveries, the possibilities inherent in a method of composition by montage of monologues. (The ending of *Der Prozess* bears a distressing similarity to Expressionist works. That both Lawrence and Kafka should have broken off texts at virtually the same time is an example of the general seismic shift caused by the turning of an epoch; one has the uncanny sense of actually witnessing a moment of great historical change). By the close of his life, virtually all Kafka's writing was taking the form of monologue, returning to the techniques of his earliest works, after the middle period of narration, in which he had learned in an experimental vacuum how to manipulate larger forms. The novel forgets its opening just as the characters forget themselves. There is pathos in Frieda's self-forgetting (forgetting her place in the hierarchy and then forgetting K.) – it is the poignancy of settled emnity against oneself, so one repeatedly sloughs off one's life, the plangent absurdity of explaining at length to people why one has left them. The later pages of *Das Schloss* are obsessed by the way people can be close and yet mutually unknowing: 'deine Naehe ist, glaube mir, den einzigen Traum, den ich traeume' (believe me, your nearness is the only dream I dream)[15] says Frieda after leaving K.. She may be speaking to a figment of her imagination, for all are separate dreams. To write novels is to know nearness only as a dream; the novel arises in a society of isolation, where the non-existent individual dreams of the non-existent. The novel as a form is anti-hierarchical, but only hierarchy ultimately secures meaning against the possible hermeticism of private languages. *Das Schloss* looks back at the lost hierarchy and finds it incomprehensible, and critically participates in the medievalism of the Expressionist by means of parody. In Kafka the gestus is not the charged pseudo-medieval woodcut[16] but the photograph, where action has no context and tantalises by tempting us to read an intended riddle into the blank neutrality of technical reproduction. The photograph is the negative of the intention that led a finger to press the trigger, it is a symptom; the invisible photographer is more important than what we see. (It is this that drives many photographers to tendentious cliché in order to inscribe their meaning legibly upon the image; in doing so, they sacrifice mystery to banality, and there is no alternative to the choice). The attraction of the unattainable is obvious: 'Seit du nicht mehr die Braut seines Herrn bist, bist du keine solche Verlockung mehr fuer ihn.' (Since you have ceased to be his master's bride you have lost your old attractiveness in his eyes)[17]. Self-doubt lets one trust others' judgements rather than one's own, so if someone has been chosen by someone else as a lover, she must be of value; such self-doubt is the root of the Oedipus complex and of snobbery.

The natural home of the monologue is the death-bed, when none dare interrupt the speaker. As a result of this, *Das Schloss* is the quest as a series of death-bed scenes. Many of the monologues have the whispering incoherence of the dying whose speech is snatches of mist, a wintry hypnagogia of words snowing within the room. K.'s quest progresses backwards, like Zeno's arrow[18], as his strength ebbs. More and more people are interposed between him and the castle, so the way grows longer with every step. First the objective is the castle; then it is Klamm as a way to the castle; then it is Frieda as a way to Klamm and thence to the castle; then Brunswick, Schwarzer, the Barnabas family and Buergel appear; and so on. Max Brod states that Kafka proposed the following ending: K. receives permission to live in the area as he dies surrounded by the villagers. Were this to have been so, the ending would have completed the reversed pattern of the whole book. Only when the whole village stands between K. and the castle can contact be established. This simultaneity of presence and absence is a parable of the nature of the book itself; reality is only meaningful in so far as it appears in the mirror of art, reversed. The more one turns away from reality, the closer it draws.

The death-bed is perhaps the basic image in Kafka's work. Gregor Samsa and Joseph K. awake in bed to the end of their lives hitherto; for the civilian bureaucrat, one's bed is the place where one will die and thus represents death in life. The machine in *In der Strafkolonie* (*In the Penal Colony*) is a public death-bed (such as the Chinese Emperor also possesses). The story about the penal colony has a slightly willed and pretentious Expressionist stasis until the frenzied death-bed scene in which the officer is destroyed by the machine, which simultaneously goes to pieces. This scene has a poetic richness the rest of the work lacks, for in it appears the powerful constellation of motifs that links writing, death and the vulnerability and unconsciousness of lying down. Writing that expresses the individual is also something that is done to him (like the Expressionist scream) – it is self-destruction and destruction of the instrument of writing – and the passage has the apocalyptic immediacy of discovery. Discovery comes whilst one is in bed, vulnerable to the insights of the unconscious, as yet uncaptured by the routine of the day. In *Der Prozess* (*The Trial*) the accused are described as beautiful, and a similar idea – the radiance of the condemned man – is mentioned in *In der Strafkolonie*. Seeing a person as beautiful is seeing him as dead, as self-sufficient, like statues with which we cannot interact. The Expressionist hero Kafka uses is also stiff, having hardened himself against the violence of reality. Is it too whimsical to suggest that the letter K represents a man holding his hand up, Canute-like, to halt the march of events? one of those stick-men Kafka drew so often? (It would thus be like a Chinese pictogram, another ramification of his interest in the East. The sign would here lose its arbitrariness.) And the gestus is a frozen frame in the narrative film arrested by the narrator, held still so as to be lifted out of the flow of events.

Such freezing of people turns them into allegories, whence the tendentiousness (instant deep thought) of so many frozen frames in recent films. A figure called K. or painted from behind (as in many of G. F. Watts's allegorical paintings) is by nature unknowable, only partly manifest. He becomes an object of frustrated allegorical meditation, like an image of a saint onto which no identifying emblem has been painted. Allegory is here fused with the utmost realism; a figure portrayed before his death (a saint before the manner of his martyrdom is known) is inevitably perceived only in part, and such partial perception accompanies the increasing temporariness of urban experience. It is in the relationships between K. and women that the allegorical element becomes most insistent, though it is an allegory rendered ambiguous by realism. Thus when Frieda mentions how K. is using her to reach Klamm, one is tempted to see in Klamm the divine; Kafka himself saw something quasi-divine in Milena's face whilst fearing that to do so was blasphemous. Women may be a help or a hindrance, and constitute the point at which allegory and realism meet, for they are not men and can be seen abstractly as repositories of all that men lack. In so far as the work is realistic, she is a hindrance – when with Frieda, K. is wasting time he could expend in seeking entrance to the castle. But in the allegorical dimension, she is a help – Klamm is a *deus absconditus* but his lover is a tangible sign of his existence. The two orders of perception are not synchronised and never can be; in realist terms, the allegorical concern with the beyond is paranoia, but it is equally obvious that not everything can be understood through immediate encounter, as K.'s baffled wanderings show. Kafka criticises both realism and allegory; realism becomes allegory when people are so remote as to take on the abstraction of a concept.

Just as Kafka creates a form intermediate between allegory and realism, so his characters are in limbo between comic-strips and novels. The assistants in *Das Schloss* are asexual mixtures of adult and child, one-dimensional working models of Chaplin one moment and real figures with a remembered past (a childhood shared with Frieda) at another moment. The officials stand in for each other and are composite lazy, sleepy figures, bedridden and surrounded by mounds of paper, yet it seems that each has a clearly-defined personality and a Sordini could never be mistaken for a Sortini. The duality of perception is typical of urban life, in which people are either parts of an undifferentiated flow of humanity or suddenly spring out of it into reality and psychological motivation. The work that most succinctly contains Kafka's ambiguities about the personality is perhaps *Die Wahrheit ueber Sancho Pansa* (*The Truth about Sancho Panza*):

> Sancho Pansa, der sich uebrigens dessen nie geruehmt hat, gelang es im Laufe der Jahre, durch Beistellung einer Menge Ritter – und Raeuberromane in den Abend – und Nachtstunden seinen Teufel, den er spaeter den Namen Don Quixote gab, derart von sich abzulenken, dass dieser dann haltlos die verruecktesten Taten auffuehrte, die aber mangels eines vorbestimmten Gegenstandes, der eben Sancho Pansa haette sein sollen, niemandem schadete. Sancho Pansa, ein freier Mann, folgte gleichmuetig, vielleicht aus einem gewissen Verantwort-lichkeitsgefuehl, dem Don Quixote auf seinen Zuegen und hatte davon eine grosse und nuetzliche Unterhaltung bis an sein Ende.

> [Sancho Panza – who, by the way, makes no boast of it – succeeded over the years in diverting his demon – whom he later christened Don Quixote – , which he did by supplying him evening and night with large numbers of tales of chivalry and banditry, and to such purpose that the demon recklessly undertook the craziest of exploits, which, for lack of a definite object (which ought to have been Sancho Panza) harmed nobody. Sancho Panza, a free man, relaxedly followed him – perhaps with a certain sense of responsibility – on his campaigns and enjoyed a considerable and edifying entertainment to the end of his days.][19]

Here Kafka, Cervantes, Sancho Panza and the reader of Cervantes (who is Kafka, to round off the circle) form a composite figure – along with other figures – whirling in a vortex round the dead centre of namelessness. The text is an evocation of the phenomenon of identifica-tion with a text as one is reading it and poses the question: just what is one identifying with? With the author – so one becomes an author oneself, as Kafka did after reading Cervantes; with Don Quixote; with Sancho Panza; with Kafka himself; with the demon, who is diverted from himself and from Sancho Panza. The creator has to follow his creation, for it is a demon, just as Kafka was reluctant to let his works into the market-place and out of his sight. In the nowhere space of the text, which furnishes common ground, contrary emotions become one (sense of responsibility' and 'entertainment', for instance). Whilst reading one is without identity, on the carousel of transformation which allows Kafka to write 'Sancho Panza' where we would expect 'Cervantes'; the reader becomes the book. The personality to emerge most clearly from the text is that of the demon; the simple reversals that provide the mechanism of Kafka's words threaten us with the possibility of losing out minds in trying to sort out the tantalising hints. It is significant that Kafka did not permit this work to be published. We fear that we have lost ourselves in the labyrinth of the page, and the demon grows in menace as his eyes glint below it. But the work is also, more trivially and comically, a parody: of the revelations rife in newspapers (here a non-revelation because about a fictional character); of the romantic habit of considering characters as real people; of the common glorification of Sancho Panza as *l'homme moyen sensuel*; and of seventeenth-century didactic notions of art ('edifying entertainment'). Yet for all its simplicity, even facility of technique, it is a whirlpool that postulates a frighteningly nonchalant interchangeability of identity and contains Kafka's concealed confession about the meaning of art for him. It terrifies because it achieves so much by such mindless means and thus suggests that some demonic force is guiding the pen of the writer, whose identity is also in abeyance. The way most of the elements are fixed whilst only a few – the names – are labile causes a frustrated *déjà vu*; except for just a few key words, the statement is banal. But these few words suffice to make one retrospectively suspicious of every single word in the paragraph.

In *Die Wahrheit ueber Sancho Pansa* (*The Truth about Sancho Panza*) the obsessive emerges as a central category of Kafka's works. His unprecedented awareness of the importance of the minute creature, the casual phrase, relates to the obsessional isolation of his prose; one isolates oneself so as to gain control over even the smallest reaction, and his concern with purity is a concern to know that his actions are really his. Yet for all one's attempts at self-isolation, one hears something on the other side of the wall: as in *Der Bau* (*The Burrow*), this noise disquiets, for the wall itself prevents one from perceiving what is occurring on the other side. Each noise is a shock after which a train of associations attempts to blot out the memory; thus Joseph K. frantically rationalises his refusal to help the warders during their whipping in *Der Prozess* (*The Trial*). In perpetual treadmill the mind returns to the scene of the shock to see if anything actually took place. Thus Joseph K. opens the door again the day after – slamming it shut on seeing the two warders still there, not simply out of callousness but also because he fears that he will be caught up in the never-ending past, trapped in the circle of self-recrimination. He drums on the door 'als sei sie dann fester geschlossen' (as if that shut it more tightly)[20] – in closing the door of the present he is also beating on the door of his inaccessible past in order to enter and change it. One feels that all the scenes of *Der Prozess* take place simultaneously in the stasis of mortified life, on different floors of the Tower of Babel. Although Uytersprot is undoubtedly right to argue for the placing of the current chapter four after chapter one[21], one's feeling that Joseph K. may have been judged and killed already prevents one seeing the false order as a radical falsification; the last chapter may even precede the first, for its surreal death may be metaphorical and occur at night before Joseph K. wakes (its artistic regressiveness also tempts one to place it before the actual first chapter). The discrete chapters would then be alternative forms of a single obsession.

Throughout Kafka's works, people speak as if the meaning of their words was clear – thus the landlady of *Das Schloss*, jealously mothering Frieda and warning K. that she tolerates him despite his stupidity. The tone is familiar but the meaning is opaque. The landlady can launch into powerful vituperation or K. can term a matter '*offenbar*' (obvious), and both are baffling, though the latter is irritating too, for nothing is self-evident; paradoxically, one sympathises at such points with the castle rather than K., who though himself excluded excludes us by his claim to knowledge. One could rationalise this as the mutual incomprehensibility experienced by society and outsider, but the concrete immediacy of the work, which discovers the metaphysical only negatively, by feeling its way to the bounds of the physical, forbids such abstraction. Kafka's greatness is not that he discovers concrete equivalents for such given ideas but that he unearths a primitive twilit level[22] on which the two are one, and the unity is extremely disconcerting to all our categorisations. This paradoxical unity has often been loosely compared with dreams. The comparison has some validity. Schizophrenia (Laing gives the salutary etymology 'broken-heartedness') has been interpreted by some psychologists as due to an overload of dream-work avalanching into everyday life. That which afflicts Joseph K. could be madness; figures wait at the bottom of his bed as they did beside Barbara O'Brien's when paranoia enfolded her (an account of this is given in her *Operators and Things*, an autobiography written under a pseudonym). The frequent flatness of his characters is dreamlike, as are the condensation of his motifs and the displacement of key phrases – such as 'er erfaehrt es an seinem Leib' (he feels it on his body) in *In der Strafkolonie* – so they occupy inconspicuous positions. Dream enables him to give flat characters depth, which is tenuously affixed to their feet like a shadow; the comic-strip hero is also an exploited archetype. Nevertheless, the comparison with dream is invidious when pressed further than the impressionism of the above remarks permits; methodologically it is disastrous, for it allows Romantic inattention to detail to combine with psychoanalytic reductivism to destroy the possibility of criticism. Romantic vagueness, assimilating all art to the irrational, is wed with psychoanalytic exactitude to produce the variety of criticism that is an exact self-analysis of the critic, who has used the multi-referentiality of dream motifs isolated from a case study as an excuse for reading his own preoccupations into Kafka. The use of Symbols suppresses the fact of narrative continuity in order to freeze the text into a lump that can be held in the hand and safely possessed; Kafka is travestied and turned into yet another cultural object. Such criticism dominates the literature on him, but its uncertain wavering between reverential exegesis of age-old Symbols and reductivist location of Kafka in the modern world of which he is 'symptomatic' is of value only as a sign of the methodological confusion one must confess to before one can say anything valid about Kafka. The tendency of the analogy is to repress his work by referring it to him alone, reading as interesting oddities what are really truths claustrophobically trapped in the concrete and tragically unable to free themselves and enter a general social discourse, for the pluralism of experience precludes such translation.

Dream is the self translated into a foreign language: 'dream-like' texts become valid when reality has become so phantasmal that to call such a text 'dreamlike' would be to repress it by assuming the existence of 'reality'. Kafka's work is deeply concerned with the extent to which translation, a metaphor for all relationship, is still possible. The small aperture through which K. observes Klamm asleep, or the door held ajar through which Gregor Samsa observes his family, is a metaphor for the eye, the single part of the self which retains awareness of another place when the rest of the body has been imprisoned in immobility; it alone can translate itself from one place to another, though only momentarily, long enough to snap up a gestus. The insertion of *Vor dem Gesetz* (*Before the Law*) into *Der Prozess* is an attempt to label its unlabelled metaphors and so translate the private language into a public one (this must be possible, because the private language of the parable is presented as public, authoritative, and only the private individual Joseph K. does not understand it); it is the conscious mind's effort at learning from its

unconscious inspirations, as the two criticise each other. To address the
self as *du* (thou) or to refer to oneself in the third person, as he often does,
is to try to translate oneself from here to there in order to create the
possibility of companionship; to see oneself as another sees one is to
create that other. But only in imagination. Thus there is beauty and
pathos in the following passage, poised between desolation and recip-
rocity:

> Findest du also nichts hier auf den Gaengen, oeffne die Tueren,
> findest du nichts hinter diesen Tueren, gibt es neue Stockwerke,
> findest du oben nichts, es ist keine Not, schwinge dich neue Treppen
> hinauf. Solange du nicht zu steigen aufhoerst, hoeren die Stufen nicht
> auf, unter deinen steigenden Fuessen wachsen sie aufwarts.
>
> [So if you find nothing in the corridors, open the doors, if you find
> nothing behind these doors, there are other floors, and if you find
> nothing above, have no fear but clamber up new flights of stairs. As
> long as you do not cease climbing, the steps will not end, they will grow
> upwards under your climbing feet.][23]

The steps respond to the person, yet he finds nothing. His energy is
endless, he is god-like and creates reality as he proceeds, yet he also
needs the consolations of this passage (whose repetitions and ritual air
make the speaker sound like a pitying god) for he is always only a step
from falling. The last sentence plays off syntax against sense, so one sees
the steps as created by the foot, only to then be left with the steps alone,
independent and empty; this disjunction is the passage's paradox. With
you will die a world but the world will continue. Upward movement is
optimistic, we seem to see a believer trotting eagerly towards his god, but
he will never reach him; nor will he die, for Kafka's Bluebeard's castle
has no final door. For all its paradoxicality, by making the paradox
concrete Kafka gives it a richness that prevents it becoming reality's
impoverished skeleton, so one can understand his capacity to live for
writing alone; out of the bitter soil of his experience arises this airy plant.
Yet although the steps the foot has created stand as proud creations at
the end – gleaming away into the distance – no one else will see them,
they exist only for the person who climbs them, and are in any case mere
means to an end that fall away once traversed. The climber has the
manic air of someone running up an elevator going down, rushing to the
top of a deserted building; in Kafka's *Amerika*, the individual builds his
own skyscrapers. The running feet and the tall building belong to the
futuristic climate of Expressionism, of, say, Fritz Lang's *Metropolis*. The

self in a perpetual present never comes into independent existence: *du* is ultimately the mirror's inconsolable face, for no one can live before it, everything passes it by. One may write that writing is impossible and seem to contradict oneself, for that statement is itself writing. Nevertheless, writing that can never find its way back to speech is lost; Kafka's writing, aware of this danger, imitates the simplicity of colloquial language in order to fit itself to become speech, and he reads out loud to friends in order to translate writing back into speech, deliberately betraying it by allowing it to provoke laughter, as private fears can do when brought out into the open. For the same reason, he begins writing with the composition of monologues and miniatures, the latter being easy to lift off the page and retell without distortions attendant upon editing or pruning. But once he realises that he is going to die and that his writing will not become speech, he lets it burgeon on the epic scale of the novels, spiralling away from us. Afflicting himself, he tries to remove his part of the taint we all share. The letter K stands in his last works for the self that is trapped in the book; the letter is a picture of a skeletal man because it is Kafka himself, pressed between pages like a dead flower. In opening his books, we open his tomb.

6 Post-Modernism

THE FADING OF MODERNISM

The great modernist novelists aimed to create structures that would be all-embracing; on the one hand, the single place of the author's youth or childhood would provide a metonymic image, or possible repository, of all other places (Joyce's Dublin, Proust's Combray, Mann's Lübeck, Musil's Vienna); on the other, they presented the imagination as its own hero, and countered the threatening fluidity of the encyclopaedic novel with the concentration of the narcissist. The single place set a boundary to the infinity of the imagination; the imagination universalised that place. The result was both an indulgence and a critique of the powers of imagination.

Modernism broke down when these two components – self-consciousness and spirit of place – suffered separation. The dialectic of inner and outer reality, fantasy and realism, subject and object, which had reached a peak of intensity in the works of Joyce, Proust, Kafka, Lawrence and Musil, became suddenly flaccid. One cannot be quite sure how or why this happened, though one can make a few informed guesses: the harsh realities of war, industrialisation and enforced mobility may have deprived the individual of the sense that an entire life could be spent in one place (which would have to be a city in order to represent the diversity of that life); perhaps the tension within the works of these writers was too great to be sustained for long; perhaps the ongoing process of democratisation whittled away the belief that a single privileged individual could stand for a world; and perhaps the belief in the permanence of cultural artefacts had been shattered by the Great War. In any case, in the course of the nineteen twenties the novel seems to have lost one or the other of its dimensions, be it the inner or the outer. I would like to present just three examples of this atrophy: Gide, Faulkner, and Beckett.

180

Gide's *Les Faux Monnayeurs*, for instance, is clearly endowed with the self-consciousness one has come to associate with modernism, but it displays this trait in a trivial manner; too little is invested in the detached exercise, which lacks the scope of Proust's great novel. It is too obviously a chic and scaled-down model of Proust, a pocket Matterhorn, Proust popularised and made portable. One can see in this the beginnings of what Adorno has termed the culture industry. Gide's novel is less the fruit of a long and unremitting search for an authentic self than an exercise in mystification. Viewed from the vantage point of *Les Faux Monnayeurs*, Gide's *oeuvre* appears to take the shape of a flight from self. He had passed already from the scrupulous desolation of *La porte étroite* – in which the contradiction between love of the human and love of God had destroyed both Alissa and Jerome, who was infatuated with her – to the admirable brittle comedy of *Les Caves du Vatican*. Lafcadio is of course derivative of Raskolnikov, and in Gide's decision to borrow from the conveniently fashionable Dostoevsky one can see the seeds of the deeper inauthenticity of *Les Faux Monnayeurs*, but at the same time the novel is wittily objective about the hero's passion for the *acte gratuit*. In the later novel, however, the figure of the novelist is so overvalued that the self-consciousness degenerates into a facile self-congratulation; and this imprecision is a natural counterpart to the evasiveness with which Gide treats homosexuality.

At the other end of the scale, one has Faulkner, who preserves the spirit of place but whose self-consciousness is largely awkwardness – pre-modernist – because it fails to take into account the position of the narrator himself. Thus in *Light in August*, although the obsessive key-word 'to know' suggests a modernist awareness of the difficulties of perception, the significance of these difficulties is reduced by the fact that only the figures secured within the story are confronted by them. The novelist himself is free of them – indeed, his Cubist fragmentation of the story establishes his status as that of the demiurgic constructionist who alone possesses the key to the puzzle. The relativity of seeing embodied in Faulkner's frequent resort to montages of monologues (for example *The Sound and the Fury*) is not an affliction from which he suffers himself – as is shown by the elements of 'Boy's Own' melodrama in *Intruder in the Dust*. When characters are first named and then enveloped in a quasi-archetypal darkness by being termed 'he' or 'she' when we next encounter them (so they resist identification by the reader), this may suggest a Proustian awareness that every man lives several lives (in *Light in August*, McEachern becomes Christmas; Burch becomes Brown; and Bunch is mistaken for Burch), but the potentially important epistemological

dilemma is really an authorial means of achieving good old fashioned
suspense. In many respects, Faulkner resembles a modernist Balzac;
there are cross-references to other novels (in *Light in August* there is
mention of Sartoris), there is an expansionist mystery-mongering, there
is the same sense of place. But the combination of Balzacian and
modernist tendencies leads to a confusion of the different stages of the
novel's evolution, rather than to a deliberate tension. The eclectic
virtuoso is less self-aware than is the agnostic.

The third alternative is represented by Beckett. The trilogy moves
from the pungent sense of locale found in *Molloy* to the intense, self-
devastating self-consciousness of *The Unnamable*, which rehearses Beckett's own earlier themes so as the better to reject them. The entire corpus
of his later work can be seen as the afterglow of this one ferocious
moment. After reading *Malone Dies*, one sees why Beckett was able to
react to his own work with such self-disgust, for the middle novel in the
trilogy is indeed the product of a mind too well acquainted with its own
iconography. The shortest and the most classical of the three novels, it
represents a belated modernist five finger exercise: Malone is a wax-
works 'Gerontion', and his death-bound career is too predictable. *The
Unnamable* is the furthest point of Beckett's novelistic development –
self-consciousness freed from the heavy labour of *Malone Dies* by its loss
of a body. The novel's rage is that of a disincarnate spirit, and it is
awsome and terrifying. It is the greatest, and the most disturbing of
Beckett's works, but unlike *Le temps retrouvé* it does not so much lift his
earlier novels into itself as bitterly cancel them out. Beckett himself
stated that this novel led him into an impasse from which it was difficult
to discover an exit. In a sense, his position here is akin to that of Larkin.
When Larkin's novelistic inspiration ran dry, he turned exclusively to
poetry; when, in the final novel of the trilogy, the story based on a single
character disintegrated into a nameless, unrealised potentiality, Beckett
turned to a form of theatre in which the self was broken up into an
assembly of dependent half-lives. For the position of the unnamable at
the centre of the moving satellites Murphy, Watt, Molloy and Malone is
the position of Hamm at the centre of the stage in *Endgame*.

In their different ways, each of these three novelists effected a disen-
gagement with modernism which at times seems to resemble a repression of the fact that it had ever been. That they did so renders questionable the view of a continuity of modernism propounded by Gabriel
Josipovici. Although his excellent *The World and the Book* is pervaded by a
sense of reverence that suggests that the canon is now closed, and
although it exudes a nostalgia for the heady days of early modernism, it

rationalises this nostalgia by allowing itself to assert that Saul Bellow and Muriel Spark are modernists too. Used in this way, the term 'modernism' becomes meaningless. One should be prepared to say 'there were Giants in those days' without indulging in wishful thinking to remove all suspicion of one's own inferiority.

THE ART OF LYING: THREE POST-WAR ENGLISH NOVELS

The degree to which modernism has withered as it has aged becomes apparent when one considers what seem to me to be the three most important post-war English novels: *Under the Volcano, Jill* and *The French Lieutenant's Woman*. One's depression over the course taken by the post-war novel in England deepens as one notes that only *The French Lieutenant's Woman* was written after 1950, outside the afterglow of modernism. *Jill*, Larkin's first novel, is superior to his second, *A Girl in Winter*, inasmuch as it is more concrete, more sharply focused; the fact that the girl in winter's native country remains unnamed indicates the debilitating lack of range that results from Larkin's notorious dismissal of 'foreign literature'. Fowles's novel is less perfect, and its deployment of European fictional modes is often awkward, but it represents a fine peak of achievement between the self-entranced glibness of *The Magus* and the too-remote beauty, the smooth creaminess, of *Daniel Martin*. Although gauche, or perhaps shaggy, Fowles's novel has aura; assurance furred with connotation. *Under the Volcano* distils Lowry's themes with an intensity he was never to recover; his later novels resemble assemblages of fragments from the floor of the cutting-room of his imagination.

These three novels have two important shared features. Firstly, they investigate the process of lying, the genesis of the self's secrecy and secretion in a realm apart from others. Their allusions to their own fictionality are thus oblique, without the common post-modernist facility (except perhaps at the end of Fowles's novel, where the alternative endings belabour a point). Secondly, because each writer is also a poet, he is able to evoke the pitfalls and fascinations of the imagination more convincingly than the ascetic, mathematically-minded post-modernists, such as Robbe-Grillet. The dialectic of poetry and prose, imagination and reality, relates them – however tenuously – to the great early modernists. Thus they avoid the sins of the English novel, which can be represented allegorically as grim philistinism (Amis), jaunty promiscuity (Burgess), forced myth-making (Golding) and pert gratuitousness (Spark). One need only add *Nineteen Eighty-Four* to this list of three novels and one has the four post-war novels I believe to be the most significant. If I omit *Nineteen Eighty-Four* from the thinly-honed peak of this pantheon, it is because it falls outside my thematic heading and can hardly be said to be poetic. It is however both a greater book than Orwell's pre-war novels, and a more fundamentally confused one. The confusion, of course, is the result of his having superimposed upon a realistic image of the shabbiness of rationed England a combined analysis of Stalinism and National Socialism, and cloudy projections for the future.

Of other post-war English novelists, Golding appears the most interesting, and yet none of his novels seems quite to succeed. His mechanical myths creak and clank along two-dimensional streets. In *Free Fall*, for instance, there is an air of mental wheels frantically churning, a frustrated medley of earthiness and religious speculation. His pungent imagism and games with the toy soldiers of history tend to tie down to earth the objects that wish to depart from it; Golding is the novel's Gulliver, finely bound by the Lilliputians. The dizzy, semi-mythical nausea of *Free Fall* pervades his work. He seems perpetually to be seeking the bludgeon into life a dead language.

This dead language is English English. When Larkin renounced the novel after *A Girl in Winter*, he made a prophetic decision: quite simply, he intuited that nothing more of interest could be done in the field in English *in England*. The springs of linguistic life had shifted to America above all. They did so when the whole world began to be 'Americanised'. And because the Anglo-Saxon world is becoming increasingly trans-Atlantic, the modern English novel can seem merely quaint, its realism further from reality than the apocalyptic fantasy of Thomas Pynchon. At a time when the consequences of technological advance are incalculable, fantasy becomes a form of realism, perhaps a speculative instrument for survival. At present, fantasy is the – often bitter – truth.

(a) *The French Lieutenant's Woman*

Riddles are concrete contradictions. If they were abstract one could simply banish them from reality and forget them; it is their insistent concrete bearing on the present that tantalises and torments. For Fowles, the concrete human riddle is called Sarah Woodruff. She is enigmatic because the world that frustrates her and the world in which her devising imagination triumphs are one and the same, because she assigns life and fiction to the same ontological plane.

John Fowles's novel is concerned with the necessity for existentialist choice, yet a strong determinist bias cryptically colours its existentialism: he writes of the *necessity* of choice. The early, existentialist Sartre confronts Marx; the freedom of the novelist, his arrogant craving for an Utopian re-arrangement or even annihilation of the existent, meets with the sociologist's exact attention to the deep-rooted flora of Victorian life. There is choice – a single duplicitous decision by Sam, Charles's manservant, redirects the intended course of events. And there is necessity – for in any case there can be no resolution of the difference between the classes, between Sarah and Charles, and he who rattles the bars of social and sexual taboo is finally driven outside the space of the English language and into the wilderness of silence, into Europe – as was Wilde. The England that exists in Fowles's sociology and non-exists in his fiction has another name however: America. In this novel, America is England displaced and replaced, the chance of a second life for the English speaker that will nevertheless communicate with his old one; that is, an Utopia(the place of fiction is 'Nowhere') that will not cut the individual off from his past and thus will not reinstitute the division within the self it promises to heal. The motif of the second (fictional) life recurs urgently and plangently throughout the book; after Sarah and Charles have made convulsive love in Endicott's hotel, Sarah interprets the event as proof that had she had a second life, she could have married Charles. Her hope of the Utopian second life is ironised at the very close of the novel, when she really has become another person (or has she?) and declines Charles's desperately proffered hand. America is Utopia inasmuch as it is the domain of the masculine feminine. It is a place where Sarah's assertion of her intellectual parity with men is a viable general style. But because the style is general it cannot express the individual, and no one is more hermetically herself than is Sarah. Utopia means 'no-place'; America is no place for Charles, for he was not born there or moulded to its ways, nor can it be a lasting abode for Sarah. It is a mirage, a place displaced and hanging in the air. The book's famous alternative endings are in one sense true alternatives: America (Bohemia) or England, fluidity or law, openness or closure. And yet in another sense they are not, for each of the proposed endings is impregnated with the same germ of burgeoning mystery. The liar who lies only part of the time (Sarah deceiving others; Charles deceiving himself) is a riddle, a Trickster, for he/she does not act 'in character' and is thus unpredictable, enforcing upon others an unremitting and dangerous choice of interpretations. To use fiction as part of one's life (Fowles insists that we are all novelists) is to attempt to force the wills of others to conform to one's own. Thus, at different points in the novel, Charles attempts to impose upon Sarah his dream-image of her, whilst Sarah strives to enmesh him in her designs, *her* novel: similarly, the proletarian Lovelace of *The Collector* had sought to pluck the strings of discord from the heart of the girl upon whose aura of connotation (wealth, freedom and so on) he was fixated.

This project to obliterate contradiction is ultimately insane, the Utopian dream-work of characters who wish to overthrow the entire structure of social and sexual contradictions that has assigned them their fixed places in existence. They prefer the invisibility and flux of non-existence, the declassed state of Ellison's *Invisible Man*. This urge is shared by Fowles as he weds the pieties of sociology to the novel's revolutionary desire to pursue an alternative reality, and as he carefully superimposes open structures upon closed ones upon open ones.... His novel is written in the twentieth century and unwritten in the nineteenth: an unwriting of the twentieth century by over- and under-writing it with a nineteenth-century evangelism and desire to instruct. Both the experimental and the didactic are seen to be equally interdependent, equally bankrupt. The writing that is unwriting (anti-writing) is the only means of representing the area of displacement. It is a palimpsest. In the most striking modern example of continental drift, several centuries ago England became America. For Fowles, this is a determining fact of life that also offers us a choice of identities; the emergence of America is the secretion of a separate identity from the hypocrisy of Albion. *The French Lieutenant's Woman*, with all its unevenness of tone and self-consciousness (a trait that partakes both of its modernism and of its nineteenth-century stuffiness), exemplifies perhaps better than any other novel the truth of Adorno's riddling dictum: 'the greatest art-works are those that succeed even at their most dubious points'. It grips with the compressed authority of an oracle – and it falls apart like a secondhand sub-modernist patchwork; it is formally ambitious and aware of literary theory in the American style, and earthbound in the English; it is aristocratic, allusive, Sphinxlike, and yet democratically blunt; and it both succeeds and fails. Of these contradictions it weaves its bewildering, engrossing web.

(b) *Jill*

When a character in a novel lies, he ceases to be a character; instead, he steps into the novelist's spare pair of shoes. As the lie is framed we witness the scandalous mystical transformation of the non-existent into the existent, of the frog into a prince. This is the theme of *Jill*, in which John Kemp invents a sister to whom he writes letters in order to win the envy of his room-mate at Oxford, an only child.

John Kemp's power, like the power of the artist, is the desperate resourcefulness of the powerless at bay. The non-existence that has crushed his own being comes to his aid as he draws upon the endless array of fictional existences resident within unbeing; he joins Sarah Woodruff in the annals of pathology and fabricates the sister, Jill, whose possession will grant him superior status in the eyes of his moneyed room-mate Christopher. (His dream-girl is compensatory and recalls the non-existent girl who haunts the poetry of the great Polish Symbolist poet Boleslaw Leśmian). But the confusion of fiction and reality he initiates eventually rebounds to his own disadvantage; he confuses his own imaginary Jill with a real Jill, the younger sister of Christopher's girl-friend.

A social world in which there is no communication between the classes is one in which members of one class cannot tell whether or not a member of the other is lying; the two worlds are so foreign to each other that each is as it were non-existent in the eyes of the other. It is the declassed, threatened member of the weaker class who first resorts to the lie. John Kemp, a scholarship boy from the North of England, is conscious of his inferiority in class to even Christopher (and here Larkin's irony is biting), the onetime pupil of a third-rate public school. He seeks to compensate for his inferiority; he cannot flee into a real artificial paradise, the paradise of drugs and travel that is open to the outsider or inferior within the upper classes. Similarly, in *The French Lieutenant's Woman*, Sam deceives Charles into believing that he has obeyed instructions and delivered a crucial note to Sarah, whilst Sarah herself leads the entire town of Lyme to believe that she surrendered her virginity to the departed French Lieutenant (and the scene of Charles's violent love-making in the Endicott hotel that unmasks this deception may itself be simply another veil: he may in fact have befallen Sarah during her period). Similarly, John Kemp devises his non-existent girl. The character who is non-existent – relegated to the domain of fiction by an author who re-enacts society's repression of that individual's right to exist – comes into being by negating himself a second time; he negates his self-negating life, not by recovering any primal assertiveness (which remains as inaccessible to him as it has ever been, and to this extent he continues acting 'in character' even when he steps outside the bounds of his character) but by leaning on and falling through a door disguised as a wall in the edifice of consciousness. He realises that in order to affect the predetermined course of a life one has to weave fictions; to weave and unweave them is to maintain control, like Penelope. But since he is by now too far removed from the reality he fears to be able to achieve the self-deceiving fictional reality that velvetly carpets the floors of most lives, he establishes a reality based on a lie in order to abolish the original reality. On becoming a liar he turns into an invisible man in a world of fluidities, departs the world whose fixed solids are detained by God's magnet. If all people really are novelists, there still remains a crucial difference between them and such weavers of fiction as John Kemp and Sarah Woodruff; most people apply unconsciously a stratagem for which John and Sarah reach out at the last moment of their existence and with the untutored hands of despair. The liar's Utopia is an anti-world that enviously apes the first world; that is why in these novels it appears in the light of pathos and accusation.

(c) *Under the Volcano*

As Peter Szondi remarks in his *Theorie des modernen Dramas*, the possibility of drama depends on the possibility of dialogue. When dialogue entered its crisis in the late nineteenth century, drama itself began a spectral after-life (as cinema?). Where dialogue is absent, so are events. The great modernist works are concerned with what happens to the voice when it speaks in a void, unassigned. The after-life of the drama is that of a burnt-out volcano. It is that of *Under the Volcano*, which rewrites the myth of Faustus and Faust in order to show why it can no longer be a drama. Throughout the novel dialogue repeatedly fails to come into being: words are related and are then described as unspoken, interchanges are punctuated by meaningless noises from neighbouring rooms, by dos Passos-like montages of the objects that distract the auditor, and statements repeatedly encounter the silences Lowry registers in the form of '–'. Events no longer occur. And the dynamic centrifugal force of Empire that has cast a man beyond his native shores recedes to leave him stranded, a token presence closer to an absence. Such is the semi-reality inhabited by the Consul.

When communication was seen by the modernist novel to have become problematic, fiction was tempted by the demon of solipsism; he whispered to the novelist that the person before him could well be less an objective fact than the product of the novelistic imagination. The temptation created a dilemma that rendered the formation of 'characters' problematic (I describe the aporia at length in my essay on 'Doubles'). Thus in *Under the Volcano* one finds both characters outside the Consul and voices within him, mocking demons. Because of the difficulty the modernist has in creating believable others – in believing that the others really are other and not, as soon as they have become writing, figures of his alienated self – in Lowry's novel only the Consul is truly credible, only his voice rings true. He represents a figure of tremendous pathos and absurdity, the least pretentious of all the encyc-lopaedic scholars who drift through modernist fiction. As Lowry's self-projection, he is both a character and the self. He is Lowry's double, and has come into being – as 'William Wilson's' double came into being – as a result of the self-destructive self-unknowing (of which drunkenness is a cipher) of his author. His semi-fictional, semi-autobiographical significance stands for the problem of Lowry's own identity.

For Lowry's dictum is *in vino veritas*; no other proverb records so strikingly the degree to which realism is fantasy; hallucination, truth. As Lowry was a compulsive liar – 'creative autobiographer' – in life, he could only divulge the truth in a form previously conceded to be a lie, a fiction. *Under the Volcano* is so laden with the burden of mythological doom as to verge on self-parody; this self-pararody corresponds to the experience of the loss of the self. That is why to tell the truth is to lie, why to love Yvonne is to seem indifferent to her; once language and gesture have ceased to express the self – the Consul's erect carriage belies his inebriation – then appearance becomes the realm of fiction. The paradox is total and terminal. Like Beckett – though far less drily – Lowry exploits the comedy of having reached rock-bottom; the Titan lies under the volcano and cannot fall any further. It is the marvellous comedy of the Consul's totally abortive encounter with Quincey in the garden, and it reverberates with tragedy when one recalls that the Consul's motive in approaching Quincey was a momentary craving for admiration. The apparently sober toper is a genius of bad faith, of anti-expressionist acting; he is the exhibitionist of a body that no longer bears any relationship to his own. That is why he can consider himself a jackdaw and a thief:

And it was as if, for a moment, he had become the *pelado*, the thief – yes, the pilferer of meaningless muddled ideas out of which his rejection of life had grown, who had worn his two or three little bowler hats, his disguises, over these abstractions: now the realest of them all was close.[1]

The remarks sound like a self-critical comment by Lowry on his own addiction to allusion. He adds:

But someone had called him *companero* too, which was better, much better. It made him happy.[2]

The company is the fellowship of the dead, whose names Lowry evokes by means of allusion; he too is a permanent inhabitant of the Day of the Dead. It is fitting that these remarks themselves should be followed by a string of allusions – to Mozart, Alcestis, Gluck, Bach.

Allusion is the mode in which the past is recovered in the form of a phantasm. It is the product of necromancy, which restores connections in the shape of mock connections when all real links with the past have been severed. This is what Faust discovers when he invokes the spirit of Helen; what the Consul discovers on invoking the ghost of Yvonne only to find that she has returned. The Consul's loss is that of all mankind: he has lost homeland and language in the drunken realm of endless transformation, in which spies become spiders, and Eve, Yvonne.

Allusions swarm over the pages of *Under the Volcano* like the insects that crawl across the walls whenever the Consul has a fit of *delirium tremens*. Thus the artistic method that distances Lowry's own delusions has its origin in them, in the experience of the crowd that overpowers the self. As one glances at an object, it seems to be itself, but slowly it starts to sprout allusions, connections; the experience is shared by the critic as he begins to write of one aspect of the novel and discovers that it is in the process of proliferating a nightmarish number of connections with the remainder of the work and is becoming overpowering. The novel is a machine for propagating the admirable delirium of the Consul. But the long trains of his thought's associations are going nowhere, are girdling Popocatapetl with smoke and lies as they climb to their fall.

THE SURVIVAL OF MODERNISM: SOME POST-WAR AMERICAN NOVELS

(a) *Invisible Man*

Ralph Ellison's *Invisible Man* is a strange, chequered book that is of key importance in the development of the American novel. It anticipates Mailer and Pynchon and the campus novel, whilst also sinking roots in Faulkner and expressionism. In the prologue to the novel there appears the image of a girl who lay in the dark and felt her face expand across the room; the darkness had no barriers to prevent her features from pouring out like molten wax. The invisible man himself is in a similar position, for his novel is equally formless; it has at least three discontinuous levels, and the transitions between them are like plunges through a trap-door.

First there is the dimension of an insane and threatening absurdism, a world of split rationality. Here there occurs Clifton's departure from the Marxist Brotherhood to sell racist dolls; his fall outside history is akin to the state of anti-paranoia into which Slothrop passes in the second half of *Gravity's Rainbow*. Similarly, when 'I' awakes in the hospital after a factory explosion to find himself the object of electric-shock therapy, the novel seems to have been gripped by a very modern paranoia (later to be vulgarised by Ken Kesey and Milos Forman). These sections throb alarmingly, like the waves in an epileptic's brain the moment before the fit.

Then there are the largely realistic sections devoted to the Brotherhood. But the conception of the Brotherhood is weak and inaccurate; a scientific, Marxist movement has somehow assumed the sort of name that suggests primitive emotional ties, as if it were in fact a Negro initiative. This confusing ambiguity relates back to the confusion about the nature of identity in the absurdist sections I have already mentioned. Thus the three levels interpenetrate and are not simply discontinuous. The confusion results from the struggle of two bodies – a white one and a Negro one – within one human frame; the result is typical of the grotesque as defined by Bakhtin. These sections are dated, realist in manner, and read more or less continuously, without any of the electric shocks found elsewhere in the novel. They represent Ellison's wish-fulfilment of a Marxist movement with popular support – obviously an absurdity during the period of the Cold War – and hence are as much fantasies as the clearly absurdist passages. To achieve this fantasy, Ellison has to suppress any mention of Marx himself. These sections are both artistically reactionary – a throwback to plodding Thirties documentarism – and an anticipation of the Negro radicalism of the Sixties. The duality appears most markedly in the figure of Ras the Exhorter, who is both the most modern figure and the one most commonly stigmatised as reactionary. The narrator's identification with the Brotherhood is total, as was his earlier absorption of college ideals, and there emerges a paranoid rhythm whereby a system is accepted in full and then spewed out in equal entirety. The Brotherhood represents system and realism; in allowing Clifton to fall outside it and outside history, the narrator decides to relinquish the flat, self-effacing idiom of the Brotherhood narrative. Where the Brotherhood talks of the inevitable laws of history, Clifton excludes himself from it: he fears that Marxist logic is really a white means of dulling black spontaneity.

Thus there are sections in which violence occurs too quickly and too shockingly to be understood (for it is seen from the perspective of the Negro, which lies outisde system), and there are others in which a turgid rationality prevails. Threaded through them are over-written, classically 'beautiful' descriptions, such as the description of the college as the narrator leaves it, in which Ellison earnestly masters the alien white mode of 'writing well':

The novel's ambiguities receive their dazzling focus in the speeches delivered by its hero, which are masterpieces of incoherence (for Ellison, speech in a crisis is simply a stammering biological eruption). During his speech on the sidewalk at the eviction one cannot decide whether he is for or against it, and finds his confusion embarrassing, only then to be surprised by the sight of him being praised for it by the leader of the Brotherhood. He is torn between toughness and tender-heartedness. And this is because he is 'both sacrificer and victim'[1] He can spend months soaking up Brotherhood ideology only then to fluctuate between the view that it is redemptive, and the suspicion that he can use it as a sophistic means of preserving his old practices. Similarly, the radicalism that says all Negroes are invisible to whites is muted by the repeated observation that the experience of invisibility began with his entry into a Northern city; the sociological rider defuses the inflammatory generalisation. And then the hero's protest against white prejudice is also an opposition to the Marxists for whom history follows a pattern and individuals are expendable. The narrative identifies the society with the articulate opposition to it, so that the only remaining possible course of action is inarticulate contestation. Ellison is both square and hip, and this is the source of his intriguing incoherence and multiple personality. Near the end of the novel he envisages in Rinehart an impossible synthesis of the two sides of his own personality: the insider and the outsider, the ambitious realist and the man spontaneously gliding through a world without boundaries. Rinehart is the invisible man's fictional version of himself, which is why his appearance heralds the end of the book. Here the invisible man becomes truly invisible, like a demon in possession of Rinehart. Once identified with Rinehart the invisible man is unmasked and revealed as a confidence man; his composition of the book has been a confidence trick that presumed the existence of a coherent personality where in fact there are only the constant shocks of death and rebirth (he is 'never the same'[2] and his legs are detachable).[3] Thus his book should be endless; endless, for one is not the same at the end of an enterprise as one was at its outset, a fact that is built into the trajectory of the novel from the very start by beginning with a prologue followed by a flashback: even at the beginning the author knew that this was not 'his' book, and his confidence trick has involved passing it off as his own story. But because he is an author, he also permits us to see through the trick; his work is presented as a novel because any claim to possess an identity is founded upon a fiction of the self. Like Rinehart, the novelist is implicated in the creation of the non-existent. He embodies nothingness in order to take ironic revenge upon those who never perceived him in the first place. He imagines how 'Jack and Norton and Emerson merge into one single white figure';[4] by superimposing them upon each other he clears the space where they had been, and into which his fictional identity can flow. One renders others invisible, swallows them up, so as to make oneself perceptible. Real people are the live bait the novelist uses to catch his unknown self, his Other. Ellison is a 'realist' novelist who seeks to 'overcome them with yesses', like his own narrator's grandfather; he seems to affirm the existence of the real world only in order more intensely to negate it. For in Ellison, as in Thomas Mann, the real world is grotesque.

(b) The Crying of Lot 49: Mirrors, Paranoia and the Senselessness of an Ending.

Despite the undoubted intelligence of much of the existing Pynchon criticism, one reads even the fine essays of Richard Poirier, Tony Tanner and Edward Mendelson with a mounting sense of disappointment. For, by placing him solely within the framework of literary criticism, they mute the radicalism of his novels, sub-dividing them into a neat series of lots and themes that prevent us from perceiving what – if any – necessity has gathered together all this exotica and information from different fields. None of them seems sufficiently to register the devastating kinetic effect exerted upon one's imagination by his montages of history and fiction and suggestions of subterranean connections between them, for none are prepared to enter the vulnerable empty space *between* intellectual partitions within which his novels situate themselves. Moreover, Pynchon's awareness of cinema and its near-mystical capacity to overwhelm the viewer is alien to them. I will try to remedy this omission in part by suggesting some parallels between The Crying of Lot 49 and two films in particular, Blow up and Vertigo. And I will try to indicate the seriousness of Pynchon's engagement with low culture by comparing him with the inventor of one of the archetypes of popular art, Edgar

Allen Poe. But one doubts that there exists anyone capable of pulling together all the threads in his work; certainly not the author of these notes. Since no one can master all the detail, one's sole hope of understanding him is to concentrate upon the system that accumulates them, to which the key is paranoia and its relation to the reader's (or viewer's) experience of plot as an authorial, authoritarian conspiracy. Paradoxically, it is the very impossibility of mastering all the esoteric domains he freely annexes that enables us to comprehend this feature of his work; it engenders within us the paranoia, the desire to split and multiply the self, of which he writes. Paranoia postulates the existence of an endlessly displaced process of signification akin to the series of self-abolishing signs described by Derrida. Here the Marxist affiliations of the French Post-Structuralist meet up with Pynchon's radicalism, for the endless displacements of paranoia obey the same laws of postponed satisfaction as an economy based on advertisements. This endless displacement is the pursuit of meaning in a system that has become irrational. Pynchon is aware – as the Post-Structuralists aren't – of the extent to which his strategies mirror those of his society. This is clear from the 'ending' of *The Crying of Lot 49*, which leaves in suspense the question of whether or not W.A.S.T.E. exists. Pynchon's decision to break off here is both an artificial evasion of the necessity of decision – a retrospective criticism of the whole book – and a brilliant image of the impossibility of rational explanation. The polymorphous desire of Oedipus become Oedipa – having undergone a sex-change to stand on both sides of sexuality – 'says everything', as 'Tel Quel' aesthetics demand, and yet stops short of saying the most vital of things.

Repeatedly critics have stressed only the black comic side of Pynchon's work, and there has been a general critical failure to confront his mixture of a cool, hip skitteriness with a paper-thin, exposed fragility. His offhand comic manner is in fruitful contradiction with the passages of plangent lament; both stem from a doubt whether or not anyone is listening, for if they were, the tone might be tidied up or cooled down. This tone is either thrown-away or intensely precious: lonely and masochistic, or preserving itself through narcissism. His heady comedy has an eerie detachedness, as if the jokes were flowing from the drink alone and not the self-alienated drinker. He sits back and watches the steady parade of cartoon thought-balloons emerge from his mouth like chewing-gum or elegant smoke rings and burst. The alienation is that of writing in a state of possession by an idea (as did Gogol), with the rending desire to escape the self's solipsism and be possessed by a plot or a lover (usually both). Oedipa's hope that 'here in San Narciso, away from all tangible assets of that estate, there might still be a chance of getting the whole thing to go away and disintegrate quietly'[5] corresponds to Pynchon's wish that his own obsessions would dissolve in the clear water of science that has injected into the water that very fluoride he fears.

For Pynchon, 'the present' is alienated from itself by the consumerism that renders it a place in which times fantastically interpenetrate; the eclecticism is that of America's pile-up on hitting the West Coast. This interpenetration takes the form of metaphor, which evokes the present's spectral distance from itself. Different cultures intertwine tropically upon one spot; in the hot house of desire, neons of different seasons flower simultaneously. Metaphor means 'travelling', the classic American experience, living in the car that screens one from objects. One's indifference to them lets them slide by in a mediocre fashion-parade, which to the X-ray eye is simply capital's homogenised army marching on the spot. His metaphors are powerful yet tremendously delicate, even precious:

> What the road really was, she fancied, was this hypodermic needle, inserted somewhere ahead into the vein of a freeway, a vein nourishing the mainliner L.A., keeping it happy, coherent, protected from pain, or whatever passes, with a city, for pain.[6]

The repetition and hesitations show how the atom of thought is split so as to give afterthought the same weight as thought, as a simile emerges and is then criticised for its divergence from the facts. Oedipa's thoughts, like those of all in an already subjugated landscape, are those of someone who has come too late. With reality already complete as a hostile system or a mist so all-pervading as to offer itself for alteration at no point, the urge to understand inevitably shades off into self-defeating fantasy. Her fate depends upon someone who has already died (Pierce Inverarity) even before the book begins. Pynchon's description hesitates because nothing sits still long enough to be depicted with accuracy. There can only be the multiple exposure of perceptions whose metaphorical blur one finally rationalises by seeing connections between the random. His nervously rhetorical phrases lean back from 'reality'; the rhetoric is the tinted windscreen and the nervousness the squinting eye trying to peer through it to things as they really are. Events are sketchy and incomplete, for in a homogenised culture so much is taken for granted that gestures are so standardised that they need only be partly carried out to be recognised; but this incompleteness is the point of dialectical reversal of sameness, for sketchy gestures give the imagination room in which to distort their nature. Fantasy begins to impinge upon nominally public languages to a far greater extent than hitherto.

In *The Crying of Lot 49* – Pynchon's finest book – the metaphors move insecurely with falling cadences. Later, in *Gravity's Rainbow*, they become more strident, but here they give off a poignant heat-haze of yearning, movement towards identity with otherness. Since the consciousness establishing the metaphors is constant (Oedipa: and since the novel is largely concerned with narcissism, the third person form does not preclude its having been written by Oedipa herself) one does not as yet have the total flux and triumph of indifference that mars *Gravity's Rainbow*, for behind each metaphor one senses her urge to make contact. The metaphors, like the lists and rows of periods that later become obsessive, embody failure to grasp objects. Unable to understand them, one imposes upon them the momentary myth that is metaphor, or suppresses them by moving to another, as in Pynchon's lists. This is the basic strategy of the criticism of Benjamin and Adorno, and their modern relevance stems from the growing frequency of such experiences. The sole difference is that Benjamin privileges the metaphor whilst Adorno relies upon paratactic construction. The metaphors' stridency in *Gravity's Rainbow* testifies to a will to force into unity elements that have come apart, whereas in the earlier novel, they are caught on the verge of fragmentation, hanging reflected in the single raindrop of Oedipa's consciousness before it tumbles to dash in a split constellation. Here in his masterpiece they vibrate poetically, and like all vibrations the novel has a centre of dispersal – Oedipa, and the American present that contains the baroque divagations that run amok in *Gravity's Rainbow*, which is set exclusively in a past not experienced by the author himself. There is here none of the sentimentality that colours the Erdschweinhoehle strand in the later novel. Pynchon projects himself into the past because of his fear that the present's annexation of the past may have soaked up all possibility of otherness. He fears that all history is linked by myth and power – the two negative components isolated by the Critical Theory of the Frankfurt School – and so tries to preserve the past by stressing its resistance to comprehension. The fault in *Gravity's Rainbow* is that it – unlike the earlier novel – takes a total leap into the past and so destroys the tension between it and the present from which he has departed, thus rendering impossible any theory of self-consciousness. Thus the reflexes conditioned in the past repeat themselves blindly in Slothrop's present experience; the fatalistic parable precludes any possibility of freedom, for 'A. and B. are unreal, are names for parts that ought to be inseparable', as the Ouspenskians say.[7] Difference has been erased, as the mathematical process of integration transforms the rocket's motion into stasis. In both novels, the concern with the past is the search for the father in an attempt to discover whether or not one's own actions simply act out a predetermined scene. The Father Conspiracy dominates the later novel. In the earlier one, Pierce Inverarity is referred to as a 'founding father'.[8] The name Oedipa underlines the relationship to the father as well as the possible unity of history stretching backwards to Greece in incarnations of an anthropological archetype. Yet it also severs links with the past, for it sounds like a comic-strip character's name, part of the forgettable, entropic everyday. In *Gravity's Rainbow*, however, the hermetic restriction of the past to a single period in the twentieth century, together with the projection of modern attitudes into that period, seems complacent in its flattening of historical perspective. In *The Crying of Lot 49*, as 'Oedipa' – Oedipus with a feminine ending – the heroine occupies two times, the time of action and the time of passivity, spanning history in a paradoxical icon. She is Oedipus before and after the blinding, the symbolic castration that renders him feminine-Oedipa.

Pynchon's concern with otherness leads to the theme of multiple personality. Fausto in *V* had remarked that 'we can justify any apologia simply by calling life a successive rejection of personalities', a credo reflected in Pynchon's own rows of stylistic parodies. Late in *The Crying of Lot 49* Oedipa's husband Mucho is described as coming into the room like a crowd of people. Pierce Inverarity was given to ringing her up and uttering imitations of various accents. And then there are the recurrent references to a Pentecostal talking in tongues. The mixed style so common among American writers, which is driven to an extreme in Pynchon, is an attempt to please everyone; it internalises the conflicting voices of a democracy that can seem to resemble a paranoid plot against the formation of any independent centre of unity. The isolated individual yearns for a community with a Pentecostal voice that will permit him to preserve his isolation within its polyphony. This two-way movement nourishes his interest in the relationship between vision and language that branches off into an obsession with movies and comic strips. The visible object is accessible to all but is also mystified until we can go behind it to perceive its roots in a system. Metaphor breaches the object's opaque resistance, garners an X-ray of its meaning by transporting us behind it to the point at which it meets up with system; and yet we can always counteract the reduction whereby metaphor inserts objects into the publicly ratified obsessions embodied in language; we can do so by returning to vision, to the uncategorised concrete fact, to silence. Oedipa achieves community at night, in the space of dream where people split and rearrange themselves. As she wanders at night, dream and reality mingle for her. As Oedipa (blinded Oedipus and a member of a cool, rationalist generation apt to scholarship) she relies on words alone, and their echoes cause paranoia. Everywhere there lie the signs of waste, and perhaps by means of a pun the dream converts these unrelated derelict objects into 'signs of W.A.S.T.E.'. The plot does and does not exist. Dream materialises language by transforming words into images – by unearthing the metaphors they conceal – and thereby both questions the private obsessions that persecute Oedipa and grants them official recognition by according them the status of external reality. Everything is waste and so can become a sign of W.A.S.T.E., for the eye that would have seen the periods between the letters and realised that it should be read as an acronym has been put out. The spoken word unites, its homonyms the basis of puns; the written one divides.

By means of his interest in multiple personality – the chameleon personality essential to a writer in whom historian and novelist are engaged in dialogue – Pynchon examines the way in which the personality's contingencies and flaws undermine the unity of 'character' constructed by the plotting imagination. In *The Crying of Lot 49*, the tension between plot and entropic irrelevance is reinforced by one between integration of all facts into a trans-historical conspiracy and the way the modern world, by experiencing all history simultaneously, breaks out of history. In the final chapter of *Mythes, rêves et mystères*, Mirca Eliade suggests the possibility of interpreting the development of a precise historiography in the twentieth century as the equivalent of memory summoning all life's details in the instant of death. This tension generates another one between tragic seriousness (a tragedy is experienced as an organic whole and works cumulatively) and the fragmenting mechanisation seen as characteristic of comedy by Bergson. But even this opposition is dialectical, for comedy can serve paranoia and need not simply fragment; the pun yokes objects together. The whole novel is a pun on the meanings of 'plot', whilst 'Tristero' refers to both *tristesse* and trysts. The sadness of all trysts would render Oedipa another 'Caballero de la Trista Figura'. No wonder Pynchon is drawn to Rilke, whose puns combine humour and pathos in similar fashion, as in *Ausgesetzt auf den Bergen des Herzens* (*Cast out on the heart's mountains*), where there is play with the resemblance between *Bergen* (mountains) and *geborgen* (sheltered). Oedipa's name focuses the duality of the pun; the allusion to Oedipus presents the possibility that she, like him, refuses to recognise the truth (consciously?), but the alteration of the name mocks any mythical significance we may be tempted to read into it, as well as satirising the way that characters in American novels are so often assimilated to mythical typologies. The name may be a parodistic overload of Meaning, like the moment late in the novel when she passes the bookshop that sold copies of Wharfinger's play and notices that it has been burnt down. This touch seems too good/bad to be true, as signs of doom monotonously phalanx to parody the massed coincidences of melodrama: that is, of the form of art that makes us most aware of its plot's manipulations. The work dizzyingly fuses thriller with parody of the thriller with a modernist critique of the imagination; high and low culture are linked in an absurd conspiratorial totality.

In its melodramatic coincidences, the novel resembles a detective story or thriller. In common with much French *avant garde* fiction – for instance, Robbe-Grillet's *Les Gommes* – it enlists the thriller's positivist, intellectual linearity to frustrate the very expectations it arouses, simultaneously preserving the classic detective story's concern with paranoia and narcissism. Yet such works do not simply undertake the kind of polemical parody of linearity ascribed to them by Post-Structuralist critics; they also use linearity to achieve their own being, to counteract the chronic doubt and tendency to helpless stasis that looms behind their lists (or series of alternative actions) that leave untouched the reality the detective seeks to penetrate. They combat the consumer's wavering before the display of equally superfluous goods. Oedipa Maas is in the long line of American detectives that ends with her lost Chandleresque figure at the edge of the sea of mystery, at the edge of consciousness, the point at which America's dream-factory had to be situated, next to the Pacific, abode of sleep and the lost moon's scar. Classically, the detective story links narcissism and paranoia, its fictional pattern anticipating Freud. The detective is usually male and alone; if he has a companion, he too is male. This friend is his narcissistic mirror and foil: Holmes is an artist and intelligent, whereas Watson is a bumbling *homme moyen sensuel*. Watson is Holmes stepping outside himself to admire the elegance of his own logic; as such, he represents and closes off the reader's identification with Holmes, who is the creator of the plot. The artistic success of the Sherlock Holmes stories stems from their ability to channel the symbolist *fin de siècle's* concern with narcissism and mirrors. The detective trails his intelligent double like his own suppressed evil or the demonic woman. He tracks himself in order to rectify the mistake in the course of his crime that he fears would permit others to find him out; he is paranoid, for he imagines that the tiniest clue will suffice to betray him. As a result of this, he detaches himself from his old fallible self and treats that self as criminal; its crime was to let him down. He relinquishes action, which is inevitably error-ridden, for God-like contemplation of the plot. In all these respects the prototype of all subsequent detectives is Dupin in Poe's *The Purloined Letter*, who is remarkably similar to the villain he entraps. The *femme fatale* attracts in Decadent iconography because she represents the mother as prostitute, someone who gave herself to another man (the father) before the son met her. (She is also a pro-stitute in the sense Laing has isolated in his brilliant chapter on 'Crime and Punishment' in *The Self and Others*: she stands for someone else. When otherness becomes immanent, as it did at the turn of the century with the death of God, one's God has to be the only earthly consciousness tinged with otherness with which one is acquainted: woman). Oedipus was the first detective and the feminine ending of Oedipa's name suggests hermaph-roditism or homosexuality; the detective's paranoia is due to a decision to turn homosexual (in his account of Judge Schreber's delusion, Freud links paranoia with homosexuality), since the mother has already betrayed him. For him, as for Pynchon, the decisive event occurs before his arrival in the world. Stripped of any companion whose similarity to himself would enable him to understand and question his own suspi-cions, the detective becomes an expressionist hero whose limbs fly off like a marionette's at the behest of the controlling father, then to assume the form of nightmarish projections; these mock the body's impotence as it is propelled through events in a manner reminiscent of a picaresque comic strip. As hermaphrodite, Oedipa embraces all knowledge, and hence everyone and no one can identify with her. Pynchon's stylistic arabes-ques also recall the *fin de siècle*, and they too embody paranoia; the arabesque stems from a belief that *everything* executed by the genius, however sketchy, is worth preserving; the stress on everything derives from every detail's affiliation to the universal plot. The ambiguous sexuality is of Decadent provenance: Slothrop too is mas-culine/feminine, with sex being as much suffered as initiated by him. The *fin de siècle*, like Pynchon, was obsessed by mirrors because the mirror both denied the difference between the sexes by implanting sameness in the place of the other *and* reaffirmed the impossibility of absolute sameness by inverting the image in the process of reflecting it. Reproducing the image in the mirror fills the world with males and so appeases the fear of castration caused by the woman's lack of a penis. The mirror image is the self's after-life upon earth. The Death of God had rendered transcendence immanent, and man who has created God becomes his own divinity.

The *fin de siècle* problematic evoked various responses concentrated in the figures of the artist-hero, the double, the vampire, the *femme fatale* and the detective. The first writer to link these themes had been Poe, the epoch's hero. This problematic of vagueness and suspense was a reaction to the fact that in the city fog of a mystified reality events ocurred with shocking abruptness, only later becoming susceptible of decipherment. The world bears the insignia of felony stamped upon it by the instant changes effected by industrialisation and urbanisation. Faced with such shock, with the suddenness that so blurs events as to give them the vagueness that characterises the style of Decadent works, the writer projects himself out of the present moment into the future – an after-life or resurrection – from which the present will take on a coherent pattern. This projection is carried out by autoscopy and its primary result is the double or Narcissus. Its positive embodiment is the detective (male); its negative incarnation, the vampirical living corpse who is usually female (writers suddenly fear women, for a generation of female writers is about to shake male supremacy); and the mediating bridge between them is the artist as hero, the writer's self-representation. Thus all Poe's works propose transformations of the same underlying problematic. The detective is like a writer putting together all the pieces of a story, searching for the principle of their unity, i.e. plot, and the majority of the work takes place in the ante-chamber before the coda that is the detective's telling of the story to its uncomprehending participants. Before this coda there is a caesura which is described by Hoelderlin as the eccentric centre characteristic of *Oedipus Rex* (*Anmerkungen zum Oedipus*): it is no accident that this play has been described as the prototype of all subsequent detective stories. This interest in the process of composition is what has led the recent *avant garde* to detective stories. Suspense is waiting for things to come right, for a pattern to emerge at the base of the kaleidoscope shaken by imagination, by inspiration's *coup de dés*. This is the reason why only almost-artists practise the genre *sensu stricto*. Chandler and Conan Doyle, for instance, are not prepared to reflect upon their own stories but flee from them into another story, the explanatory coda, which provides a wish-fulfilment of how things should come right. Pynchon's seriousness, by way of contrast, is shown by his willingness to reflect upon his fiction and by his refusal to prick the bubble of suspense with an anti-climactic explanation. *His* coda is the silence after the text's unresolved final dissonance. For the detective, a story is not given – his own life cannot be recounted – but has to be found, as do the scattered components of the lives of a mobile society's inhabitants. His own experience has been annihilated, and so he is hard-boiled, a mere cog in the machine of system, the ghost in the machine. He descends from Peter Schlemiel (is it significant that detectives are termed 'schlemiels'?), the man who lost his shadow. He shadows the criminal. This loss causes his narcissistic isolation. It is no mere coincidence that both *The Crying of Lot 49* and Hitchcock's *Vertigo* are set on the West Coast, at the brink of mystery represented by the veiling ocean. In Hitchcock's film there is also the theme of narcissism (Madeleine sits before her own portrait) and there too this narcissism reaches into the past (the girl in the portrait is really her grandmother). The detective's black-outs due to vertigo match Madeleine's spells of amnesia and stand for the unconscious, the other place behind/below one that is inaccessible to one's vision (for this is a *film*) and so threatens, for no partner provides a pair of covering eyes. Spinning around in a split second to look in two directions almost simultaneously, one suffers the vertigo due to imminent loss of identity, of one's situation; one splits the second and so destroys time's successiveness. The detective is a camera; the double-look is shot/reverse shot. As such, he is also the megalomaniac maker of the film herself. He 'makes Judy up', buying her clothes that will reveal her similarity to Madeleine, as one makes up a story, the nightmare wish fulfilment of her identity with the lost lover. Only if one identifies the detective with the narrator can one understand his purpose in this making her up; otherwise, his motivation seems – as it is, fixated upon the living dead – perverted and opaque. The living dead are people who have become interchangeable in a social system that seeks to eradicate difference; their paranoia is a fear that they will be sacrificed and replaced by an identical neighbour. The moments of unconsciousness endured by Hitchcock's detective are the blanks filled in in earlier detective stories by the appearance of his companion. These moments symbolise sleep, our apprehension about the possibility that events crucial to our fate are in motion unbeknown to us. Macbeth's murder of sleep is in the child's desire to enjoy perpetual wakefulness and stay awake with the adults; it is a rebellion against authority's limiting of knowledge. (The cruellest form of authority's mystification is the prophecy of the witches). The detective is a paranoid pilgrim whose destination – in a secularised environment, where everything is important – has to be everywhere and nowhere. This is why Pynchon withholds the end.

The mirror preserves and inverts the image. In *Gravity's Rainbow* the relation between mirror and image is that between American and English English. Does the relation and divergence involve a sexual paradox, as would be suggested by the name 'Oedipa' and by Henry James's interest in Americans in Europe and choice of mostly female central figures? The Latin for 'mirror' is *speculum*. *The Crying of Lot 49*'s investigation of the mirror unearths the multiple meanings of 'speculation'.[9] Speculation may involve narcissism, a paranoid neurosis; the free imagination may be determined by an invisible prior Gestalt, which lies below the horizon of awareness in the same way as Pierce Inverarity's life precedes the story of Oedipa, so that we cannot know whether or not *he* devised its plot. He is invisible like the writer-god, whose tracing of the theme of the double is an attempt to see himself, to confirm his own existence and, more importantly, to see God himself. To see oneself is to be as God, free of constrictions. Mental and capital speculation may be interdependent, as Marxism asserts when in terms all intellectuals *petit bourgeois*; Pierce Inverarity's capital speculations may finance the plot that fuels Oedipa's speculations. When she imagines herself trapped in a tower, she resembles the Lady of Shalott before the mirror breaks. The self-relationship enshrined by the mirror results in the impossibility of either love or death, a constant feature of Pynchon's fiction. Love is impossible, for there is no other; and so is death, for the murderous other is oneself. As a mirror to the self, speculation traps it in solipsism, but as 'mere speculation' it is an hypothesis that may be discarded, so all knowledge hovers between romantic self-projection and science. When Oedipa pronounces W.A.S.T.E. as one word, is she right to see the initials as connoting entropy, or is she entirely mistaken, as the technician's negative reaction would suggest? If she is wrong, so were we when we read it as a reference to the theme of entropy – Pynchon is right to disturb our self-satisfaction by demonstrating that even a detail that appears blandly to illustrate 'a typical Pynchon theme' is in fact more complex than that. Tony Tanner has remarked on the connection between rubbish and fantasy pointed to by W.A.S.T.E. This connection should be understood as the reassertion of nature at the very heart of culture as its artefacts decompose, pass out of society's totality. By doing so they evade system and so become amenable to the dreaming imagination's pursuit of private significances. Similarly, the whole novel grows out of society as parasitic fantasy and yet also criticises that society in the name of the otherness it suppresses.

It is probably no accident that at roughly the same time during the 'Sixties' there appeared both *The Crying of Lot 49* and Antonioni's *Blow Up* (as well as the Cortazar story upon which the latter is based). Both works are about the way a bored milieu or person manufactures a mystery to relieve tedium and keep itself going. At the point of society's maximal affluence, development carries on only in the sphere of the imagination; the sated body lies still and safe and only the smoke of a marijuana hallucination moves in the air above it-the hippies colonised mystery. Thus both works in question grow with an almost obsessive force in the mind after their experience, for their unfinished search for a decisive event hands the torch to us when they break down; Pynchon's text goes silent and Antonioni's photographer is wiped off the screen, leaving only serene green grass, an instant moss over his gravestone. The detective turned ghost passes through the walls of the book and into our minds. The text dies and its nails and hair carry on growing.

Questioning the imagination, Pynchon implicates the reader in a searching inquisition of his own imagination, and this shock effect has been too little considered by critics. Historical fact ought to offer firm bedrock, but Pynchon's pop tones stem from awareness that history's relevance to the present is dubious. Certainly there have always been apocalyptic moods parallel to our own, but were these moods ever validated by the facts to the extent that they are now? And the imagination that recreates history for us does not so much transmit it as make it new. Fiction is a relief from the positivist world, whose weight it momentarily lifts by dematerialising it and so freeing the subject; but this freedom can itself become the prison-house of unvalidated delusion. Pynchon is concerned with the extent to which we can and cannot control reality – his eremitic isolation is an attempt to control how much is known about him, to resist easy integration into society's computer-bank. The attraction exerted upon him by spies and secret societies is obvious, since if his subject matter is secret, how can one be sure it is fictional? At moments whilst reading him one is tempted to interpret his works as a Secret Gospel; he taps the side of supposedly respectable intellectuals that hankers for the hidden numinous worlds of U.F.O.s and parapsychology. He undermines the illusion of a unitary consciousness whilst also recognising his project's danger–destructuring is madness as well as liberation. Thus the increasing number of ellipses near the end of *Gravity's Rainbow* accompanies both Slothrop's disintegration and a possible revelation. Pynchon's passion is strong enough to turn us all into paranoid scholars like Oedipa, reaching for encyclopaedias to check whether or not a particular detail in his texts is factual. The modern lack of common knowledge due to specialisation allows us to read history as novel, the unverifiable fiction of an unknown scholar.

The last pages of *The Crying of Lot 49* hang agonisingly between either and or, whilst the rest granted us once the book closes may be tense expectation or the blanking out of a consciousness no longer able to sustain the pressure of paradox. The text's sudden silence, veering off into the unspeakable, may be the blinding of Oedipus, the symbolic castration that would render him Oedipa; the last sentence's quotation of the title suggests a circularity whereby the beginning and the end are one in an instant of compressed mystical time. In the threatening atmosphere immediately before the auction, where the pale men recall the gaunt murderers of *The Courier's Tragedy* and the closing of doors is like the sealing off of an execution chamber, there is the paranoid possibility that all this has been arranged to achieve Oedipa's ritual murder. The last sentence refers to the book's beginning and so invites us to re-read in order to rectify the mistakes that caused it to break down at this crucial moment. The collapse may be due to the plot's origin in Oedipa's personal fantasy *or* to its actual endless ramifications – the last pages consider the problem to be no less than America itself – which would make it unimaginable, as if it had never been. In that case, in order to perceive it one would have to select an Archimedean point outside the country and the plot, and since the plot is inextricably interwoven with the book, one can pass outside it only by entering silence. Near the close there is mention of a mysterious C. M. S. Schrift; in German, his name means 'writing' and hints at the possibility that writing itself, being the medium of the underground postal system, is the prime source of threat. Were that to be so, Pynchon would join Lévi-Strauss in locating the origins of enslavement in the invention of writing. If history has a plot, its hieroglyphs indicate a God who lives in a cloud of unknowing.

The unimaginable and unspeakable, nameless as horror, are the subject of the entire book. If there is a secret organisation, how can we be sure it doesn't exist? This aporia is the self-fulfilling source of all paranoia. It affects the 'Sixties' and the West Coast – the home of the Underground – in particular. How can the Underground present an alternative to existing society if it is amenable to consumption by the mass media? It is culture's dream of freedom and an impossibility, like a paradise among rubbish dumps. Hence all evocations of otherness must, like Pynchon's, be self-mocking, aware that they probably destroy what they purport to record. The text's silence at this point crowns Pynchon's structure of ambiguities. Nothing is richer or poorer or more indeterminate in meaning than silence, as in the novel's final tableau; as Gombrich has stressed, the image without a context established by language is inherently ambiguous. Silence constitutes a romantic attack upon authority; it is utopian and independent of our demands, like the taciturn Christ of Dostoevsky's Grand Inquisitor parable. Ambiguity reflects Pynchon's radicalism, for there can be no unitary, authoritative reading, only the clash of diverse interpretations. Books favour the hidden; they are read and written by those who feel invisible, for to read is to step outside the social circuit, to dematerialise oneself from the face of the present earth. Thus the book opposes society's growing centralisation. At its close, Pynchon's book freezes between contraries, giving way to the mechanical demands of an either/or symmetry in a manner that helps one to realise that for him machines can live because people can think as digitally as machines. (The symmetry is also a formal rider of the mirror theme.) People think thus in states of affluence, when there is no pressing imperative for choice; the affluence of fantasy reflects the impossibility of action. The radicalism that assigns to a woman the traditionally male role of the detective becomes ambiguous as one recognises that she obtains this role only because *her* stereotyped helplessness equips her for it. As Pauline Kael remarked of Marlowe in Robert Altman's version of *The Long Goodbye*, the detective has become Miss Lonelyhearts. The imagination of the traditional detective who relates the story at the end has broken down. Hence the absent final page retails unimaginable events that can be shrugged off as immaterial or feared as invisibly omnipotent. The only contemporary *lingua franca* is silence, and this is why throughout the 'Sixties' radical thought laid emphasis on the silent speech of the body. As picaresque fantasy filling out the polymorphous realm of both/and, the book is excluded from the space of either/or, of choice; its approach to this space signals its own demise. The ending is both relaxed and terrifying. A modest historian, Pynchon admits that the facts will not bear the interpretation he has imposed on them, as he hides the rickety framework of his narrative with an embarrassed smokescreen of silence; a hellfire preacher, he claims that the smoke swirls up from the maw of the abyss; it is the threat of growing monopoly by an advancing system.

For Pynchon, the novel is a paradoxical point of consciousness between contrary definitions of truth: the naturalistic/realistic and the purely fantastic. *The Crying of Lot 49* is Pynchon's most conscientious embodiment of this dialectic. The interaction occurs because the first premise of realism is the fantastic belief that one can know everything important about a person, whilst the basis of fantasy is the sceptical conviction that one cannot. With two definitions of truth, reality is decentered. Day and night are superimposed the one upon the other. But this decentering is not the total displacement envisaged by 'Tel Quel', for the notion of centre is preserved, as well as criticised, by duplication. *The Crying of Lot 49* has a central consciousness, but its naming as *Oedipa* relativises it, partly because the name extends a mythological series and so undoes the primacy of the individual, partly because its comic-strip improbability (compare Phoebe Zeitgeist) functions as an alienation effect. The comic-strip name evokes the frustration of the blinded that is part of the Oedipus motif; we hanker for the cartoon of her that has been suppressed, and in its absence cannot tell whether or not she should be treated as a one-dimensional woman.

Mary Douglas has remarked that marginal areas, since they resist categorisation, are sources of purity and danger. The purity and danger emanated by Pynchon's characters is that of sexual taboo, as a result of which all sexual encounters are momentary; waves of shock carry one away from each lover. His incredible sensitivity to fleeting detail and to the poignancy of its loss is part of his interest in unofficial history. There is the sadness of isolated facts, which seem as eccentric outside their native contexts as do the majority of Pynchon's characters. At a time when the main streams of tradition freeze over, the writer cannot draw large draughts of water; he can only chip small particles from the ice, or seek further afield. Like the hero of Antonioni's *Blow Up*, he and Oedipa enlarge the image of reality to render visible the hidden. Nevertheless, since the concealed healing element can only be obtained after hard labour, having been preserved only by the unconscious (which, as the complexity of Freud's analyses demonstrates, is adept at hiding anew), it resists the grasp of the conscious mind. It resembles that species of fish that bursts upon touching the surface. Hence both Oedipa and Antonioni's hero are helpless in the face of their own findings. If the text goes silent at the close it does so as Oedipa's disavowal of her experience.

Pynchon's light-sensitive mind records the detail at the edge of the retina as an insurance policy on the meaningfulness of the central image. This is a means of rejecting its centrality even as that image provides the text's organising structure. The shapeless, half-perceived detail is likely to be moulded in accordance with unacknowledged desires that seize upon it as their sole outlet; its fleetingness precludes its return to deny the validity of those desires. Thus paranoid systems are self-validating; the desire to believe in something is identical with the desire to believe in nothing, in mere fiction (hence the emergence of Negative Theology out of Christianity was inevitable: God's remoteness above the clouds was always the expression of belief in a supreme, unverifiable fiction that gave the believer the total freedom of 'unbelief'). That which will not return cannot be disproved. Thus Oedipa cannot establish contact with the reality that might disconfirm her hermetic system; silence stops its last gap. Can she know whether or not the modified final couplet of *The Courier's Tragedy* was uttered on the night of the performance she attended? Was the original Tristero a madman, an honest rebel, a confidence-man, or not a man at all, merely a trick deriving from Pierce Inverarity's fear of death and desire for posthumous life in the form of an unsolved riddle? Or rather, in the formlessness of a riddle. The riddle congeals in our mind to resist consumption; the impossibility of forgetting the unease it provokes leads to a suppression of its actual details. This is why Poe's stories are so different to recount; their baroque complexity is the means whereby the narrator asserts that despite appearances and despite the degree of his Romantic alienation he is not superfluous, for he possesses a skill which cannot be transmitted. If he is then allowed to live forever, it is however as the Sibyl in the bottle who would rather die. A similar desire for after-life drives writers since Poe to the detective story; and Pynchon in his virtuosity selects the most memorable form of the detective story, the story without an ending. In the tension between reality and fantasy his art outlives death by embracing it; the artist's disappearance indicates the necessity of his presence, the necessity of language. The final silence drives the reader to words. He becomes the ghostly *alter ego* of the writer himself.

(c) *Gravity's Rainbow: 'Nullpunkt', 'Brennschluss'*

'*Nullpunkt*' and '*Brennschluss*' mark the two ends of the rocket's parabola. One is the zero that completes a countdown; the other, the moment when the rocket's engines cut out and it drops through an eerie silence onto its unwitting target. But Pynchon's zero-hour is more than just the moment the precedes the rocket's lift-off or fall: it is also the '*Nullpunkt*' of Germany in 1945, the primal chaos from which reconstruction begins (a chaos in which the only perceptible patterns are statistical ones); the razed cities are the *tabula rasa* of a new writing, for which beginning and end are mystically one, for which temporality has dissolved. The simultaneity of this writing seeks to fulfil Leni Pökler's dream of 'not A before B, but all together'[10] it is the indifference to time that obtains in the dimension of the dead, those who frequent the White Visitation. For '*Nullpunkt*' and '*Brennschluss*' are also one and the same: once the engine cuts out, a second countdown begins, the countdown to impact.

In Pynchon's mammoth novel, beginning and end are one. *Gravity's Rainbow* opens and closes with the imminence of the rocket's fall, the immanence of destruction within its targets: the beginning records Pirate Penzance's fear of the silently screaming projectile, and the close of the novel balances this with a raucous, cheer-leader's countdown to the endlessly deferred moment of detonation. One notes this symmetry as evidence that the novel is far less chaotic than it seems. But beginning and end are interdependent over and above the matter of formal counterpoint; their simultaneity is the ambiguous phenomenon that furnishes the book with its nightmare and its Utopia. On the one hand, all may co-exist, as it does in the ideal community of the dead (the simultaneity is woven into Pynchon's style itself as his sentences envelop recurrent lists of items and events, passing over them with a deft hand, stapling them together, dissolving them into each other like the frames of a film, just as each phrase dissolves within the long, meticulously tacking sentence that contains it into a series of dots . . .). But on the other hand, the dead themselves are threatening, and the Other World provides no alternative to the nightmarishness with which I. G. Farben and the other multinationals proliferate; for simultaneity is also a feature of the process whereby they homogenise and repress a variety of cultures. This is borne out by Walter Rathenau's speech from the grave:

> The more dynamic it seems to you, the more deep and dead, in reality, it grows. Look at the smokestacks, how they proliferate, fanning the wastes of original waste over greater and greater masses of city. Structurally, they are stongest in compression. A smokestack can survive any explosion – even the strongest shock wave from one of the new cosmic bombs – a bit of a murmur round the table at this – as you all must know. The persistence, then, of structures favouring death. Death converted into more death. Perfecting its reign, just as the buried coal grows denser, and overlaid with more strata – epoch on top of epoch, city on top of ruined city. This is the sign of Death the impersonator.[11]

Thus beginning and end, life and death, interlock. Because of this, Pynchon's novel is one in which both life and death are impossible. Apocalyptically it collapses the beginning of what he defines as the modern age into its end; the result is a totalised image of the age of plastics, of I. G. Farben, of multinationals that work on both sides of any border and so perpetuate the anarchy of the Zone. (One recalls that during the last war I.T.T. supplied both the Allies and the Axis; similarly today, the multinational concerns that construct cars in Eastern Europe for sale in the West both cut the costs of their own capitalism and provide the nominally socialist Eastern Bloc with indirect support.)

The ambiguous employment generates paranoia on both sides, a fear that nothing is happening, that the polarisations that dictate official policies are illusory – and thus one's actions are illusory too. The secret. all-embracing dictatorship exercised by the cartels and monopolies evokes in Slothrop a paradoxical sense of security: he 'is almost sure that whatever They want, it won't mean risking his life, or even too much of his comfort. But he can't fit any of it into a pattern, there's no way to connect someone like Dodson-Truck with someone like Katje'.[14] The pattern has been subverted by the simultaneous discontinuity and continuity between Katje and Dodson-Truck.

In Pynchon's eyes, 1944 and 1973 are not simply part of the same process; there is no fundamental difference between them. The solvents of his novel melt fiction into history, history into fiction. None of the characters can distinguish the one from the other. 'The Plot' that underlies and unifies history may be just a fiction, the characters' collective hallucination, Pynchon's own fiction, the firework of specula- tion that goes up but never comes down, is never either disconfirmed or confirmed. But in reaching this conclusion and asserting the identity of history and fiction (compare *Nineteen-Eighty-Four*) – in asserting that any and every fact is malleable – he dismisses the scrupulous tension between fact and fiction that had prevailed in *The Crying of Lot 49*. In the earlier novel Oedipa Maas had functioned as a Maxwell's Demon, mediating between paranoia and the reader; she was both a cartoon figure and an intellectual, so even as he derided her, Pynchon sympathised with her quest and dilemma. The novel's decision to occupy a position both inside and outside her consciousness engendered a fruitful doubt as to whether she was snuffling out a hidden history or simply projecting a nervous private obsession onto the reified blankness of her environment (which would be one means of conjuring life from a dead world). But *Gravity's Rainbow* is a novel of pure exteriority, of gliding surfaces, and Slothrop is only seen from outside; we never see with his eyes. Thus the work is less a logical step on from the previous novel than a regression; for all that has been written of the spiralling difficulty of the later novel, it is fundamen- tally simpler than *The Crying of Lot 49*. If Pynchon's middle novel activates a dialectic of high and low seriousness, in *Gravity's Rainbow* this dialectic has frozen into a stalemate; and the sombre, apocalyptic notes with which it is threaded stem less from the writer's earnestness than from his despair over his incarceration in the condemned playground of his writing. If *V* distinguished between history and fiction, so that the history became simply the backdrop of a shimmering, wilful mosaic, and if *Lot 49* achieved a fruitful tension between them, *Gravity's Rainbow* homogenises them. If history and fiction are ultimately one, then narrative is a bad joke, and the three hundred odd characters (and some of them are *very* odd) can be allowed to fade out as fast as they multiply; why bother to follow them when there exists no chance of establishing their truth? In the place of Oedipa, the detective truth-seeker who finds herself unwittingly led into her own mind, which may well be the only scene of the crime, one has Slothrop the tortured marionette; the interdependence of detective, patient and psychiatrist (Oedipa's own name alludes to Freudian psychoanalysis) gives way to the sado-masochistic mutuality of victim and behaviourist experimenter. The interplay of sign and signifier which is the basis of interpretation is replaced by a sinister, monotonous carnival of opaque and unreadable signs. Pynchon's own relationship to Slothrop appears to be sado-masochistic; he identifies with Slothrop, but also seems at times to abhor him. Part of Pynchon's own East Coast background has gone into the archaeology of the New England Slothrop, but at the same time his protagonist is made to blurt 'that' in front of every proper noun as if he were a character from Sinclair Lewis; he is half Cabot, half Babbitt. In him are compounded the genteel culture of the East and the notorious cultural blankness of the Mid-West. He is protected by the omniscient narrator (shielded from castration and rocket fall), but he is also subject to continual threats from Them, who are similarly omniscient (if They exist) and may well represent the narrator's phantom limbs. Although in many respects Pynchon transposes modern attitudes to 1944, he has transposed one 1944 attitude into the present. Now that the moon-landing has taken place, a rocket is something that lifts clear of the pull of gravity; to identify it with the parabolic movement gravity imposes is to believe, like a man of 1944, that 'what goes up must come down' – usually upon one's own head. Nevertheless, in another respect, the nature of the modern rocket determines the course of the book; the modern rocket can stay up for ever, and so does Pynchon's narrative. It never comes down, never resolves itself into a denouement.

The gradual hardening of the arteries of Pynchon's imagination can be seen in the stylistic differences between *The Crying of Lot 49* and *Gravity's Rainbow*. In the former the writing has an urgency tempered by lightness, a power balanced by a rapidity of movement, which make it seductive and compulsive. This compulsiveness draws us into the circle of Oedipa's obsessions and signals the book's sympathy with the pop speed of a detective story, and with the hot-gospelling articulacy of the best disc jockeys (one recalls that Mucho Maas is a disc jockey, as was Pynchon himself for a while). Look at the suppleness of this passage:

Yet at least he had believed in the cars. Maybe to excess: how could he
not, seeing people poorer than him come in, Negro, Mexican, cracker,
a parade seven days a week, bringing the most godawful of trade-ins:
motorised, metal extensions of themselves, of their families and of
what their whole lives must be like, out there so naked for anybody, a
stranger like himself, to look at, frame cockeyed, rusty underneath,
fender repainted in a shade just off enough to depress the value, if not
Mucho himself, inside smelling hopelessly of children, supermarket
booze, two, sometimes three generations of cigarette smokers, or only
of dust – and when the cars were swept out you had to look at the
actual residue of these lives, and there was no way of telling what
things had been truly refused (when so little he supposed came by that
out of fear most of it had to be taken and kept) and what had simply
(perhaps tragically) been lost: clipped coupons promising savings of 5
or 10c, trading stamps, pink flyers advertising specials at the markets,
butts, tooth-shy combs, help-wanted ads, Yellow pages torn from the
phone book, rags of old underwear or dresses that already were period
costumes, for wiping your own breath off the inside of a windshield
with so you could see whatever it was, a movie, a woman or car you
coveted, a cop who might pull you over just for drill, all the bits and
pieces coated uniformly, like a salad of despair, in a grey dressing of
ash, condensed exhaust, dust, body wastes – it made him sick to look,
but he had to look.

There is a combination here of a telegraphic style, nervously lingering
on the edge of breakdown in the face of what it sees, and the heady
continuousness of an aria. The short interpolated clauses allow both for
sovereign comic asides and express Mucho's fundamental stammering
unease. At points the linguistic wit has almost Shakespearean reverberations; when Pynchon states 'there was no way of telling what things had
been truly refused', he relates 'refusal' to 'refuse' (rubbish, waste,
W.A.S.T.E.), and the poor become those who have no right of refusal.
'What had simply (perhaps tragically) been lost' shows an awareness
that at this level of destitution any and every loss can be shattering. The
sweeping out of the cars becomes like the inspection of a corpse after
death – the moment of death, and of the change of gear within the prose
from a style of exasperation to a style of grand lament, being marked by
the dash after 'dust', as a result of which the cigarette smokers themselves become dust, cigarette ash.

Compare the following paragraph from *Gravity's Rainbow*, which is
similarly self-contained:

He left the dodoes to rot, he couldn't endure to eat their flesh. Usually, he hunted alone. But often, after months of it, the isolation would begin to change him, change his very perceptions – the jagged mountains in full daylight flaring as he watched into freak saffrons, streaming indigos, the sky his glass house, all the island his tulipomania. The voices – he insomniac, southern stars too thick for constellations teeming in faces and creatures of fable less likely than the dodo – spoke the words of sleepers, singly, coupled, in chorus. The rhythms and timbres were Dutch, but made no waking sense. Except that he thought they were warning him . . . scolding, angry that he couldn't understand. Once he sat all day staring at a single white dodo's egg in a grass hummock. The place was too remote for any foraging pig to've found. He waited for scratching, a first crack reaching to net the chalk surface: an emergence. Hemp gripped in the teeth of the steel snake, ready to be lit, ready to descend, sun to black-powder sea, and destroy the infant, egg of light into egg of darkness, within its first minute of amazed vision, of wet down stirred cool by these southeast trades. . . . Each hour he sighted down the barrel. It was then, if ever, he might have seen how the weapon made an axis potent as Earth's own between himself and this victim, still one, inside the egg, with the ancestral chain, not to be broken out for more than its blink of world's light. There they were, the silent egg and the crazy Dutchman, and the hookgun that linked them forever, framed, brilliantly motionless as any Vermeer. Only the sun moved: from zenith down at last behind the snaggleteeth of mountains to Indian ocean, to tarry night. The egg, without a quiver, still un-hatched. He should have blasted it then where it lay: he understood that the bird would hatch before dawn. But a cycle was finished. He got to his feet, knee and hip joints in agony, head gonging with instructions from his sleep-walkers droning by, overlapping urgent, and only limped away, piece at right shoulder arms.

This passage embodies a facile mystique of the power of Nature, of the Archetype; there is a complacent anti-colonialism (the warning, un-heeded voices) that relishes the colonialist's discomfiture; and there is even a certain melodramatic self-congratulation: 'brilliantly framed' the picture may be, but the framer is none other than Thomas Pynchon. The Dutchman is 'framed' in a different sense too, frozen in the dock before the tribunal of Nature. Below the fine phrases and the mysticism lurks a knot of hard-bitten torpor; the phrases are often self-consciously porten-tous ('It was then, if ever'; 'Only the sun moved', and so on) and even

obvious, ennui-laden. The customary exteriority of the novel comes close
to a philistine cartoon. There is flat-footed play with 'Dutchness' – 'all
the island his tulipomania'; 'brilliantly motionless as any Vermeer' (at
times one feels that the bird Pynchon sympathises with is less the dodo
than the culture-vulture). There are over-explicit 'cosmic' overtones: 'it
was then, if ever, he might have seen how the weapon made an axis
potent as Earth's own between himself and this victim' (the lack of a
definite article before 'Earth', as later before 'world', is a danger-signal
indicating the presence of the pseudo-poetic). There is an insistent
inflation of individual details in a manner one is tempted to call
'Teutonic' – the silent staring Dutchman suggests a scene from a film by
Werner Herzog. This Teutonic manner clearly reflects the book's sat-
uration with Germanic references, which range from the pretentious to
the camp. In this context I feel that Pynchon's engagement with the
work of Rilke has had a detrimental effect upon his own imagination. He
has adopted the portentousness of the Angel (the first sentence of the
novel echoes the 'scream' with which the 'Duineser Elegien' open), and
although he also quotes from the 'Sonetten an Orpheus', their pleasing
ease is foreign to *Gravity's Rainbow*, a novel whose very title suffers from
an overload of unclarified allusions. All in all, one is surprised at
Bergonzi's damning-with-mispraise description of the work as 'beauti-
fully written'; as often, the exclamation that an object is 'beautiful' serves
to preserve the critic from the difficult task of evaluation and interpretation. In one's more pessimistic moments, one may fear that the *Nullpunkt*
of my title may prove to be that of Thomas Pynchon himself.

But Pynchon alone is not to be blamed for this, and I do not wish these
remarks to be construed as a diatribe. *The Crying of Lot 49* was buoyed
up by a certain mid-Sixties energy, and is appropriately enough set in
California, which promised for a while to be less the factory of tooth-and-
mind-corroding dreams than a workshop of liveable fantasy. If this novel
ends inconclusively, this is in part because events had not yet run their
full course. But by the late Sixties and early Seventies, when Pynchon
was stitching (or to use a term borrowed from Derrida's translator,
'basting') *Gravity's Rainbow* together, the possibilities had closed. The
pop revolution had proved a pseudo-revolt, easily assimilable in the form
of fashion to the capitalism it nominally opposed, and the USA seemed
mired in the horror of the war in Vietnam. Thus although the novel is a
tract for the post-war era in general, it is also a tract for the few years
during which it was written – as one would expect in a writer as
politically aware as Pynchon. Thus in making the rocket a V-2, he is
doing more than reconstructing the past; the fact that the V-2 is a rocket

that is also a bomb provides a concise icon of the link between the space race and the proliferation of arms. And by integrating the multinationals into his schema, he shows how the immanent force of technological advance interlocks with the self-perpetuation of military complexes – a self-aggrandisement that is pursued even into a vacuum, as in the frontierless Zone of 1945, in which V-2s are launched in defence of a nation that no longer even exists. The novel's political perspective even encompasses the revolt of the negroes against colonialism, of the *Schwarzkommando* against their German masters. It thus presents all the salient aspects of post-war political reality. But the fullness of the vision has its drawbacks.

The novel's main failure is due to the impossibility of its attempt to create a totalised vision; the attempt to bring everything in bursts the seams of the novel, which pays for its fecund suggestiveness by degenerating into a series of garishly lit individual scenes, frames in a film. (At one point in the novel, Pynchon speculates that this discontinuous perception may be essentially Germanic, but since America is the home of the film industry, may it not be American too? Or even more American? Pure experience, unencumbered by 'theory'.) Each lurid composition gives a quick glimpse of the social and psychological contradictions that rack the frames in which people are trapped, but the vision of the totality disappears into the gaps between the scenes. It is because the totality is imageless that it evokes paranoia; its threat is as imminent as that of the silent rocket whose explosion is heard only by the survivors. And this imagelessness eludes Pynchon's intense sense of tactility, thus demonstrating the unfeasibility of his project, a project to show within a novel what it is that makes a system a system. Perhaps this can be done only by enlisting theory, or rather, anti-theory, which submerges itself in the individual moment so as to reveal the presence of the contradictory totality inscribed in that moment. I have in mind the negative dialectic of Adorno, as pre-figured by the work of Benjamin, which uses individual feelings to record the extent of the individual's '*Beschädigung*' (damage) by the totality. In Pynchon's novel, however, the individual scene is less a microcosm of the social macrocosm than a bit of flotsam discarded by the centrifugal movement of the system – individuals themselves persist in a sentimentalised isolation from it. Thus the system is left outside the novel, a mystified It or They – and the false mystery seduces Pynchon into the debilitated mysticism of the Rocket-as-Angel. He shows too little awareness that They are also We.

This consciousness of the importance of an anti-theory is not restricted to philosophers but can be found in novelists too – specifically, in the great modernists. Thus when I criticise *Gravity's Rainbow* it is because it dissolves the essay into the novel rather than setting them in the kind of tension found in the works of Proust or Musil. And Musil's *Der Mann ohne Eigenschaften* is of particular relevance here. It is aware of the extent to which They are We, and like Pynchon's work it is concerned with relationships between the individual, bureaucracy and the multinationals (for which Arnheim is the main agent; one notices a point of direct contact between the two novels in the fact that Arnheim was modelled on Walter Rathenau). For Musil, individual and system are homologous, and his novel documents the similarities between Ulrich, the chief protagonist whose identity has evaporated, and a series of people opposed to him. The main resemblance lies in the way the same thoughts pass through their mind; They are We, the unwitting protagonists are one with the omniscient narrator, the novel's collective subject. Musil registers depth-soundings in the ideology of his era, compiles notes towards a collective depth-psychology, whilst Pynchon simply observes the criss-crossing of froth in the surface storm. Musil juxtaposes characterisation and narrative with lengthy cross-sections through the protagonists' thoughts – and they are all thinking the same thing, the thought that dominates *The Crying of Lot 49*: something must happen. Thus the complicity between individual and system is revealed; from without, all the characters appear to be discrete, but they evince the same inner structure of ideology. In this mental space they are all '*eigenschaftslos*' (without qualities).

In *Gravity's Rainbow*, however, there is no dimension but that of mystified interpersonal exchange; there is no intra-personal or mental space. All is exterior; for Pynchon, the ice age has already descended. Things are no longer extensions of people (as in the passage I have quoted from *The Crying of Lot 49*); people are things. Or rather, as in the schizophrenic vision of Barbara O'Brien, they are *Operators and Things*. The privilege he accords vision gives him a bracing empathy with films and comics, an instinct for the pull of sensuous surfaces, and for the beauties of technology – but it also condemns him to the behaviourist viewpoint, the view from without, the sentimental prospect of the perennial outsider. *Gravity's Rainbow* is both a witting parody of existentialism and its helpless slave. All too often it uses materialist and dialectical theories – theories implicit in its own politics of experience – as a basis for allusive charades. Thus its politics and its poetics are in contradiction. The politics maintain that a system exists (even if it is only perceptible statistically), but the fragmented narrative method trivialises the political insight by reducing it to the status of paranoia. The systematic dislocation renders the system invisible. One of the most ambitious books of this century, *Gravity's Rainbow* is also a resounding failure, and this is because its chosen means are inappropriate to its ends. One needs means resembling those of Benjamin, Musil and Adorno – the means of Weber, with which there is much casual play ('routinisation of charisma' and so on), will not suffice. Pynchon comes close to writing the Great American Novel, only to fail because in many respects the work is not American enough; it avoids the pain of confronting felt social and psychological contradictions in the manner of *The Crying of Lot 49*. The transposition to Europe of all the events (even *V* was half and half) functions less as an alienation device than as an evasively luxuriant metaphor. Even so, he remains the greatest living English novelist. His books are in themselves historical events.

(d) *The Public and the Private Burning*: Coover and Doctorow

Robert Coover's *The Public Burning* and E. L. Doctorow's *The Book of Daniel* cry out for comparison. They share the same subject matter – the electrocution of the Rosenbergs during the collective delusion of the McCarthy era – whilst treating it in totally different manners. Perhaps comparison is unfair inasmuch as it juxtaposes Coover's best work with a book that is far from Doctorow's best (*The Book of Daniel* founders on its gauche inability to distance and order its material, and is far inferior to *Ragtime*, which I also intend to consider): but in every other respect the books call for a parallel analysis. Where Coover resorts to political cartoon, places the electrocution in Times Square, and stages it as a hucksterist ritual, Doctorow reviews the private life of the Rosenbergs, alters the names of the protagonists, and considers the effects of their orphanage upon the Rosenberg children (whom he makes a brother and a sister rather than two brothers) and its relevance to the changing nature of the American radical tradition. Coover's book constitutes a brash, direct, love-hateful attack on the redneck mentality, which it sees as gloriously and horribly undying; Uncle Sam reincarnates himself from generation to generation in a series of presidents who form a lurid typology of deformity. He shows Vice President Nixon wrapped in masochistic fantasies of which the most passionate is the dream of possession (and penetration) by Uncle Sam; Coover thus bridges the gap between the early Fifties and the late Sixties, in which Nixon actually became President, and so justifies his belief in the unchangingness of the rites of American politics. If his book has a flaw, it lies in its frivolous, emigré's assumption that a super-patriot Republican is somehow more truly American than a Democrat. Doctorow's work, by way of contrast, is more introverted, and participates in a dialogue within the American Left itself; it is scrupulous, but can seem a little provincial. Where Coover stages a public burning, a satyr feast, Doctorow's perspective is more intimate. Coover deals with the mechanisms of demagoguery and apocalypse, with the shamelessness with which the individual erupts within the confines of a crowd; Doctorow considers the individual in a plaintive isolation.

Coover is a fundamentalist journalist, a chameleon and paradoxical being; a Trickster. In *The Origin of the Brunists* the polarisation between the embryo fanatical sect and the sceptical newspaper editor reflected a split within the mind of the author himself; but in actuality the two opposites were interdependent, as became apparent when the sect found in the journalist its sacrificial victim. In *The Public Burning*, Coover presents Uncle Sam as an Old Testament God, the tribal, unforgiving deity of the frontier mentality whose power is efficacious only within the vicinity of the tribe. Uncle Sam is locked in combat with the Communist Phantom, the shadowy comic book villain who foments anti-Americanism throughout the world. Coover himself is involved in an intense love-hate relationship with the vitality of Uncle Sam's philistinism; he appreciates his quasi-Elizabethan linguistic inventiveness, but he is also aware of the terrible crassness of the hillbilly court at which 'TIME' is the poet laureate. The ambiguity that pervades Coover's relationship with 'TIME''s jargon is a source of one of the major weaknesses in his novel; one is often unsure whether or not the repeated slogans (America the joke of the world – America the poke of the world, and so on), which also recall early futurist novels, are intended as satire, or as the kind of wide-eyed homage to the force of the new in which the futurists themselves indulged. This ambiguity in Coover's feelings about the vulgar vitality of American idiom is focused more satisfactorily in the figure of Uncle Sam himself – partly because Uncle Sam's corrupted Biblicisms are further from everyday American usage, and are thus unlikely to be confused with the language of the novelist himself. Uncle Sam speaks neologistically, or rather, the twang of his accent deforms the language in such a manner that it appears neologistic when transcribed. This is a crowd-pleasing tactic, for Sam Slick likes nothing better than 'showin' off'. In transcribing Sam's language as he does, Coover ironises it: 'we reap what we sow' becomes 'we rips what we sews', and 'graven image' becomes 'craven image'; the writer reveals the extent to which everyday speech is studded with the parapraxes of the American collective unconscious. Coover both imitates Uncle Sam and undermines him: on the one hand, he demonstrates that the grandstanding orator and freedom-fighter is an illiterate, demagogic hick; on the other, he savours Sam's terse sense of humour and dry word-play.

But the brilliant heart of Coover's novel is his depiction of the character of Nixon. He grants Nixon a series of monologues in which to express his aspirations, fears, memories, sense of identity with and difference from the Rosenbergs, lust for Ethel, political theories and low high-mindedness. Nixon is Coover's ideal target, both because of the scandal of the Watergate cover-up and because his later presidency forges the link between the mentality of the Fifties and that of a more recent era. Thus the novel indicates that the sins of the past are still with us. And the fiasco of Nixon's appearance on the stage in Times Square shortly before the execution, trousers down and 'I AM A SCAMP' lipsticked on his backside, is a marvellous myth-making explanation of the disfavour into which he fell after the Fifties, which so delayed his accession to the presidency. In *The Public Burning*, much as in life, Nixon sees himself as a thinker politician who has to work hard for what comes easy to others; he sees his catastrophic encounters with ordinary people as signs of an idealistic preoccupation with higher forces. The scenes with Nixon are the finest and most inventive in the book, and make the up-to-the-minute political reports that punctuate them seem two-dimensional. Nixon in a cab with a cabbie whose mocking humour leads the Vice President to see in him an incarnation of the Phantom; Nixon 'the farting Quaker' chugging along butt-end first (playing Anus to Ola's Dildo in a school production of *Dido and Aeneas*); Nixon fulminating inwardly against the Commie demonstrators who are milling around him, only to discover them to be Government supporters bearing placards that rejoice in the prospect of 'TWO FRIED ROSENBER-GERS' – these comic scenes are the most successful in the book. And they are so because Coover is both fascinated and appalled by his subject – because Nixon the loser evokes in him an amused charity. Especially in the chilling final scene in which Uncle Sam sodomises him.

The Book of Daniel is a far less vociferous and assured piece of work. Its worst fault lies in the yawning gap between its mundane details and its apocalyptic overtones. It opens with paragraphs that shift back and forth between a first-person and a third-person account of a visit by Daniel, his wife Phyllis, and his foster parents to Worcester State Hospital, in which his sister Susan is being detained after an attempted suicide in a roadside café. Daniel and Susan are the children of the Isaacsons, electrocuted fifteen years earlier on a trumped-up espionage charge. Neither has ever recovered from the sense of radical isolation into which they were thrown by that event. The 'he'/'I' alternation with which Doctorow begins his novel can be interpreted as an image of Daniel's sense of bifurcation (he and Susan are the two components of one being: 'they were like the compensating halves of a clock sculpture that would exchange positions when the chimes struck'); nevertheless, the parallel feels forced, and the modernist device is simply strained decoration. Moreover, one notices that the shifts are always from 'he' to 'I': this is an expression of Doctorow's fundamental objectivity, which carefully sets the scene in which the 'I' is to appear in such a way as to deflate in advance all its claims to apocalyptic primacy, utter unique-ness. The disturbed, revolutionary overtones of the narrative seem detached because that is just what they are: *The Book of Daniel* should really be called *The Book of Susan*. If Daniel were in the hospital instead of Susan, then the parallels between his state of mind and the unbalanced condition induced in the Biblical Daniel by persecution would seem more convincing than they are. As it is, the title has the ring of portentous afterthought. For Doctorow's novel is a square work masquerading as a hip one. Thus its intermittent dirty talk is self-conscious and forced. Doctorow is even capable of bromides like 'they must know we mean them no harm except the harm in our love for them' or of cacophonous phrases like 'a blanket of burned space about my ears', which fling ill-fitting words together in the hope that the dissonant awkwardness will seem intense. But the intensity is merely contrived. His work improves immeasurably in *Ragtime*, when he admits his inability to speak in the name of a radical figure (Susan is the true radical here, whereas Daniel is half-radical; whence the half-heartedness of the book). His temper is too sober to enable him to frame believably inflammatory statements.

Where Coover is brash, Doctorow is muted and discreet. This is why, unlike Coover, he needs to create a distance between himself and his subjects. His temper is almost classical; *Ragtime* is arranged in four deft sections. *Ragtime* is a revised version of Kleist's *Michael Kohlhaas* (the name 'Coalhouse' is surely Doctorow's tribute to his mentor); it is a study of the violence of principle that leads Coalhouse Walker, Jr, a negro ragtime pianist, mercilessly to revenge himself upon the firemen who insulted him, to burn down their firehouse, shoot several of them, and demand that the city authorities restore the prized model T Ford destroyed by the firemen. Doctorow is quieter than many American writers, but his stillness nourishes a studious, almost dapper intent; nevertheless it is only very distantly akin to the principled violence of his negro protagonist. One recalls that *The Book of Daniel* did not deal primarily with real anarchists, but with people wrongly accused of subversion. For Doctorow can treat real anarchists (Emma Goldmann, for instance) only at the historical remove of *Ragtime* (here he is like Kleist, whose Kohlhaas appears in the sixteenth century); the implausibility of such violence of principle leads one to locate the moment of its eruption in the past, in a mythological age in which humans were capable of such inhuman absolutism. Moreover, Coalhouse is a negro; thus his rage becomes comprehensible. *Ragtime* is more successful than *The Book of Daniel* because the greater formality of manners in the nineteen twenties, the period in which it is set, accords with Doctorow's own luminous, understated sobriety. This sobriety is evident in the crisp perspectivism of the narrative, which juxtaposes vignettes of scenes with Houdini, Freud, Coalhouse Walker, Henry Ford and others. Doctorow's perspectivism (itself a trait of much fiction in the Twenties, a multisidedness that shows him to lack the monomania of a Coalhouse, a Kohlhaas, a true radical) is further justified by the theme of death and reincarnation that reverberates through the novel: Pierpont Morgan sees in Henry Ford a reincarnation of an Egyptian pharoah; Sarah's baby is heard crying underground and then rescued; Younger Brother is transformed into a revolutionary (and blacks his white face, a sign that the boundaries between negro and white have been eroded by Coalhouse's refusal to slip into the mould of negro servility); and the impoverished Jewish artist Tateh adopts a new name and identity, becoming the Baron Ashkenazy, sole proprieter of the Buffalo Nickel Photoplay, Incorporated.

Doctorow's work is unusual in recent American fiction in that much of it is narrated from the position of a child; most of *The Book of Daniel* is devoted to Daniel's childhood memories, and *Ragtime* is recounted by a young boy. The power of *Ragtime* stems from the grace of its indirection, of a viewpoint that stands outside the overwhelming events by which others are submerged, and that criticises the engrained prejudices that determine the fates of Paul and Rochelle Isaacson and Coalhouse Walker, Jr. In elevating family concerns to the level of the public world, Doctorow is pleading for a world in which one's judgement of another person will be based on close knowledge rather than upon hearsay. But his perspectivism recognises the unlikelihood that one will ever know anyone but the members of one's family sufficiently closely; encounters are fleeting in the city world in which perspectivism was born (compare Musil and Proust). For him, there exists an intimate link between political life and private life. Coover may perhaps be the more realistic writer, for he sees the two spheres as irrevocably split, but this view deprives his work of the poetic resonances that accrue to the work of a writer engaged with reality as perceived by a child. Where Coover brilliantly chronicles myths and their public making, Doctorow – at his best – has the committed exactitude of a poet.

Notes

INTRODUCTION

1. J. Hillis Miller, *The Form of Victorian Fiction* (Notre Dame and London: University of Notre Dame Press, 1968) p. 140.
2. S. Prickett, *Victorian Fantasy* (Brighton: Harvester, 1979) p. 79.
3. Ibid.
4. M. Bakhtin, 'Das Wort im Roman', in *Die Aesthetik des Wortes*, ed. Rainer Grübel (Frankfurt a.M: Suhrkamp., 1979) p. 166.
5. Ibid.

2. CLARISSA, DIALECTIC AND UNREADABILITY

All references to *Clarissa* itself are to the Everyman edition (London: Dent, 1962), which has the advantage of accessibility. There is, however, no adequate edition; the nature of the book is such as to preclude it.

1. F. Jameson, *Marxism and Form*: (New Jersey: Princeton University Press: Suhrkamp, 1971) p. 308.
2. T. W. Adorno, *Gesellschaftstheorie und Kulturkritik* (Frankfurt: Suhrkamp, 1975) p. 8.
3. Speculation was first privileged by German Idealism, and the self-unfolding of the Absolute as it manifests itself in the dialectic of history closes with the arrival of philosophy in the same way as *Clarissa* ends with abstract maxims.
4. C.f. I. Gopnik, *A Theory of Style and Richardson's 'Clarissa'* (The Hague and Paris: Mouton, 1970) p. 115: 'But as the network like quality of the verbal structure, painstakingly articulated as the editorial notes make it out to be, constantly juxtaposing present contexts with past and future ones, insisting that significance inheres in no less a domain than the total structure apprehended at once, frees the novel from the captivity of a sequential plot.'
5. *Clarissa*, vol. 4 (London: Dent, 1962) p. 277.
6. T. W. Adorno, *Negative Dialektik* (Frankfurt: Suhrkamp, 1966) p. 15.
7. C.f. *Negative Dialektik* p. 13: 'Once philosophy broke the promise that it would be one with or immediately bring about reality, it became necessary for it ruthlessly to criticise itself.'
8. *Negative Dialektik*, p. 16.
9. T. W. Adorno, *Minima Moralia*, (Frankfurt: Suhrkamp, 1978) section 152.

10. vol. 4, p. 530.

11. This demand covers the entire artistic spectrum, emcompassing both engaged and hermetic works, both Brecht and Celan.

12. R. Musil, *Der Mann ohne Eigenschaften*, (Hamburg: Rowohlt, 1957) p. 729.

13. T. Pynchon, *The Crying of Lot 49* (London: Cape, 1967) One may experience such a feeling of paranoia most often during films, when a modern medium exerts a total control over one; unlike books, films allow the receiver no rest and combine his inscription into the 'plot' (audience response calculated in advance) with his exclusion through a refusal to halt should he demand this. The shock of cutting contributes to this sense of paranoia, of another reality taking its course 'over the head' (as the ray passes over it) of one's wishes. Each new image is a door in Bluebeard's castle. Whilst watching the scene in *The Godfather*, Part II, in which a cake was sliced, I was convinced it was going to explode. Cutting prepares one's thought to make such irrational leaps, and is allied to Surrealism; everything can be linked with everything else, and the images have the dwarfing hugeness of childhood experience. One can combine everything only because everything is already dead.

14. I. Gopnik, *Richardson's 'Clarissa'* chapter IV, Verbal Structure and the Role of 'Editor' in 'Clarissa', pp. 107–16.

15. C.f. Ann Doody's *A Natural Passion* (Oxford, Oxford University Press, 1974). Miss Doody traces *Clarissa*'s affinities with Restoration tragedy: Lovelace's illness stems from Fowler's ruse in *The Wittie Faire One* (1633), also employed by Valentine Legend in Congreve's *Love for Love* (1695). Nevertheless, the parallels tell us little: 'the closest parallels suggested so far lack the distinctive feature of Richardson's conception of Clarissa's tragedy, the reversal in which she rises above her seducer by refusing to marry him.' (T. C. Duncan Eaves and Ben D. Kimpel, *Samuel Richardson* (Oxford: Oxford University Press 1971) p. 235) In fact, Lovelace's comi-tragedy more closely recalls that of Chah Abbas in Andreas Gryphius's *Catherina von Georgien*. C.f. M. Szarota, *Kuenstler, Gruebler und Rebellen* (Bonn and Munich: Francke, 1967) especially p. 359 note 6, in which the critic's strictures of Chah Abbas replay exactly the tone of Richardson's denunciations of Lovelace.

16. One can, of course, take a less charitable view of dialectic's Baroque traits. Thus W. R. Beyer *Vier Kritiken: Heidegger, Sartre, Adorno, Lukács*, (Koen: Puhl-Rugenstein/VVA 1970), 'negative dialectic' recalls the era of the Baroque, for which even disorder was order.... The pyrotechnician himself knew that he was only an illusionist, though he also knew that he understood more than the audience' (p. 156). Since Beyer's book is a negation of Adorno's practice, his insistence that thought must be affirmative is self-contradictory and falls into the common confusion of the everyday with the philosophical meaning of 'negative'; this conceptual confusion needs to be understood dialectically.

17. See Karl-Heinz Birkele, *Mythos und Aufklaerung – Adornos Philosphie gelesen als Mythos, Versuch einer kritischen Rekonstruktion* (dissertation, Wuerzburg 1977) for an acid comment on dialectic's mythical dimensions. One should add, that although Birkele can easily find quotations to support his view, quotation is the one procedure to which a dialectical text is not susceptible,

for it stops its development: to ascertain that dialectic is concerned with myth hardly proves that it is itself mythical. However much there may be about stasis in Adorno, the dialectical movement gives it more historicity than Birkele's book, which repeats itself continually and so turns into a myth about dialectic.

18. F. Copleston, S. J., *A History of Philosophy*, vol. III, (London: Burns and Oates Limited, 1960) p. 272–3.
19. Hence the restlessness of the tyrant in *Catherina von Georgien*:

Halt hin! Komm her! Ja geh! Es muss doch endlich sein! (Stay there! Come here! Well, go! This thing must be at last!)

Here the structure of the line itself has the fatality that determines that something must happen; the rhyme and alexandrine draw action on, whilst the reversal after the caesura imposes change on Abbas. Syntax becomes fate. With relation to the tyrant's restlessness, c.f. E. Canetti on the survivor in *Masse und Macht* (Munich: Carl Hanser Verlag, 1973).

20. M. Kinkead-Weekes, *Samuel Richardson, Dramatic Novelist* (London: Methuen, 1973) p. 421.
21. Coleridge, *Table Talk* 15 July 1834.
22. Elspeth Nachtigall, *Die 'Memoires' der Marguerite de Valois als Quelle zu Samuel Richardsons 'Clarissa'*, Romanisches Seminar (unpublished dissertation Bonn 1960) p. 82.
23. Kinkead-Weekes, *Samuel Richardson* p. 491.
24. W. Benjamin, *Ursprung des deutschen Trauerspiels* (Frankfurt: Suhrkamp, 1972), p. 182: 'the contemplative calm with which allegory lets itself down into the abyss between being and meaning has none of the self-satisfied indifference found in the superficially similar intention of the sign.' Most semiology suffers from this self-satisfaction in that it simply inverts Romanticism by privileging the signifié above the signifiant, the goal above the journey. Barthes's antidote is their complete separation to open to language the field of Utopia, but although this provides room for a brilliant and mellow speculation, it is basically absurd.
25. In a preface to *The Meaning of Contemporary Realism* (London: Merlin, 1963).
26. Adorno, *Negative Dialektik*, p. 41.
27. Ibid., vol. 4, p. 103.
28. Ibid., p. 145.
29. Adorno, *Negative Dialektik*, p. 15–16.
30. Adorno, *Gesellschaftstheorie . . .*, pp. 125–6.
31. Freud's remarks on narcissism in the essay 'Ueber libidinoese Typen', in (*Gesammelte Schriften*, Band 11 (Vienna: Internationaler Psychoanalytischer Verlag, 1934) p. 119), are very suggestive when brought into contact with the complexion of Richardson's characters: 'a great deal of aggression lies in the hands of the Ego and manifests itself in readiness for action; where the love-life is concerned, loving is preferred to being loved. People of this type impress others as 'personalities' and are especially suited to provide others with a stable point of reference, to become leaders, to give new stimulus to cultural development, or to damage the established order.' These remarks

seem most obviously applicable to Lovelace, but we should remember that Clarissa is seen as criminal by her family, yet is also presented as exemplary. The desire to impress often noted in Richardson himself may well result in the writing of letters: selecting the best of oneself for appraisal, creating the illusion of an integral self speaking without breaks in argument or hesitations. Psychoanalysis of texts must both analyse characters individually and demonstrate the extent to which they are all versions of the same person. They are dialectical, images of the self that expels them.

32. Adorno, *Gesellschaftstheorie . . .*, p. 8.
33. e.g. J. Derrida, 'La structure, le signe et le jeu' in: *L'Écriture et la Différence* (Paris: du Seuil, 1967) p. 426: 'Le jeu est la disruption de la présence. La présence d'un element est toujours une référence signifiante et substitutive incrite dans une systéme de différences et le mouvement d'une chaine . . .'. This ceaseless substitution is the source of the engaging fervour of Derrida's style.
34. *Clarissa*, vol. 1 (London: Dent, 1962) p. 71.
35. Mark Kinkead-Weekes, *Clarissa Restored*, RES, NS, X (1959) pp. 156–71.
36. C.f. T. Adorno, *Aesthetische Theorie* (Frankfurt: Suhrkamp, 1970) p. 541: 'It is purely and simply a matter of it following from my thesis that there is nothing philosophically "primary" that one can no longer build up the context of an argument in stages as one usually does.'
37. T. Adorno, *Philosophie der neuen Musik* (Frankfurt a.M., Berlin, Wien: Vllstein, 1972) p. 27. The Baroque and Richardsonian subject's feeling of superfluity and alienation causes its readiness to leave the world.
38. *Clarissa*, vol. 1, (London: Dent, 1962) p. v.
39. Nachtigall, *Marguerite de Valois*, p. 31: 'The evident confidence required by the new is still lacking. It is characteristic that the writers of this era who stem from Puritanism all come late to creation, after first overcoming their initially negative attitude. Defoe writes his first secular novel when he is sixty, Lille is forty and Richardson over fifty when they produce their first works. And even then, Defoe and Richardson start by publishing anonymously.' One's readiness to depart the world may induce a preparedness to forsake one's own form of life hitherto.
40. Adorno, *Negative Dialektik*, p. 19: 'to oppose Wittgenstein and say what cannot be said'.
41. *Clarissa*, vol. 4 (London: Dent, 1962) p. 7. In Belford's words, the Biblical style is 'that truly easy, natural and simple one which we should admire in other authors excessively' (as he does Clarissa's). His ironic strictures concerning people who learn morality 'from undercurrents, perhaps muddy ones too' in preference to the 'pellucid fountain-head' can be applied to those who read *Clarissa* rather than the Bible. Richardson here shows the lack of self-knowledge that made of his work a titanic study of, and monument to, self-delusion.
42. Jameson, *Marxism and Form* p. 10: 'the language of causality gives way to that of analogy or homology, of parallelism'.
43. *Clarissa*, vol. 1 (London: Dent, 1962) p. 25. 'My uncles never stir out without arms and armed servants.' The enmity of households resembles that in Verona, and James Harlowe is as fiery as Tybalt and as much a 'king of cats'. And Death, described by Lovelace as Clarissa's beloved (vol. 3,

p. 495) is the lover Romeo suspects of keeping Juliet's complexion fresh in the tomb. Both he and Lovelace envy Death his favour.

44. *Clarissa*, vol. 1 (London: Dent, 1962) p. 59.
45. Here lies the limitation of the sociological criticism of Ian Watt or Christopher Hill.
46. Nachtigall, *Marguérite de Valois*, p. 139.
47. Quoted by Gopnik from the Shakespeare Head edition, *Clarissa*, vol. 4 (London: Dent, 1962) p. 319.
48. vol. 3, p. 210: 'O Lovelace, you are Satan himself; or he helps you out in all you do, and that's as bad!'
49. vol. 4, p. 487.
50. C.f. Adorno, *Minima Moralia*, section 9, on lying.
51. vol. 3, p. 462.
52. Philip Slater, *The Pursuit of Loneliness* (Harmondsworth: Penguin, 1971) 'Love at first sight' can only be transference, in the psychoanalytic sense, since there is nothing else on which it can be based. Romantic love, in other words, is Oedipal love.... It is fundamentally incestuous, hence its emphasis on obstacles and non-fulfilment, on tragedy and trespass. Its real object is not the actual parent, however, but a fantasy image of that parent which has been retained, ageless and unchanging, in the unconscious.' (p. 98–9).
53. e.g. vol. 3, p. 400, or his repeated statements about her exceptional nature near the end.
54. vol. 1, p. 201: 'Sometimes we have both thought him one of the most undesigning *merely* witty men we ever knew; at other times, one of the deepest creatures we ever conversed with.' It is interesting how the switch from 'men' to 'creatures' leaves open the chilling possibility that Lovelace is not a man, but rather sub- or super-human.
55. vol. 3, p. 231.
56. vol. 2, p. 316.
57. vol. 1, p. XIV.
58. C.f. Szarota, *Kuenstler, Gruebler und Rebellen*, the chapter on 'Das saekularisierte Maertyrerdrama', pp. 267–340.
59. vol. 3, p. 491.
60. For Barthes, who sees neologism as erotic, this would be the result of Lovelace's nature as a seducer. See R. Barthes, *Sade. Fourier. Loyola.* (Paris: du Seuil, 1971 p. 87.
61. Warren G. Bennis and Philip E. Slater, *The Temporary Society* (New York: Harper and Row, 1968).
62. vol. 3, p. 400.
63. Stefan Morawski, 'Czytanie Adorna', *Miesiecznik Literacki*, (Pazdziernik (October) 1974) p. 55. Lovelace as an adolescent gang-leader is also a precursor of Burgess's Alex in *A Clockwork Orange*. Downs writes: Lovelace is not Lucifer 'but a type as perennial and common and odius as Pamela, that of the over-grown schoolboy: a schoolboy soaked in the lust of adolescence, intoxicated with the sense of power and of immense superiority (soi-disant genius) which a careful preference for the society of inferiors confers'. (B. W. Downs, *Richardson*, London: G. Routledge and Sons, Ltd., 1928 p. 116). The Sixties flattered youth to extend the market. The Roman-

tic idealisation of the child anticipated a society in which the family disintegrates to turn every member into a potential consumer. Adorno sums up the dialectic of regression: 'the more modern, the earlier the stage to which one regresses' (*Philosophie der neuen Musik*, p. 147). Whence the ambiguity of being a precursor.

64. vol. 3, p. 376.
65. vol. 3, p. 251.
66. vol. 1, pp. 84–5.
67. Eaves and Kimpel, *Samuel Richardson, A Biography* (Oxford 1971) pp. 247–8.
68. vol. 3, p. 152.
69. N. Mailer, *Marilyn* (London: Coronet Books Hodder Paperbacks, 1973) p. 106.
70. C.f. the doctoral thesis of Miss Rosemary Bechler of Girton College, Cambridge, in which Lovelace's role as a precursor of the Romantics is documented (unfinished at the time of my writing).
71. vol. 3, p. 169.
72. vol. 3, p. 191.
73. vol. 3, p. 204.
74. vol. 3, p. 393.
75. C.f. John Fraser, *Violence in the Arts* (Cambridge: Cambridge University Press, 1974) p. 59: 'The same kind of difficulty arises in a particularly poignant form in the case of individuals of one's own culture whose faces have been hideously mutilated in war or in civil accidents: the very thing that cries out for the deepest sympathy serves in some measure to inhibit that sympathy, namely the conversion of the sufferers into "monsters".'
76. Phillipe Sollers, 'Sade dans le texte' in: *L'Ecriture et l'Experience des Limites* (Paris: Points, 1972) p. 57.
77. vol. 3, p. 175.
78. vol. 3, p. 495.
79. A. Storr, *The Dynamics of Creation* (London: Secker and Warburg, 1972), p. 25 (quoted from Helene Deutsch's 'The Psychology of Women' (Grunt and Stratton, 1945)): 'Because of the temporal coincidence of the yearning for ideal love and the genital urge, it is difficult for the boy to deny the connection between the two./Girls, however, do not so easily discover that their genitals are the executive agents of their yearning for love.' And Storr (Ibid.): 'To the psychiatrist, the world of the romantic novel resembles rather closely the world of the hysterical patient. In psychoanalytic terminology, hysterical patients have remained at a childhood pre-genital stage of development known as the "phallic" phase. They have not been able to progress emotionally beyond the predominance of an attachment to the parent of the opposite sex; and, since sexual excitement really implies to them incest, they tend to repress physical manifestations of sex as much as possible. This has two results. First, they tend to be frigid in actual sexual intercourse .... Second, they tend to intensify, and live in, a world of fantasy, because they are unable to find satisfaction in the real world.' Whence Clarissa's inability to enjoy her femininity or leave the family; she is caught in a double-bind whereby she can neither leave the family, for to do so would precipitate her into the clasp of a husband or lover and so activate the sexuality she finds sinful (to leave the family is to be guilty of incest!), nor can she stay within it, for she is subject to the sexual advances of suitors, and

it is moreover possible that an incestuous feeling for her father exists: the mother has to mediate between the two, as if the one were taboo for the other. For Lévi-Strauss, incest occurs when a riddle is solved, when 'the answer succeeds, against all expectations, in getting back to its question.' (C. Lévi-Strauss, *The Scope of Anthropology* (London: Cape, 1967) p. 39.) One's inability to solve the riddle of the book, to resolve its dilemma, (which is also Richardson's inability to find a way out of the dilemma created by mingling fiction with didacticism) is the very force that prevents incest from taking place in the book. The book represses the rape, situates it in the realm of horrified silence: otherwise, in the darkness of so monstrous a trangression (symbolic incest), Time would stop. Returning to Storr (p. 26), 'Idealisation also is characteristic of both hysterics and romantic fiction.' In this perspective, the Lovelace who idealises Clarissa *is* Clarissa: they must be identical, for they are both 'Richardson'. It is possible that there is a link between hysteria and all fiction that turns upon love; Freud's first patients were hysterics and recounted imaginary seductions, non-existent events, whilst at the same time appearing 'normal'. This might explain how the novelist can have access to a non-existent world and yet be able to return to *this* world.

80. vol. 3, p. 233.
81. vol. 3, p. 199.
82. vol. 1, pp. 51–2.
83. C.f. Karl Marx, *Grundrisse zur Kritik der politischen Oekonomie* (Berlin: Dietz Verlag, 1974) p. 5.
84. F. Hoelderlin, Kleine Stuttgarte Ausgabe, (*Collected Works*) abridged version compiled by Friedrich Beissner, pp. 14–15.
85. R. S. Brissenden, *Virtue in Distress* (London: Macmillan, 1974) p. 183.
86. vol. 1, p. 83.
87. Ibid.
88. Eaves and Kimpel, *Richardson* pp. 240–1: 'His [Fiedler's] identification of Lovelace with the head, the Enlightenment, and of Clarissa with the heart, the sentimental view of Christianity, threatened by reason, is not so easy to see – it is, after all, Lovelace who, like a romantic hero, follows his passions.'
89. vol. 1, p. 88.
90. Ibid., p. 89.
91. Ibid., p. 90.
92. Th. Mann, *Bekenntnisse des Hochstaplers Felix Krull* (Frankfurt: Fischer, 1974).
93. Max Byrd, 'Madhouse, Whorehouse and Convent', *Partisan Review*, no. 2 (1977) p. 271.
94. The following remarks owe part of their inspiration to Robert Warshow's classic essay 'The Gangster as a Tragic Hero' (in *The Immediate Experience*, New York: Atheneum, 1970), part to discussions with Miss Bechler.
95. C.f. Adorno, *Minima Moralia*, section 59 'Seit ich ihn gesehen', on 'the feminine nature'.
96. E. A. Poe, *The Complete Poems and Stories* (New York: Knopf, 1946) pp. 593–607.
97. Edmund Wilson, *A Literary Chronicle* (Garden City, New York: Doubleday Anchor, 1952) p. 325.
98. Barthes, *Sade. Fourier. Loyola*, pp. 22–3.

3. THE NINETEENTH CENTURY

Four Germans: Hoffmann, Kleist, Goethe and Büchner

1. T. W. Adorno, *Negative Dialectics* (London: Routledge and Kegan Paul, 1973) p. 6.

The illustrated novel: Thoughts on the Novels of Dickens

1. Patrick Swinden, *Unofficial Selves* (London: Macmillan, 1973) p. 38.
2. J. R. Harvey, *Victorian Novelists and Their Illustrators* (London: Sidgwick and Jackson, 1970) p. 8.

Reading signs: Hawthorne and the characters of allegory

1. See W. Benjamin, *Ursprung des deutschen Trauerspiels* (Frankfurt a.M.: Suhrkamp, 1972) pp. 174–210.
2. A. D. Nuttall, *Two Concepts of Allegory* (London: Routledge and Kegan Paul, 1967) p. 48.
3. Nathaniel Hawthorne Centenary Edition, Ohio State University Edition, vol. XI *The Snow Image/Uncollected Tales* p. 166 (all further references to Hawthorne's texts will be to the Ohio State Press edition).
4. Kenneth Dauber, *Rediscovering Hawthorne* (New Jersey: Princeton University Press, 1977) p. 31.
5. Hawthorne, *Snow Image*, p. 97.
6. Hawthorne, *The Scarlet Letter*, vol. 1, p. 64.
7. Ibid., p. 54.
8. Benjamin, *Trauerspiels*, p. 197.
9. Hawthorne, *The Marble Faun*, vol. IV, p. 35.
10. Ibid., pp. 22–3.
11. Gabriel Josipovici, *The World and the Book* (London: Macmillan, 1971) pp. 155–78.
12. Hawthorne, *Mosses from an Old Manse*, vol. 10, pp. 74–90.

4. THE TEXT AGAINST ITSELF

The dialectics of enlightenment: *Elective Affinities* and *Women in Love*

1. K. Alldritt, *The Visual Imagination of D. H. Lawrence* (London: Edward Arnold, 1971) p. 178.
2. Ibid., p. 181.
3. P. Stöcklin, 'Stil und Geist der "Wahlverwandtschaften"', in *Wege der Forschung*, Band CXIII; Goethes Roman *Die Wahlverwandtschaften*, ed. Edwald Rösch (Darmstadt: Wissenschaftliche Buchgesellschaft, 1975) p. 218.

4. Hans Mayer, *Goethe* (Frankfurt a.M: Suhrkamp, 1973) p. 76: 'Noch in Goethes Tagebuch vom II. April 1808 werden sie als "kleine Erzählung" qualifiziert. Im August jedoch wird vor Riemer bereits über "den neuen Roman" gesprochen,'
5. Ronald Gray, *Goethe* (Cambridge: Cambridge University Press, 1967) p. 218: 'in view of the later developments in depth psychology we may well suppose that he was midway between superstitiousness and a germinating awareness of unconscious motivations'. (In this context, compare the narrator of *Die Elixiere des Teufels*.)
6. Mayer, *Goethe*, Ibid.
7. W. Benjamin, '*Goethes Wahlverwandtschaften*' in: *Illuminationen* (Frankfurt a.M: Suhrkamp, 1977) p. 75.
8. T. W. Adorno, *Minima Moralia* (Frankfurt a.M.: Suhrkamp, 1978) p. 108.
9. Ibid., p. 109.
10. e.g. Mephistopheles' self-definition as 'Ein Teil von jener Kraft/Die stets das Böse will und stets die Güte schafft'.
11. B. Bergonzi, *The Situation of the Novel* (Harmondsworth: Penguin, 1972) p. 251.
12. Adorno/Horkheimer, *Dialektik der Aufklärung* (Frankfurt a.M.: Suhrkamp, 1969) p. 18.
13. Ibid., p. 15.
14. Solger, quoted in Mayer, *Goethe*, p. 80.

Utopias: Butler and William Morris

1. W. Benjamin, Letter to Adorno, Paris, 9 Dec. 1938, in *Schriften*, 1, 3 (Frankfurt a.M.: Suhrkamp, 1974) p. 1106.

A note on Metonymy in Proust

1. Paul de Man, *Allegories of Reading* (Yale University Press, 1981) p. 63.

Doubles: Conrad, Irzykowski, Poe, Hawthorne

1. R. Rogers, *The Double in Literature* (Detroit: Wayne State University Press, 1970) p. 2.
2. Ibid., p. 29.
3. Ibid., pp. 31–2.
4. K. Irzykowski, *Metamorfozy Mojskiego*, in *Spod ciemnej gwiazdy* (Warsaw: Czytelnik, 1958) p. 57.
5. Ibid., p. 61.
6. J. L. Borges, *Labyrinths* (New York: New Directions, 1964) p. xxii.
7. Julia Kristeva, *Semiotike* (Paris: du Seuil, 1969) p. 246.
8. 'William Wilson', in: *The Complete Tales and Poems of Poe* (New York: Random House, 1938) p. 631.

9. Ibid., p. 639.
10. Allen Tate, *Essays of Four Decades* (Chicago: Swallow Press, 1968) p. 391.
11. Poe, *Complete Tales*, p. 641.
12. Nathaniel Hawthorne, Centenary Edition, Ohio State University Press, vol. III *The Blithedale Romance/Fanshawe*, p. 246.
13. Ibid., p. 160.
14. Ibid., p. 170.
15. Ibid.

Józef Konrad

1. F. R. Leavis, *The Great Tradition* (London: Chatto and Windus, 1948) p. 180.
2. C.f. the relationship between Lena and Heyst in *Victory*.
3. J. Conrad, *Lord Jim* (London: Dent, date unknown) p. 208.

The Late Henry James: Substitution, Projection and the Guilty Eye

1. Edel (ed.) *The Complete Tales of Henry James*, vol. IX (London: Rupert Hart Davis, 1962).

5. FICTIONS OF IDENTITY: MODERNISM IN GERMANY

Thomas Mann: The myth of 'Doktor Faustus'

1. See his essay on Mann in *From Prophecy to Exorcism* (London: Longmans, 1965).
2. T. Mann, *Die Entstehung des Doktor Faustus* (Frankfurt a.M.: Suhrkamp 1949) p. 36.
3. Ibid., p. 33.
4. Ronald Gray, *The German Tradition in Literature 1871–1945* (Cambridge: Cambridge University Press, 1965).
5. Mann, *Die Entstehung*, p. 36.
6. Ibid., p. 32.
7. T. W. Adorno, *Noten zur Literatur I*, (Frankfurt a.M.: Suhrkamp, 1975) p. 68.
8. T. Mann, *Doktor Faustus*, (Frankfurt a.M.: Fischer Taschenbuch Verlag, 1977) p. 57
9. Mann, *Die Entstehung*, p. 36.
10. Mann, *Doctor Faustus*, p. 487.

Some aspects of *The Man Without Qualities*

1. K. Laermann, *Eigenschaftslosigkeit, Reflexionen zu Musils Roman 'Der Mann ohne Eigenschaften'* (Stuttgart: Metzler, 1970).
2. R. Musil, *Der Mann ohne Eigenschaften The Man without Qualities*, ed. A. Frisé (Hamburg: Rowohlt, 1957).
3. Ibid., p. 1161.
4. F. G. Peters, *Robert Musil: Master of the Hovering Style* (New York: Columbia University Press, 1978).
5. R. Musil, op. cit. p. 251.

Franz Kafka: The Impossibility of writing

1. F. Kafka, *Sämtliche Erzählungen* (Frankfurt a.M.: Fischer Verlag 1976), p. 299. All further references to Kafka will be to the paperback versions of this edition.
2. Ibid., pp. 18–19.
3. Ibid., p. 320.
4. F. Kafka, *Der Prozess*, pp. 66–7.
5. T. S. Eliot, *The Waste Land* (London: Faber and Faber, 1969) p. 61. lines 5–6: 'Winter kept us warm, covering/Earth in forgetful snow'.
6. Kafka, *Sämtliche Erzählungen*, p. 138.
7. F. Kafka, *Das Schloss*, p. 12.
8. T. W. Adorno, *Aufzeichnungen zu Kafka*, in: *Gesammelte Schiften* 10,I (Frankfurt a.M.: Suhrkamp, 1977) p. 262: 'the wounds with which society brands the individual are read by him as ciphers of its social falsity, as negatives of the truth'.
9. Ibid., p. 254.
10. Kafka, *Der Prozess*, p. 11.
11. Kafka, *Das Schloss*, p. 206.
12. Ibid., p. 144.
13. Ibid., p. 169.
14. F. R. Leavis, *D. H. Lawrence: Novelist* (Harmondsworth: Penguin, 1973) pp. 169–73.
15. Kafka, *Das Schloss*, p. 212.
16. C.f. Adorno, *Kafka*, p. 278, where Kafka's work is likened to a description of an expressionist painting.
17. Kafka, *Das Schloss*, p. 209.
18. J. L. Borges, '*Kafka and his Precursors*', in: *Labyrinths*, (Harmondsworth: Penguin, 1970) p. 234.
19. Kafka, *Sämtliche Erzählungen*, p. 304.
20. Kafka, *Der Prozess*, p. 68.
21. H. Uytersprot, *Zur Struktur von Kafka's 'Der Prozess': Versuch einer Neu-Ordnung* (Brussels: Didier, 1953).

22. W. Benjamin, *Franz Kafka*, in: *Angelus Novus II* (Frankfurt a.M.: Suhrkamp, 1966) pp. 258–9: 'we do not know exactly how this unknown family of men and animals is constituted. It is only clear that it is the force which drives Kafka to move aeons in his writing.' And Ibid., p. 260: 'Every forgotten thing mingles with the oblivion of the primeval world.'
23. Kafka, *Sämtliche Erzählungen*, p. 323.

6. POST-MODERNISM

The Art of Lying: Three Post-war English Novels

1. Malcolm Lowry, *Under the Volcano* (Harmondsworth: Penguin, 1969) p. 374.
2. Ibid.

The Survival of Modernism: Some Post-war American Novels

1. Ralph Ellison, *Invisible Man* (London: Gollancz, 1953) p. 382.
2. Ibid., p. 36.
3. Ibid., p. 253.
4. Ibid., p. 384.
5. Thomas Pynchon, *The Crying of Lot 49* (London: Cape, 1967) p. 109.
6. Ibid., p. 26.
7. Thomas Pynchon, *Gravity's Rainbow* (London: Cape, 1973) p. 30.
8. *Crying*, op. cit., p. 26.
9. I owe this idea to an unpublished dissertation for Cambridge English, Part II, by Jeffrey Seroy.
10. *Gravity's Rainbow*, op. cit., p. 159.
11. Ibid., p. 167.
12. Ibid., p. 207.

Selected Critical Bibliography

The following bibliography is meant to serve a dual purpose: to suggest further reading, and to indicate my most important debts. It is in no way comprehensive.

Adorno, T. W.: *Gesammelte Schriften* (Frankfurt a.M.: Suhrkamp, 1970 ff.), especially:
  Band 6: *Negative Dialektik. Jargon der Eigentlichkeit* (1973)
  Band 7: *Aesthetische Theorie* (1970)
  Band 11: *Noten zur Literatur* (1974)
Anders, G.: *Kafka, Pro et Contra* (Munich: Beck, 1951)
Bakhtin, M.: *Problemy poetyki Dostojewskiego* (Warsaw: P.I.W., 1970)
  Die Aesthetik des Wortes, ed. Rainer Grübel, (Frankfurt a.M.: Suhrkamp, 1979)
Barthes, R.: *Mythologies* (Paris: du Seuil, 1957)
  Sade. Fourier. Loyola. (Paris: du Seuil, 1971)
Benjamin, W.: *Schriften* (Frankfurt a.M.: Suhrkamp, 1974)
Bergonzi, B.: *The Situation of the Novel* (Harmondsworth: Penguin, 1972)
Coates, P.: *Cinema, Symbolism and the Gesamtkunstwerk*, in:
  Comparative Criticism Yearbook 4 (Cambridge University Press, 1982)
Dauber, K.: *Rediscovering Hawthorne* (New Jersey: Princeton University Press, 1977)
Deleuze, G.: *Proust and Signs* (London: Allen Lane, The Penguin Press, 1973)
Doody, A.: *A Natural Passion* (Oxford University Press, 1974)
Douglas, M.: *Purity and Danger* (London: Routledge and Kegan Paul, 1966)
T. C. Duncan Eaves and Ben D. Kimpel: *Samuel Richardson, A Biography* (Oxford University Press, 1971)
Eliade, M.: *Les mythes, les rêves et les mystères* (Paris: Gallimard, 1957)
Freud, S.: *Gesammelte Schriften* (Vienna: Internationaler Psychoanalytischer Verlag, 1934)
Furbank, P. N.: *Reflections on the Word 'Image'*, (London: Secker and Warburg, 1970)
Genette, G.: *Figures III* (Paris: du Seuil, 1972)
Gopnik, I.: *A Theory of Style and Richardson's 'Clarissa'* (The Hague and Paris: Mouton, 1970)
Hamburger, M.: *From Prophecy to Exorcism* (London: Longmans, 1965)
Harvey, J. R.: *Victorian Novelists and Their Illustrators* (London: Sidgwick and Jackson, 1970)
Heath, S.: *The Nouveau Roman* (London: Elek, 1971)

Hochstätter, D.: *Sprache des Möglichen* (Frankfurt a.M.: Akademische Verlags-gesellschaft, 1972)

Josipovici, G.: *The World and the Book* (London: Macmillan, 1971)

Kermode, F.: *The Sense of an Ending* (New York: Oxford University Press, 1967)

Kinkead-Weekes, M.: *Samuel Richardson, Dramatic Novelist* (London: Methuen, 1973)

Kristeva, J.: *Semiotike, Recherches pour une semanalyse* (Paris: du Seuil, 1969)

Laermann, K.: *Eigenschaftslosigkeit, Reflexionen zu Musils Roman 'Der Mann ohne Eigenschaften'* (Stuttgart: Metzler, 1970)

Leavis, F. R.: *The Great Tradition* (London: Chatto and Windus, 1948)
D. H. Lawrence: Novelist (Harmondsworth: Penguin, 1973)

Lukács, G.: *Die Theorie des Romans* (Darmstadt: Luchterhand, 1965)
Kunst und Objektive Wahrheit (Leipzig: Reclam, 1977)

Müller, G.: *Ideologiekritik und Metasprache* (Musil-Studien 2) (Salzburg-München: W. Fink, 1972)

Nachtigall, E.: *Die 'Memoires' der Marguérite de Valois als Quelle zu Samuel Richardsons 'Clarissa'* (Bonn: Romanisches Seminar, 1960)

Nuttall, A. D.: *Two Concepts of Allegory* (London: Routledge and Kegan Paul, London 1967)

Peters, F. G.: *Robert Musil: Master of the Hovering Style* (New York: Columbia University Press, 1978)

Poirier, R.: *The Performing Self* (London: Chatto and Windus, 1971)

Prickett, S.: *Victorian Fantasy* (Brighton: Harvester, 1979)

Rogers, R.: *The Double in Literature* (Detroit: Wayne State University Press, 1970)

Salaman, E.: *The Great Confession* (London: Allen Lane, The Penguin Press, 1973)

Sandauer, A.: *Liryka i logika* (Warsaw: P.I.W., 1969)

Sartre, J.-P.: *L'Imaginaire* (Paris: Gallimard, 1940)
Situations I (Paris: Gallimard, 1947)

Shaffer, E.: *'Kubla Khan' and 'The Fall of Jerusalem'* (Cambridge: Cambridge University Press, 1975)

Slater, P.: *The Pursuit of Loneliness* (Harmondsworth: Penguin, 1971)

Sollers, P.: *L'écriture et l'expérience des limites* (Paris: Points, 1972)

Swinden, P.: *Unofficial Selves* (London: Macmillan, 1973)

Tanner, T.: *City of Words, American Fiction 1950–70* (London: Cape, 1971)

Uyttersprot H.: *Zur Struktur von Kafkas 'Der Prozess'* (Brussels: Didier, 1953)

Walser, M.: *Was zu bezweifeln war* (Berlin and Weimar: Aufbau-Verlag, 1974)

Index of Names

Index of Themes